Caribbean Discourse

SELECTED ESSAYS

Caribbean Discourse

SELECTED ESSAYS

By Edouard Glissant

Translated and with an Introduction by
J. Michael Dash

CARAF BOOKS

University Press of Virginia

CHARLOTTESVILLE

F
2081
.G5313
1989

This is a title in the C A R A F B O O K S series

THE UNIVERSITY PRESS OF VIRGINIA

Le Discours Antillais Copyright © Les Editions du Seuil 1981
This translation and edition Copyright © 1989 by the Rector and Visitors
of the University of Virginia

First published 1989

Library of Congress Cataloging-in-Publication Data

Glissant, Edouard, 1928–
    [Discours antillais. English]
    Caribbean discourse : selected essays / by Edouard Glissant :
translated and with an introduction by J. Michael Dash.
        p.   cm. (C A R A F books)
    Translation of: Le discours antillais.
    ISBN 0-8139-1219-9
    1. Martinique—Civilization.   2. Martinique—Dependency on France.
3. Blacks—Race identity.   4. Nationalism and literature—West
Indies, French—History—20th century.   5. Caribbean literature
(French)—History and criticism.   6. West Indies, French—Relations—
France.   7. France—Relations—West Indies, French.   I. Dash, J.
Michael.   II. Title.   III. Series.
F2081.G5313   1989
972.98'2—dc19   89-5469
                                                                                       CIP

Printed in the United States of America

1926 4886   10/22/90 RB

To describe is to transform.

Then Chaka shouted to them: "You murder me in the hope of taking my place after my death; you are mistaken, that is not to be, for Oum'loungou (the white man) is on the move and he will be the one to dominate you, and you will become his subjects."
>
> Thomas Mofolo
> *Chaka, Bantou Epic*

Between Europe and America I see only specks of dust.
>
> Attributed to Charles de Gaulle
> on a visit to Martinique

But the most powerful language is the one in which all is said without a word being uttered.
>
> Jean-Jacques Rousseau
> *Essay on the Origin of Language*

Acoma fall down, everybody say the wood rotten.
>
> *Martinican proverb*

A black man is a century.
>
> *Martinican saying*

An enormous task, to make an inventory of reality. We amass facts, we make our comments, but in every written line, in every proposition offered, we have an impression of inadequacy.
>
> Frantz Fanon
> *Black Skin, White Masks*

Contents

Contents

Introduction

I and We
Either I am nobody or
I am a nation.
Derek Walcott,
The Schooner Flight

Edouard Glissant's *Caribbean Discourse* is an unflaggingly ambitious attempt to read the Caribbean and the New World experience, not as a response to fixed, univocal meanings imposed by the past, but as an infinitely varied, dauntingly inexhaustible text. In its effort to plumb this deeper psychic truth of the Caribbean, Glissant's work examines everything. Its reach extends from the trivial to the portentous, from windshield stickers to the first document promising the abolition of slavery. To this extent *Caribbean Discourse* follows in the wake of essays of similar scope and originality, which examine with equal attention the humblest artifact or the popular game of cricket or the familiar ritual of the fiesta, by intellectuals and artists such as Alejo Carpentier, Octavio Paz, Frantz Fanon, C. L. R. James, Aimé Césaire, Jean Price-Mars, and Wilson Harris. In a series of essays, lectures, anecdotes, and prose poems, which are often as scientific in conception as they are poetically digressive in execution, Glissant shifts our attention away from the conventional reduction of Caribbean history to a racial melodrama of revenge or remorse and toward a close scrutiny of the obscurities, the vicissitudes, the fissures that abound in Caribbean history from slavery to the present. In so doing he calls into question a number of received ideas on creativity, colonization, and the Creole language. In no area is his challenge more thoroughgoing than in the revaluation of the notion of the self. Like so many modern critics and philosophers, Glissant affirms that the era of naive faith in individualism is over.

Glissant's oeuvre in general and *Caribbean Discourse* in particular are predicated on a dislocation or deconstruction of the notion of individual agency in a post-Cartesian, post-Sartrean sense. There is a constant deflation of the solemnities of the self-certain subject in Glissant's critique of the longing for inviolable systems and pure origins, the sovereignty of self-consciousness, the solipsism of the structuring ego. For him, true beginnings and real authority are lowly, paradoxical, and unspectacular. To this extent his work marks a significant departure from the Caribbean's fixaton with prelapsarian innocence, an origin before the Fall of the New World. This is the source of his criticism of Saint-John Perse, who is presented as an example of the constructive subject who desperately attempts to impose order, structure, on a world in a continuous state of flux. "But the world can no longer be shaped into a system. Too many Others and Elsewheres disturb the placid surface. In the face of this disturbance, Perse elaborates his vision of stability." The Caribbean is the realm of the unspeakable. In this rejection of Perse's yielding to the temptation to "totalize," Glissant is a natural deconstructionist who celebrates latency, opacity, infinite metamorphosis.

Such an insistence on formlessness, latency, mutation, or (to use Glissant's favored expression) "une poétique de la Relation" (a cross-cultural poetics), has always been at the heart of his creative enterprise. His very first novel, *La Lézarde* (The ripening, 1958), is as much as anything a parable of the Cartesian *cogito* in reverse. The main characters, willingly or reluctantly, leave their solitude to become part of a political group or to open themselves to the vitalizing force of sea and land. In this novel politics opens the door to communion. In *Caribbean Discourse* Glissant is equally explicit on the limitations of the structuring, transcendental ego: "man is not the privileged subject of his knowledge; he gradually becomes its object. . . . He is no longer the mind probing the known-unknown." Or again: "The author must be demythified, certainly, because he must be integrated into a common resolve. The collective "We" becomes the site of the generative system, and the true subject." This demythification of the self-certain subject is remarkable in the ideological and aesthetic context of Caribbean writing. The point of departure of Caribbean literature has been the effort to write the subject into existence. Its master theme has been the quest for individual identity. The heroic prodigal, the solemn demiurge, the vengeful enfant terrible, outspoken Caliban—these are some of the pervasive images of the transcendental subject in Caribbean literature. However, Glissant's work treats the subversion of the ordering ego and attempts to transcend the monomania of Caliban. What Glissant emphasizes is the structuring force of landscape, community, and collective unconscious.

Aimé Césaire was the first Caribbean writer to consciously examine the notion of the subject as a disembodied self seeking incarnation. His *Cahier d'un retour au pays natal* (1939, 1947, 1956) (Notebook of a return to the native land) documents a journey from "ex-isle" to union with the "native land," from solitude to solidarity, from felt to expressed. For him, the subject was not privileged but simply the site where the collective experience finds articulation. In the *Cahier* we do not find the apotheosis of the subject, more characteristic of conventional literature of protest, but the decentered subject, central to the poetics of the cross-cultural imagination as conceived by Glissant. Glissant's focus on the decentered subject and the process of *Relation* seems to emerge logically from his own personal experience.

Just as Glissant's writings encompass a wide range of topics and include as well as combine most literary genres, so his experience points to a life lived as a cross-cultural process and to an insatiable investigation of all areas of human inquiry and artistic creativity. He was born in 1928, not in the oppressive lowlands of Martinique, dominated by the grim reality of the sugarcane plantation, but in the hilly commune of Sainte-Marie, noted for its retention of local traditions from both the pre-Columbian and the African past. Like the character Thaël in the novel *La Lézarde,* who shakes himself free from the paralyzing beauty of his mountain landscape, Glissant himself followed the course of the Lézarde River down to the plains of Lamentin, where he entered school. In 1938 he began classes at the Lycée Schoelcher, from which he retains memories of the francophile excesses of various teachers and the suppression of the Creole language and culture. In 1939, however, Aimé Césaire was appointed to a post in modern languages at the Lycée Schoelcher. Glissant, along with his contemporary Frantz Fanon, was exposed to Césaire's ideas on black consciousness and the value of literary creativity as an exemplary activity for the dispossessed colonial imagination. These ideas were reinforced by the leader and theorist of the surrealist movement, André Breton, who arrived in Martinique in 1941. The forties were a period of intense political and cultural activity in Martinique, in spite of the isolation imposed by the Allied fleet because of the occupation of France by Germany during the war. Glissant had his first experience of collective action and group solidarity through his involvement in the group "Franc-Jeu," which played a part in Césaire's electoral campaign in 1945. His distance from his origins in the highlands of Martinique increased in 1946, when he left for France on a scholarship.

The capacity of the writer to descend, like Orpheus, into the underworld of the collective unconscious and to emerge with a song that can reanimate the petrified world has a shaping force on Glissant's conception of artistic activity. This idea was reinforced in Paris through his exposure to the phenomenologists, the "new novelists," and in the late fifties he associated with Barthes, Sollers, and avant-garde literary circles in Paris. In this post-Sartrean atmosphere where the notion of man as "free spirit" was gleefully debunked and the importance of being "in situation" was given a fuller application than Sartre ever intended, Glissant composed his first novel, *La Lézarde*, which transcends authorial omniscience and a simplified didacticism to explore Martinican time and space through the crack (*lézarde*), or fertile insight, provided by the river, the true protagonist of the novel.

However, his intellectual activity in the fifties was also affected by the increasing importance of black literary and cultural activity promoted by the publishing house connected with the magazine *Présence africaine*, which was founded in 1947. He maintained his links with the Caribbean through a particularly close association with Frantz Fanon and read intensely the works of Saint-John Perse. He participated in the First Congress of Negro Writers and Artists in 1956 but it would be wrong to see him as simply another negritude writer. Along with Fanon, he had already begun to look beyond the simplifications of the negritude movement. Aesthetically, he had started his examination of the specificities of a Caribbean sensibility in *Soleil de la conscience* (The sun of consciousness, 1956). This early collection of essays treats his disorientation with respect to Parisian intellectual circles. In it Glissant's keen sense of the shaping power of place is already observable. It also contains Glissant's first meditations on a Caribbean worldview based on a convulsive, unregimented ideal and not on the ordered symmetry associated with Europe. This elaboration of a Martinican sensibility is more fully treated in *Le quatrième siècle* (The fourth century, 1965). In the same way that his literary explorations were centered on the Caribbean, so were his politics. Following riots in Fort-de-France, he helped form in 1959 the "Front Antillo-Guyanais," which called for the decolonization of the French overseas departments (DOM) and the cultural integration of the French territories in the Caribbean region. This group was disbanded by De Gaulle in 1961, and Glissant was kept under surveillance in France.

The link between individual activism and collective destiny was reinforced when he returned to Martinique in 1965. This return marks another phase in the refusal to isolate himself from the world around which all his activity is centered. As he says in *Soleil de la conscience:* "J'écris enfin près de la Mer, dans ma maison brûlante, sur le sable volcanique." ("So I write near the sea, in my burning house, on the volcanic sands.")[1] Too often Caribbean intellectuals had led other people's revolutions—Fanon in Algeria, Padmore in Ghana, Garvey in the United States, and Césaire's role in African decolonization—but had had little or no impact at home. In Martinique, Glissant founded the Institut Martiniquais d'Etudes (Martinican Studies Institute) in order to promote educational and cultural activities. He started the journal *Acoma* in 1971 to disseminate the ideas of a research group attached to the institute. Unlike Césaire's journal *Tropiques* in the forties, Glissant's journal did not concentrate on the revaluation of Martinique's African past. Rather, *Acoma* stressed the problem of the psychological and cultural dispossession of the Martinican mind and elaborated a poetics of the Americas in investigating the work of Carpentier, Guillén, and Neruda. However, the corrosive power of the phenomenon in Martinique that Glissant calls *colonisation réussie* (successful colonization) made any kind of cultural activity superfluous. Glissant's despondency is reflected in his novel *Malemort* (1975). There is a sense of collective impotence and official corruption that is depressingly different from his earlier writing. The atmosphere of expectancy and the moments of sensory plenitude in *La Lézarde* are absent in this later novel, in which the contemporary agonies of Martinique are depicted in the stagnant and polluted trickle that the Lézarde River has become. The theme of a people destined for a painless oblivion persists in his most recent novel, *Mahagony* (1987), whose title underlines the theme of a people's agony. In this work Glissant plays on the name of the tree "mahogani" to suggest "my agony." In the story the tree, from which the names of three protagonists are taken—Mani, Maho, and Gani—is threatened and so is an entire people.

1. Edouard Glissant, *Soleil de la conscience* (Paris: Seuil, 1956), p. 43.

Introduction

Glissant left Martinique for Paris to become editor of the UNESCO journal *Courrier,* which to some extent still continues the struggle against cultural dispossession begun in the now-defunct *Acoma.*

In the postcolonial Caribbean situation, the artist, intellectual, leader attempts to give definition to an existential void, to impose a total, transcendental meaning on the surrounding flux. Glissant has always insisted that the problem has traditionally been that the intellectual has looked outside of the land and the community for a solution. He is critical of the Martinican's pre-Oedipal dependence on France, which manifests itself in an anxious quest for paternity. This dependence is persuasively illustrated in the cult surrounding the French abolitionist Victor Schoelcher. Glissant's early play *Monsieur Toussaint* (1961) examines the Haitian revolutionary's similarly disastrous fascination with France and his dismaying lack of faith in his own community. This degree of insecurity in the group unconscious is cleverly exploited in the French government's policy of assimilation. Again and again Glissant treats the anxieties resulting from the unresolved contradictions of the group unconscious in *Caribbean Discourse.* It is, to this extent, an elaboration of the theme of psychic dispossession treated by Fanon in *Black Skin, White Masks,* (*Peau noire, masques blancs* 1952).[2] The problem of the dissociated Martinican self is even more acute for Glissant, writing nearly three decades after Fanon. The image of the Martinican as happy zombie, as passive consumer, is pervasive in *Caribbean Discourse.* Its most moving incarnation may be found in the novel *La case du commandeur* (The foreman's cabin), also published in 1981. The protagonist Mycéa, after being taken to a mental asylum, exists in a state of suspended animation, staring unblinking and uncaring at a color television set (bought on credit) that broadcasts French programs. A com-

2. Frantz Fanon, *Peau noire, masques blancs* (Paris: Seuil, 1952); the English translation by Charles L. Markmann was published by Grove Press in New York in 1968.

Introduction

munity, living off French welfare and mesmerized by French consumerism, is epitomized by Mycéa's painless zombification. "Les Antilles heureuses," the happy islands of travel posters, are indeed societies in extremis.

Caribbean Discourse offers a historical perspective on the unchecked process of psychic disintegration in Martinique. History—or, to use Glissant's term, "nonhistory"—is seen as a series of "missed opportunities," because of which the French West Indian is persuaded of his impotence and encouraged to believe in the disinterested generosity of France, to pursue the privilege of citizenship and the material benefits of departmental status. Glissant consistently points to the erosion of the economic base, the division of the working class, the absence of a national bourgeoisie and the suppression of local self-supporting productivity, which make the disintegration of a collective identity and creative sterility inevitable. The mimetic impulse is the final stage of this process: "The process of total dislocation (the destruction of all productive capacity) aggravates the impulse towards imitation, imposes in an irresistible way an identification with the proposed model of existence (the French one), of reflection, and unleashes an irrational reluctance to question this model, whose 'transmission' appears as the only guarantee of 'social status.'" In the Caribbean Departments, life is dominated by the Social Security building and the airport. The choice can often be dependency or escape. The French Caribbean predicament lies in this collective abdication of identity and the inescapable degradation of folk culture, Creole language, and any sense of being Caribbean.

As Glissant points out, Martinican history is simply a reflection of French history. The temporary abolition of slavery in 1794, the end of slavery in 1848, adult male suffrage in 1877, and departmentalization in 1946 are the result of events in French history. Glissant concludes: "There is therefore a real discontinuity beneath the apparent continuity of our history. The apparent continuity is the periodization of French history. . . . The real discontinuity is that in the emergence of

Introduction

the periods we have defined, the decisive catalyst of change is not secreted by the circumstances but externally determined in relation to another history." Departmentalization is the ultimate manifestation of this unceasing experience of dislocation and alienation. Within departmentalization, economic dependency is acute; political impotence is increased through a tertiarization of the economy and the power of the prefect; social imbalances are produced by massive migration to France ("genocide by substitution," as Glissant puts it) and an influx of metropolitan French; and cultural dislocation is induced by an artificial affluence and a new consumer culture. The end result is mental alienation such as that of Glissant's heroine Mycéa. In such a situation the destruction of the collectivity undermines the emergence of individual mental structures: "But we have here the embattled, impossible group that makes the emergence of the individual impossible. The question we need to ask in Martinique will not be, for instance: 'Who am I?'—a question that from the outset is meaningless—but rather: 'Who are we?'"

In a situation where the group is ignorant of its past, resentful of its present impotence, yet fearful of future change, the creative imagination has a special role to play. Martinicans need writers to tell them who they are or even what they are not. A collective memory is an urgent need for the Martinican community if oblivion is to be avoided. Glissant's return to this community is indirectly conveyed through the character of Mathieu in *La case du commandeur.* Mathieu, who first appeared in *La Lézarde,* is, along with Thaël, part of that ideal cultural and intellectual whole that is sadly lacking in Martinique: the composite of hill and plain, mythical and political, intuition and intellect. Mathieu is described as "le Grand Absent" since he leaves the island at the end of *La Lézarde* as Glissant himself did. In *La case du commandeur* Mathieu, who has been traveling widely, writes to Mycéa from Europe, Africa, and the Americas. But letters written by Mycéa to Mathieu are not adequate to maintain the latter's sense of belonging. The dialectic of withdrawal and return needs to be reactivated. The answer is perhaps suggested in *Caribbean Discourse*. Twice he declares, at the beginning and the end of this work, "I still believe in the future of small countries." As Glissant explains in his essay "Reversion and Diversion," this wandering, this solitary self-fulfilment is pointless if we do not return to the point from which we started: "Diversion is not a useful ploy unless it is nourished by Reversion . . . [as] a return to the point of entanglement, from which we were forcefully turned away; that is where we must ultimately put to work the forces of creolization, or perish." The individual self has no future without a collective destiny. The "unhoused" wanderer across cultures must be "rehoused" in the fissured history, the exposed sands, before the surging sea.

Language and the Body
Each time we try to express ourselves
we have to break with ourselves.
Octavio Paz, *The Labyrinth of Solitude*

In his perceptive essay *Black Orpheus* (1948) Jean-Paul Sartre observed that black poetry was essentially a fierce response to the inadequacy of language: "this feeling of failure before language . . . is at the source of all poetic expression."[3] Language for the black writer was, not a neutral, transparent instrument, but the determining medium of thought itself. In his pursuit of self-definition, the black artist saw the inherited colonial language as a pernicious symbolic system used by the European colonizer in order to gain total and systematic control of the mind and reality of the colonized world. In the face of Prospero's hubris, his signifying authority (*langue*), the African or Caribbean Caliban deployed his own militant idiom (*langage*).

Like many of their iconoclastic counterparts in the Dada

3. Jean-Paul Sartre, "Orphée noir," in Léopold Sédar Senghor, ed., *Anthologie de la nouvelle poésie nègre et malgache de langue française* (1948; Paris: PUF, 1972), p. xix. (Trans. J.M.D.)

Introduction

and surrealist movements, black writers yearned for an almost Mallarméan purity. Language was so contaminated and debased that they longed for an a-historical, prelinguistic world of pure presences, the realm of the unspeakable. The full margins and calculated short-windedness of the first exponent of negritude, Léon Damas, can be seen as manifestations of this minimalist impulse. The cult of feeling and expressivity is a provocative feature of the 1932 manifesto *Légitime défense* and is given poetic expression in the critique of language pervasive in Damas's *Pigments* (1937). In the spirit of this radical scepticism, Damas felt that language had to be destroyed in order to be saved.

If some dreamt of an Eden before the fall of language, others saw the real enemy as the written word and attempted to revitalize the latter through the energies of the spoken word. The written word was seen as a degenerate outgrowth of speech. To Césaire, for instance, the rationally censored world of the written had to yield to something more intuitive, more verbose, and less restrained. Radical art must do more than subvert. It must transcend. What Césaire advocated was, not Damas's strident silence, but the passionate expression of the agitated unconscious. Art would not be polished and finished, not mere expression, but the unregimented and unedited flow of the collective unconscious. In attempting to devise a new discourse, a new representation, for those who had been condemned to silence and to being represented by others, the watchwords were opacity and orality. *Discours antillais* is Glissant's meditation on language "in situation." Language is utterance exchanged between speaker and listener, conqueror and conquered, who together create speech according to given social and political contexts.

Caribbean Discourse is, among other things, an exploration of a poetics of the Martinican unconscious. To Glissant the Martinican unconscious is one in which contradictions and humiliations, denied in the everyday world, exist in a state of intense repression. If this process of domestication and containment did not take place, life would be a waking night-

mare. The intolerable truths of chronic economic dependency
and the reality of cultural oblivion are subjected to collective
denial and systematic camouflage. It was this conformist silence that led Aimé Césaire earlier to describe the Martinican
people as "so strangely garrulous yet silent." It is the writer's
responsibility to break this silence. The problem faced by the
French Caribbean writer is his awareness that the repercussions of assimilation are not only economic but also linguistic.

It has been customary to single out the French language as
the contaminated instrument of communication. In assessing
the linguistic situation of the French Caribbean, Glissant sees
Creole as equally debased. In his essay "Poetics and the Unconscious" Glissant states: "The official language, French, is
not the people's language. This is why we the elite speak it so
correctly. The language of the people, Creole, is not the language of the nation." Creole is constantly being eroded by
French. Creole is no longer the language of responsibility nor
of production. This he sets out to prove in "Man gin-yin an
zin." In this essay Glissant concludes that Creole: "has stopped
being a functional language: it is being undermined by a
dominant language. . . . All that the Creole language has
achieved . . . risks being lost in this process of marginalization, produced by both an absence of productivity and an absence of creativity." Creole is not the language of the hollow
modernity of the new departmentalized Martinique. It does
not belong in shopping malls and luxury hotels. "Cane, bananas, pineapples are the last vestiges of the Creole world."
As Martinique produces less and less, Creole is doomed to extinction. Glissant observes that in order to compensate for his
real impotence, the Martinican speaker, either of French or
Creole, resorts to a kind of baroque excess. The deformation
of French and Creole in the French Caribbean is illustrated by
the ornate excesses of the former and the verbal delirium of
the latter. An elaborate French is the highest achievement
of the *assimilé* (assimilated) speaker. "Had we not observed
that, in the evolution of our rhetoric, the baroque first appears
as the symptom of a deeper inadequacy, being the elaborate

ornamentation imposed on the French language by our desperate men of letters?" In this, Glissant follows closely his compatriot Frantz Fanon, who devoted a chapter in *Black Skin, White Masks* to language as a symptom of Martinican neurosis. But this verbal excess is also true of Creole in Glissant's estimation. Creole is similarly afflicted by verbal delirium: "We can also state, based on our observation of the destructively nonfunctional situation of Creole, that this language, in its day-to-day application, becomes increasingly the language of neurosis. Screamed speech becomes knotted into contorted speech, into the language of frustration." Creole is marked by its defensive reflex. It was the secretive means of communication. Its predominant characteristic became extreme or intense sound. Creole needed to be spoken both loudly and quickly, producing an "accelerated nonsense created by scrambled sounds." Creole cannot be murmured, it is the language of either the urgent whisper or the frenzied shriek. Like the Haitian novelist Jacques Roumain, who saw collective labor (the *'coumbite*) in terms of its power to release the repressed imagination, Glissant makes a close association between productivity and creativity, labor and language. According to Glissant's definition "a national language is the one in which a people produces." Since Martinique is crippled by an absence of self-sustaining productivity, it is a community without a national language. French is the *langue imposée*— the imposed language—and Creole is the *langue non-posée*— the nonsituated language.

In this situation of extreme cultural and linguistic erosion, it is the writer who must locate a zone of authentic speech. Glissant's search for linguistic authenticity takes him beyond both French and Creole, beyond writing and verbal delirium. *Caribbean Discourse* contains a catalog of static cultural forms that depressingly demonstrate the crisis within the French Caribbean imagination. For instance, Glissant examines music in Martinique, only to find that, unlike jazz and reggae, which are shaped by communities struggling to assert themselves, Martinican music has not evolved from the music of the plantation. What local music is produced is exploited by the tourist industry. The vacuum that remains is filled by Haitian and Dominican music. Similarly, the folktale is investigated to determine its capacity to sustain an authentic imaginative discourse. In this medium, the degree of dispossession is even more marked. In the use of space and the function of landscape, in the folktale, Glissant notes that the world belongs to someone else. The tale simply verifies the existing system. What Glissant describes as its "pathetic lucidity" focuses on a world of nonproductivity, a world of absence or excess, communicative reticence or calculated shrillness. It is a precise representation of the alienated world of the Martinican.

When Glissant does locate the metalanguage he is seeking, it is discovered in forms outside of Martinique and outside of the conventions of writing. It is in painting and sculpture that he locates the liberated poetics of the Caribbean. Glissant's comments on Haitian painting are pertinent here. He sees Haitian Creole as secreted in the symbolic discourse of painting. "It is the symbolic notation of a seldom seen side of reality. It is both a means of communication and a transfer of knowledge for the very people who cannot write. It demonstrates by its visual form the specific nature of orality." The Haitian writer can therefore draw on this visual language in order to depict his world. The subtleties of color, the principles of composition, and the conception of form allow the writer to visualize his world. In Haitian society, dominated by mass illiteracy, imagery or the symbolic language of painting was the main agent of nonoral narrative. As Glissant asserts— "Haitian painting is derived from the spoken." In an extension of his observations on Haitian painting Glissant traces a Caribbean and New World sensibility in the work of the painters Wifredo Lam and Matta as well as the sculptor Cárdenas. In Lam, Glissant senses "the poetics of the American landscape" and in Matta the multilingualism central to the American experience. He sees in Cárdenas's work a privileged site where the voices of an entire continent find sustained articulation. His duty as a writer would be to forge a similar symbolic language through words in order to represent his world. Graphic and plastic narrative provide exemplary forms in this pursuit of an authentic poetics.

Language not only reflects but enacts the power relations in Martinican society. Neither French nor Creole are the true languages of the community. If, as most militant writers are tempted to do, the artist resorted blindly to Creole, he could fall into an empty "folklorism." "Literature cannot function as a simple return to oral sources of folklore." He warns against the use of an *extrême créolité* (a self-conscious Creole) a *doudouisme de gauche* (a leftist folksiness) to conceal an inadequate analysis of the lived reality of Martinique. Similarly, he cautions against the use of techniques of realism and objectivity in depicting the Caribbean experience.

> The surface effects of literary realism are the precise equivalent of the historian's claim to pure objectivity. . . .

> Now realism, the theory and technique of literal or "total" representation, is not inscribed in the cultural reflex of African or American peoples. . . . Western realism is not a "flat" or shallow technique but becomes so when it is uncritically used by our writers. The misery of our lands is present, obvious. It contains a historical dimension (of not obvious history) that realism alone cannot account for.

In *Caribbean Discourse* not only language but literary conventions are demystified. To use Glissant's playfully cerebral formulations, the literary act must not be prescriptive but prescriptive, not describe but de-scribe. In the written language the creative writer is forced to devise, orality has a significant place.

The French Caribbean writer must forge a new discourse that transcends spoken languages, written conventions, liter-

Introduction

ary genres, traditional notions of time and space. The writer is described by Glissant as a "forceur de langage" (one who forces a language into existence). The deconstructive thrust of his poetics isolates the French Caribbean writer from the language of his world and from the average reader. Indeed, his success can even be measured in the resistance to his strange language, to the defamiliarizing force of his poetics. "In the face of the numbed linguistic sterility imposed on Martinicans, the writer's function is perhaps to propose language as shock, language as antidote, a nonneutral one, through which the problems of the community can be restated." In an attempt to create writing "at the edge of writing and speech," Glissant realizes that the written text is primarily experimental. Its main attribute is not destined to be clarity or accessibility. It is the articulation of a collective consciousness trying to be, to find expression. Inevitably there is something forced about this kind of writing in its striving to avoid the trap of eroded forms and self-consciously reaching for the realm of the unsaid and perhaps the unsayable. This project is easier for the painter or sculptor, whose nonoral narrative plunges with an enviable directness into physical reality. The book is always a more contrived medium in its dependence on contaminated materials to transmit meaning and in its temptation to freeze what is shifting and elusive: "The book is the tool of forced poetics; orality is the instrument of natural poetics. Is the writer forever the prisoner of a forced poetics?"

In this attempt to voice the unvoiced, the writer is precariously poised—particularly so in multilingual postplantation societies. He is poised between light and dark, self and other, felt and expressed, hill and plain, and ultimately between solitude and solidarity. A Caribbean discourse seems inextricably tied to a form of creative schizophrenia, as the poet Derek Walcott has suggested. The idiom sought by Glissant is androgynous, the speech of a twilight consciousness. The need to break with self to understand community, to break with self-consciousness in order to understand the collective unconscious is traced by Glissant in one of his most provocative essays, "Natural Poetics, Forced Poetics." Here Glissant indexes the relationship between oral and written, between the ecstatic *cri* (cry) and the static *corps* (body) in order to demonstrate the difficulty in establishing a natural kind of writing in the postplantation world. The body or corporeal images provide an insight into the psychic condition of the enslaved individual.[4] The body—like the mind in the world of the slave—is numbed, impotent, inert, ultimately someone else's possession. Consequently, self-assertion is inevitably linked to a sensuous physical presence, to an active body, to standing "upright and free," in the words of Césaire's *Cahier.* Freedom for the enslaved is seen in terms of unrestricted physical movement. The problem, as Glissant puts it in "Natural Poetics, Forced Poetics," is that "the written requires nonmovement."

The natural reaction for the freed body of the slave is the explosive scream, the excited gesture. The immobility of the body, which is a necessary condition for writing, is unnatural in such a situation. Glissant traces this ideal of speed, shrillness, of physical excess in various aspects of Martinican Creole and folk narratives. Writing that follows the natural voice and posture of postplantation societies must yield to the stridency, the frenzy, that is historically determined. The experimental writer's goal is the inflexible body and the flexible mind. The creative writer should aim for a forced immobility out of which the true writing that transcends present contradictions can emerge. A Caribbean discourse favors a sober, reflective, indirect treatment of lived reality. The value of the immobile body combined with the animated senses is graphically presented by Wilson Harris, who in *Tradition, the Writer, and Society* sees the writer as a Ulysses who has deprived himself of movement on the deck of the ship, "since the muse of death calls for an involuntary tread which is the dance of the ves-

---

4. Sartre also makes a similar observation: "We are in language just as we are in our body; we feel it as we feel our hands and feet." *Qu'est-ce que la littérature?* (Paris: Gallimard, 1948), p. 27. (Trans. J.M.D.)

sel."[5] Similarly, Glissant sees the crew or community as deaf but following an involuntary movement. The creative imagination, chained to the same vessel or island, is the lone, immobile figure, voluntarily bound to the ship's mast, and sensing through it the shudder of the vessel and the energy of the crew. He cannot command. His audience is deaf. He must both refuse the call of the Sirens and believe that the journey ends in freedom.

Time and Space

> Vegetation is slowly reemerging in a confusion which is all the more deceptive since it preserves, beneath a falsely innocent exterior, memories and patterns of former conflicts.
>
> Claude Lévi-Strauss, *Tristes Tropiques*

In the same way that Glissant undermines traditional faith in the sovereign individual and rational subjectivity, he sets out to unmask history as a coherent, progressive system. *Caribbean Discourse* singles out as the culprit the "totalizing" pretensions of the historical approach. For Glissant human experience is not to be seen as a tale of inexorable Progress, from the shame of Fallenness to the glory of cosmic Perfection. It is precisely such a vision of mankind moving forever upward and onward that fixes the Caribbean on the margins of world history, that dooms the powerless to extinction. Instead, Glissant sees the world and the Caribbean in particular in terms of an intricate branching of communities, an infinite wandering across cultures, where triumphs are momentary and where adaptation and *métissage* (creolization) are the prevailing forces.

In Glissant's vision of ceaseless Creolization, it is the synchronic relations within and across cultures that matter more than the rigid diachrony of orthodox historicism. It is the anthropologist's sense of fragmentation and diversity that re-

5. Wilson Harris, *Tradition, the Writer, and Society* (1967; London: New Beacon Press, 1973), p. 54.

Introduction

places the falisfying symmetry of history as linear progression. Indeed, he makes a difference between the "totalizing" impulse of a transcendental History (with a capital *H*) and the true shapelessness of historical diversity.

"History is fissured by histories; they relentlessly toss aside those who have not had the time to see themselves through a tangle of lianas." History has no monopoly over the past. Historians are not its privileged interpreters. Glissant quotes with approval the observation by the St. Lucian poet Derek Walcott that "History is Sea," with its constantly changing surface and capacity for infinite renewal. For Glissant and for Walcott there is no sense of passing judgment on the past. No one has been unambiguously right or wrong. It is the collective experience that matters.

In his demystification of the "totalizing" pretentions of History, Glissant focuses on the destructive and disfiguring effects of this form of overdetermination on the non-European world. Because no truly total history (in all its diversity) is possible, what History attempts to do is to fix reality in terms of a rigid, hierarchical discourse. In order to keep the unintelligible realm of historical diversity at bay, History as system attempts to systematize the world through ethnocultural hierarchy and chronological progression. Consequently, a predictable narrative is established, with a beginning, middle, and end. History then becomes, because of this almost theological trinitarian structure, providential fable or salvational myth. As examples of such closed, absolute systems, which are ultimately more mythical than rational, Glissant points to the notion of "Absolute Spirit" in Hegel and "Historical Necessity" in Marx. History ultimately emerges as a fantasy peculiar to the Western imagination in its pursuit of a discourse that legitimizes its power and condemns other cultures to the periphery.

Glissant is acutely aware of the effect of this imaginative construct on such areas as the Caribbean. He points to Hegel's division of History into ahistory, prehistory, and History as essentially discriminatory in its attitudes toward non-European cultures.

History is a highly functional fantasy of the West,
originating at precisely the time when it alone
"made" the history of the World. If Hegel relegated African peoples to the ahistorical, Amerindian peoples to the prehistorical, in order to reserve History for European peoples exclusively, it
appears that it is not because these African or
American peoples "have entered History" that we
can conclude today that such a hierarchical conception of "the march of History" is no longer
relevant.

Such a deeply flawed and ethnocentric view of the world can
also be located in Marxist historicism. Marxist thought has
been forced "to concede that it is not in the most technically
advanced countries, nor in the most organized proletariat,
that the revolution will first be successful. Marxism has thus
used objective reality and its own viewpoint to criticize the
concept of a linear and hierarchical History." It is precisely
such "totalizing" and hierarchical master texts that relegate
the Caribbean to the noncreative, nonhistorical periphery—
"la face cachée de la Terre" (the earth's hidden face).

If History is essentially a system of signs that are part of a
discourse of domination and control, literature can also har-
bor an equally pernicious narrative strategy. For instance, the
parallel between the pretention to objective interpretation on
the part of the historian and the belief in the power of the real-
ist narrative is examined by Glissant. As he observes in "History and Literature," "each conception of the historic" is accompanied by its own rhetoric. Indeed, the desire to reduce
reality, to transform the fleeting and the elusive into an all-
encompassing system finds its foremost literary exponent in
the poet Stéphane Mallarmé. To visualize the world as only
existing to become a text, the definitive book that would provide "the Orphic explanation of the world," was Mallarmé's
almost megalomaniacal ambition. Glissant sees this temptation to devise such total systems as a failing in European

Introduction

literature. It is the great weakness of Saint-John Perse, who is blindly driven to assert stability in the face of formlessness, to impose an architecture of words in the face of flux, to seek elegant clearings in a forest of conflicting signs: "The last herald of world-as-system; and no doubt Hegel would have loved the passion for "totality" in Perse. . . . The stubborn attempt to construct a house of language (from the word, a reality) is his response to the world's 'lack of structure.'" The Argentinian writer Borges yields to a similar temptation to transcend "cultural diversity" in terms of a "universal absolute." However, Glissant is careful to point out that this blind faith in a total system or in *Le Verbe* (The Literary Word) is not shared by some of the more adventurous writers in the twentieth century, who have broken away from this fascination with transcendent meanings. Instead, they yield more willingly to the infinite diversity of the world. In the works of Loti, Segalen, Claudel, and Malraux, there is a turning away from the West and its homogenizing sameness and a concern with knowing the East.

However, this notion of a single History has had a devastating effect on the non-European world. Glissant sees the brutal political rivalry in Latin America and Africa as the consequences of the imposed values of a system based on power and domination. A striking literary evocation of the desire to dominate and systematize the postcolonial world on the part of non-Europeans is Aimé Césaire's depiction of Haiti's Henry Christophe. The king sees his role as redemptive and the world he has inherited as hopelessly defiled. He attempts to impose his own discourse on this world to make it intelligible. Christophe's hubristic discourse is built on a rhetoric of honor and regimentation, on symbols of grandeur and finery. Césaire's play is ultimately about the inappropriateness of Christophe's script and the tragic limitations of the king's belief in his power to master and transform. The king's failure is symbolized in the incomplete monument to freedom—the Citadelle. Christophe's journey to freedom comes to an untimely end in the frozen, stone vessel of his fortress. In the wake of the failure of Haiti's king, Glissant constructs his ideal of the role of writer who is capable of an imaginative reconstruction of the past in the void left by History.

The Caribbean in general suffers from the phenomenon of nonhistory. No collective memory, no sense of a chronology, the history of Martinique in particular is made up from a number of psuedo-events that have happened elsewhere. What is produced is a lack of any historical continuity or consciousness. Consequently, Martinique, as an example of an extreme case of historical dispossession in the Caribbean, is caught between the fallacy of the primitive paradise, the mirage of Africa, and the illusion of a metropolitan identity. Glissant's early epic poem *Les Indes* (The Indies) (1955) recalls the brutal encounter between the misguided adventurer and the New World. The "West" Indies were the result of Columbus's perverse insistence that he had found the route to the Indies. The history of greed and exploitation that follows is not the history of those who inhabit these islands. For them, it is "une histoire subie" (a history of submission), and orthodox history sees in them nothing but "the desperate residue of the colonial adventure." Their history remains to be written. The project of evolving a history through imaginative reconstruction persists in an explicit way in Glissant's novels, in which the character Mathieu, a trained historian and archivist, attempts to complete his formal chronology of Martinican history through the subjective and intuitive memories of the old *quimboiseur* (healer) Papa Longoué. Mathieu learns that the truth does not emerge explicitly or in a flash of insight, but slowly and indirectly like the accretions of the Lézarde River. However, the specter of Martinique as a community that has lost a sense of its past persists, and the inability to relocate the primordial track (*la trace*) is central to the events in *La case du commandeur*. Within the disappearance of *la trace*, not only a sense of the ancestral past is lost but the land is so transformed that it no longer allows for the exploration of past associations. Martinican man is dispossessed in time and space.

Introduction

Glissant examines this dispossession not only in the context of Martinique but in the New World longing for *le désiré historique* (the ideal of a history). He is particularly interested in writers of what he calls "the Other America"—novelists from Latin America, the Caribbean, and the American South who construct an alternative imaginative history in defiance of the regulative assumptions of causality, orderly succession, and hierarchical system. The rejection of a linear and "totalizing" historicism leads invariably to strategies of narrative deficiency in their novels. Perhaps, when considered in this light, *Caribbean Discourse* in its use of the essay form achieves the ideal narrative construct. It allows the author to escape the conventions of plot, characterization, and chronology. Glissant is to this extent freer to track down, explore, and linger over the peculiarities, paradoxes, and multiple intricacies of his experience of the world.

Glissant, through a critical comment on Joan Didion's heroine in *A Book of Common Prayer*, points to the naive and complacent view of history that believes in "progress, learning, the ever-ascending evolution of Mankind." This innocent reduction of history to "a sequence of events, to which there will always be an *outcome*" is precisely the kind of smugness and credulousness that the most innovative writing in the New World eschews. It is precisely what Glissant himself struggles against in the French Caribbean mentality. The truth is far more complex. For example, he points to the way in which "linearity gets lost" in the tangle of relationships and alliances that cloud the history of the Sutpen family in *Absalom, Absalom* by William Faulkner. The whole quest for origins, for legitimacy, is doomed to failure in the New World context. In Faulkner, history is not seen as "encounter and transcendence," but his novels are built on what Glissant describes as "the assumption of history as passion." The same theme of the inability to establish pure origins is demonstrated in the life story of Thomas Jefferson's slave concubine Sally Hemmings, where the biblical model of a clear line of descent cannot be established. This quest for history is, perhaps, best

represented among Southern novelists in Shelby Foote's novel
Jordan County (1954), with its many-tiered visualization of
time, reaching back towards the first contacts between whites
and Indians in America. Glissant's interest in these American
novelists is clear. He identifies closely with the technical and
moral dilemma that these "kindred spirits" face. Interesting
points of comparison could also be made between the work of
Flannery O'Connor and that of Glissant in their common concern with fallenness, the need to surrender to the unconscious,
and the psycholiterary obsession with the mirror images of
self. Similarly, a novel such as Djuna Barnes's *Nightwood* contains interesting parallels to Glissant's *La Lézarde*—especially
in the denouement of both novels.

This search for *le désiré historique* and *la trace primordiale*
is at least as important in Latin American writing. Here we
are not simply concerned with historical fiction but with a
thoroughgoing investigation of the concept of time in the New
World imagination. In Alejo Carpentier's *The Lost Steps* and
Gabriel García Márquez's *One Hundred Years of Solitude*,
Glissant traces similar preoccupations with journeys through
time. In the case of Carpentier's novel, the quest is not for
legitimacy but for innocence. It is doomed to failure from the
outset. His protagonist's return upriver to a primal innocence
that he once knew is impossible. He must confront this loss
in the here and now. Carpentier's main character is no different from Thaël in *La Lézarde,* who cannot return to his
secluded mountain Eden. He is forced ultimately to face a
blood-spattered Eden and the necessity of returning to the
world of the everyday. García Márquez also treats a return
through time. In his novel the movement is circular, not the
"spiral ascent" of Didion's heroine but "a return down the
spiral." To Glissant the essential "modernity" of the writers
from "the other America" lies in their need to compose a new
history for the region. It is this element that differentiates
Faulkner from Henry James. It is precisely this anxiety that
lies at the heart of the work of the Haitian novelist Jacques
Stephen Alexis, who feels the need to transcend the dialectical

materialism of his Marxist ideology to create the concept of a marvelous realism. Glissant's own definition of the novelist's need to rewrite the past shows his affinity with novelists from Faulkner to Carpentier. The exploration of history is: "related neither to a schematic chronology nor to a nostalgic lament. It leads to the identification of a painful notion of time and its full projection forward into the future, without the help of those plateaus in time from which the West has benefited, without the help of that collective density that is the primary value of an ancestral cultural heartland. That is what I call *a prophetic vision of the past.*"

The crucial link with landscape is made when Glissant observes that the impossible dream of innocence, the unfulfilled return to the secluded Garden is indexed through a peculiar use of landscape by these novelists. Nature is not simply *décor consentant* or pathetic fallacy. Land is central to the process of self-possession. In this regard, Glissant seems close to the Proustian belief in the link between the material world and immaterial time, between sensation and memory. Glissant too observes that it is not the rational mind that restores the past, but that the past resides in material objects that only release their hidden meanings when encountered imaginatively or sensuously. Landscape in the imagination of New World writers functions in the same way. In its uncharted profusion it translates the intricate and polysemic nature of collective experience. In contrast to the cataloged, monolingual, monochrome world that Glissant identifies with Europe, New World landscape offers the creative imagination a kind of metalanguage in which a new grammar of feeling and sensation is externalized. The artist must translate this multilingualism into his work. In the paintings of Lam and Matta, Glissant locates a poetics of landscape where a linguistic pluralism is consciously developed.

The land provides precisely such an opaque and daunting matrix in the novelists of "the Other America." Glissant focuses on the presence of the primordial forest in the latter: "Sutpen clears it in vain. Aureliano crosses it, . . . the narrator of *The Lost Steps* "goes down" through it and down through time as well. . . . Conquering it is the *objective,* to be conquered by it is the true subject." It is further observed that this is not the biblical notion of "the Eternal Garden" nor the European ideal of "the Spring and the meadow"; the space of the "American novel" is convulsive and overwhelming. When it is entered, it is seen to be the realm of the unsayable where infinite metamorphosis prevails. It is the direct opposite of "the Eternal Garden." Here no Creator provides the text that makes this world intelligible, and perhaps there is no Creator for Adam to ape. The problem for the New World Adam is how to inhabit such a world, which in the past has defeated all who tried to possess it. Glissant notes that the use of space in the Martinican folktale indicates the extent to which this space is ignored and uninhabited. Landscape in the folktale is a *terre de passage* (a land of wanderers), a zone in which no one seeks permanence, a bitter premonition of the fate of Martinique. It is the writer's role to animate this space, to attempt to articulate its hidden voice.

Glissant in *Caribbean Discourse* says almost nothing about Aimé Césaire's contribution to the expression of a poetics of Caribbean landscape. This link is given greater attention in an earlier work, *L'intention poétique* (1969), in which Césaire's evocation of Martinican topography is treated. However, Césaire's entire oeuvre can be seen as an attempt to produce a *cadastre* (a survey) of Martinican space. Beneath the *décor consentant* (the balmy natural setting) which is the traditional stereotype of the Caribbean, Césaire presents a dense field of relationships that allows the individual consciousness to grow with the discovery of landscape, akin to Claudel's notion of *co-naissance* (in which observer and observed coexist). His *Cahier d'un retour au pays natal* breaks free from the silence of a world clogged with accumulated mud and coagulated blood through verbal revelation. In his play *Une tempête* the voices of Prospero and Caliban are drowned by the sounds of the surf and the cries of birds. In Césaire's imagination the island space always prevails. One could say that Glissant's "discourse" is a thoroughgoing expression of Césaire's cry.

Introduction

Glissant's main contention is established unequivocally when he declares that it is not enough simply to describe the landscape. The world to Glissant is not anthropocentric, and landscape is not the externalizing of the individual's state of mind. Glissant prefers to think of the authorizing power of landscape into which the subject is immersed: "The relationship with the land, one that is even more threatened because the community is alienated from the land, becomes so fundamental in this discourse that landscape in the work stops being merely decorative or supportive and emerges as a full character. Describing the landscape is not enough. The individual, the community, the land are inextricable in the process of creating history. Landscape is a character in this process." To the same extent that the Cartesian ego is decentered and traditional historicism demystified, Glissant elevates landscape to a central position in his discourse. This phenomenon he identifies as a central feature of the textual discourse of the American novel.

This peculiar literary discourse is derived directly from the "mobile structures of one's landscape." As Glissant declares: "the language of my landscape is primarily that of the forest, which unceasingly bursts with life." The ever-changing nature of this landscape is especially significant when it comes to the question of time. It is through the constantly shifting quality in nature that Glissant focuses on the issue of duration. As opposed to the falsifying notion of the fixed instant, Glissant sees time in landscape as duration, where past and future are linked, as are the notions forward and backward: "We have seen that the poetics of the American continent, which I characterize as being a search for temporal duration, is opposed in particular to European poetics, which are characterized by the inspiration or the sudden burst of a single moment. It seems that, when dealing with the anxiety of time, American writers are prey to a kind of future remembering." It is the continuous flow that is emphasized and not the short-lived event; the collective memory and not clinging to individual dates. The *intention poétique* replaces the *intention historique*. The imagination must unearth unofficial truths that official history has suppressed. This unregimented ideal of space and time is realized in the symbol of the banyan tree in *La Lézarde* with its "network of down-growing branches . . . winding about the sea."[6]

This ideal New World landscape exists in microcosm in Martinique: "our lands share three common spaces: the heights of the Andes, where the Amerindian world passionately endures; the plains and plateaus in the middle, where the pace of creolization quickens; the Caribbean Sea, where the islands loom! . . . Martinican landscape (the mountains in the north, the plains in the middle, the sands in the south) reproduces in miniature these spaces." The three dimensions of Martinican, Caribbean, and American space correspond to three chronological periods—past, present, and future. But it is not the division between these time zones that is emphasized, nor their linear progression. The sea holds memories of the past, but it is the future toward which the Lézarde River flows. The *morne* (hill) is the world of the maroon, but remains the only path for future action. The center, the known, the sayable is constantly threatened on the inside and the outside by the unknown or the unspeakable. This dialectical relationship between stable and unstable, voiced and unvoiced, that is inscribed in Martinican space is indicative of a process of "becoming," of inexhaustible change that Glissant identifies as predominant in the American conception of time and space.

Glissant's novels focus on the intersection of known and unknown, of acceptance and denial. This is not a poetics of *refus* (rejection), of inaccessible space, but of synthesizing space, of "relation." It can become evident in the pairing of opposing characters, historical forces, and narrative forms. These ideas are enclosed in Wilson Harris's notions of exterior and interior in the Guyanese landscape. It can also be seen in the fictional world of Alejo Carpentier, where the delimitation between vegetable and animal, animate and inanimate, is abol-

6. Edouard Glissant, *La Lézarde* (Paris: Seuil, 1958), p. 204. (Trans. J.M.D.)

Introduction

ished. It is in this untamed spectacle that Glissant locates the poetics of the cross-cultural imagination. It is a matter, not of searching for origins, but of immersing the self in this exemplary synchrony. In this vision of American time and space, Martinique is not simply a "speck of dust" upon the water but the essential point of reference for an entire continent.

Antillanité—from Matouba to Moncada
Carnival was the true feast of becoming, change, and renewal.
Mikhail Bakhtin, *Rabelais*

Universality paradoxically springs from regionalism. Thomas Hardy saw the world in Wessex, R. K. Narayan the world in Malgudi, García Márquez the world in Macondo. Edouard Glissant similarly locates in the Caribbean a process of global dimensions. Glissant's vision of the world is centered on the displacement of communities, the relocation of peoples, on the individual driven across languages, frontiers, cultures. To him it is pointless to look for remote origins, to establish hierarchies of great and small civilizations, since the process of metamorphosis is unceasing and inevitable. To this extent, the Caribbean is seen in *Caribbean Discourse* as an exemplary instance of intense patterns of mutation and creolization. In "Reversion and Diversion" this process of transformation is examined in great detail. In his essay "Cross-Cultural Poetics" Glissant poses this question:

> What is the Caribbean in fact? A multiple series of relationships. We all feel it, we express it in all kinds of hidden or twisted ways, or we fiercely deny it. But we sense that this sea exists within us with its weight of now revealed islands. The Caribbean Sea is not an American lake. It is the estuary of the Americas.

In the same way that the condition of the Caribbean is shared globally, Martinique within the Caribbean is presented as a solitary and absurd denial of the cross-cultural imagination by its desperate attachment to metropolitan France. Assimilation has meant for overseas departments like Martinique a denial of collective memory, of regional identity. Glissant points to the elemental intimacy that once existed in the Caribbean, binding Martinique to the history of an entire region: "Until the war of liberation waged by Toussaint Louverture, the peoples of Martinique, Guadeloupe, and Saint-Domingue (which then became Haiti) struggled together in solidarity. This applied as much to the colonizers as to the slaves in revolt and the freedmen (generally mulattoes). . . . Such was the case for Delgrès, of Martinican origin, who fell with his Guadeloupean companions at Fort Matouba in Guadeloupe, and whose example was so dear to the heart of Dessalines, Toussaint's lieutenant." But this history has been deliberately obscured. The victories of Toussaint and Martí came to be seen as local events, peculiar to Haiti and Cuba. Bolivar's stay in Haiti was another example of a regional event that has left no trace in the consciousness of Martinique. From this potential for a "global Caribbean history" the departure has been gradual and real. Colonization has successfully balkanized the region, creating divisive loyalties and a corrosive fragmentation. It is the writer's duty, as Glissant explains, to restore this forgotten memory and indicate the surviving links between the diverse communities of the region, to demonstrate the continuity, across time and space, between Delgrès's stand at Matouba and Castro's victory at Moncada. In the case of Martinique and Cuba, it is a matter of creating a nation in the Caribbean as well as of visualizing a Caribbean nation. The writer's role in inextricably tied to *le devenir de la communauté* (the future of the group), as Martinique's fate is tied to that of the Caribbean "one is really Caribbean because of wanting to be Martinican."

This ideal movement from insular solitude to regional solidarity in the Caribbean, from complacent denial to the generous acceptance of the archipelago, the "Other America," is the political manifestation of a deep-seated and pervasive mechanism in Glissant's thought and may even be an important re-

flex in the Caribbean sensibility. The flight from the plantation, the defiance of confinement, the movement away from
stasis is central to the imaginative discourse of the Caribbean.
Ex-stasis, or *marronnage* (escape), is the phenomenon with
which Glissant is constantly preoccupied. Perhaps this flight
from an enclosed world is expressed in the images of the ship,
the spiral, the journey that recur in Caribbean art. It can be
associated with the poetics of exuberance, of ecstasy, that is an
imaginative departure from the shipwrecked, petrified condition of the colonized mind. If the Caribbean imagination bal-
ances on this axis of shared images of mobility, Glissant's contribution may well be seen as an attempt to transcend the ideal
of flight to conceive of a new solidarity or *métissage* (creolization). It is the composite reality of the bastard that obsesses
Glissant, not the longing for a remote paternity.

Caribbean Discourse presents the Caribbean in terms of a
forest of becoming in the untamed landscape, in the human
carnival, in the interplay of linguistic and aesthetic forms. Un-
fettered by an authoritarian language or system, the human
forest of the carnival becomes an exemplary Caribbean space.
Individual and community, tree and forest, *parole* (individual
utterance) and *langue* (collective expression) interact as old
hierarchies are dismantled and old associations erased. In the
sculpture of the Cuban artist Cárdenas, Glissant senses this
creative disorder: "we do not acclaim the overwhelming stature of any one tree, we praise this language of the entire forest. Cárdenas's sculpture is not a single shout, it is sustained
speech: unceasing and deliberate, which is forever creating
and at every turn establishes something new." He sees it as
part of the "tradition of oral festivity" and corporeal rhythms.
In Cárdenas Glissant locates the use of the carnival model that
he prescribes as an essential component in a Caribbean sensibility: "the camouflaged escape of the carnival, which I feel
constitutes a desperate way out of the confining world of the
plantation."

Carnival, because of its baroque irreverence, its creative excess, represents the very opposite of the plantation or the Gar-

Introduction

den of Genesis, with its regulated and regimented space. In this new carnival aesthetic Glissant seems to both reaffirm the need for the individual to be immersed in the group and yet be interested in individual differences within the community. It is not simply a matter of the collective shaping force of *langue* overwhelming the individual utterance. Individual idiosyncrasy and choice is a vital part of this process of interaction. The essence of the carnival is its demonstration of a cross-cultural poetics, a joyous affirmation of relativity. There is in Glissant a reaction against the single-minded determinism of the modern structuralist devaluation of individual agency, while recognizing the need to valorize the inarticulate and the valid skepticism about the individual will, which is part of the modern linguistic approach to interpretation. For instance, on the subject of language he feels the need to assert that "we are collectively spoken by our words much more than we use them," but a popular revoluton in Martinique would allow Martinicans "to choose either one of the two languages they use, or to combine them into a new form of expression." Subjective autonomy is never free from, but never completely erased by, the everchanging context in *Caribbean Discourse.*

In this regard Glissant's ideas overlap with those of Octavio Paz from Mexico and Mikhail Bakhtin from Russia. No doubt the Soviet Union in the 1920s was a world in turmoil in which the old lines of authority were removed and had been replaced by a mixing of languages, cultures, and social groups. Bakhtin develops through his vision of the carnival an aesthetics of incompleteness in which a new exuberant relationship between body, language, and politics emerges and replaces an old and rigidly confirming order. Octavio Paz examines the Mexican fiesta as a plunge into the chaotic, the primordial. As an experiment in disorder the fiesta becomes, in Paz's words, "a revolution in the most literal sense of the word."[7] Glissant has similarly insisted in his various works on the importance of

7. Octavio Paz, *The Labyrinth of Solitude* (Harmondsworth: Penguin, 1985), p. 43.

Introduction

this plunge into primordial chaos as a means of both confronting self and interacting with the community. In particular, the novel *La Lézarde* depicts characters who leave their self-centered worlds, whether in the consoling shadows of the hills or on the inhibited lowlands. Knowledge lies in walking away from these complacent mental spaces and plunging into the vortex of ritual. This creative disorientation of the individual is evident in the town's festivities, in Thaël's immersion in the sea, in the victory procession after the elections.

In this tangle of new forms, this verbal carnality, Glissant visualizes the poetics of *Antillanité*. This idea stands in clear opposition to the longing for the virtues of clarity and the disincarnate aesthetic of those who wished to suppress the cross-cultural imagination. It also is opposed to the demiurgic reconstruction of the world in terms of some master text: Prospero's as well as Christophe's imposition of their high-minded rhetoric on the polyphonic voices that threaten their grand project of rehabilitation. *Antillanité* does not stress the static confrontation of cultures that is central to the ideas of negritude. The poetics of carnival is highly valued because it is a form of *révolution permanente* (permanent revolution), of ceaseless change. Immobility and alienation are the necessary consequences and the facilitating circumstances of exploitation. In the case of Martinique it might mean repossessing the carnival, which has been appropriated by the official media as a kind of local eccentricity. It might mean giving it both direction and a new expressiveness through a popular theater. Whatever the form, there is a need to move from the intuitive sense of being Caribbean to a conscious expression of Caribbeanness.

> We cannot deny the reality: cultures derived from plantations; insular civilization (where the Caribbean Sea disperses, whereas, for instance, one reckons that an equally civilizing sea, the Mediterranean, had primarily the potential for attraction and concentration); social pyramids with an Af-

Introduction

rican or East Indian base and a European peak; languages of compromise; general cultural phenomenon of creolization; pattern of encounter and synthesis; persistence of the African presence; cultivation of sugarcane, corn, and pepper; site where rhythms are combined; peoples formed by orality.

The vision of *Antillanité* remains for Glissant a precarious but persistent one. The French overseas departments are vulnerable because of their lack of local self-supporting productivity, their self-inflicted cultural alexia, making their world unintelligible, and the absence of responsible leadership. A recent spate of bombings (1983) suggests a growing impatience among the young. The intervention of larger nations also undermines the possibility of regionalism, yet the dream remains, and there are moments when it is fulfilled—for a short time. In the essay "Carifesta 1976" Glissant, after experiencing in Kingston a sense of a collective Caribbean consciousness during Carifesta celebrations, asks the question "Is Martinique a cyst in a zone of Caribbean civilization?" The answer might still be dismaying to Glissant. In his recent novel *Mahagony*, he describes Martinique as a museum, isolated from its cultural and political context.[8] However, in *Caribbean Discourse* he offers to a society in extremis, yet smugly certain of its metropolitan heritage, a Caribbean and American identity that it so far seems reluctant to claim. *Caribbean Discourse* is "the account of an expedition into the universe of the Americas," but the sad truth, as he admits in *Malemort*, is that the *lecteurs d'ici* (local audience) are still less receptive to this message than the *lecteurs d'ailleurs* (foreign audience).

ACKNOWLEDGMENTS

I wish to thank Edouard Glissant and James Arnold for their encouragement and assistance. I am also grateful to Marcia

8. Edouard Glissant, *Mahagony* (Paris: Seuil, 1987), p. 178.

Lawrence, who typed the manuscript, and to Cynthia Foote, who read the manuscript with special care and consideration.

J. Michael Dash
University of the
West Indies
Mona

Bibliography

PRINCIPAL WORKS BY EDOUARD GLISSANT

Poetry

Un champ d'îles. Paris: Editions du Dragon, 1953.
La terre inquiète. Paris: Editions du Dragon, 1954.
Les Indes. Paris: Seuil, 1955. Reprinted 1985.
Le sel noir. Paris: Seuil, 1959.
Le sang rivé. Paris: Présence Africaine, 1960.
Poèmes: Un champ d'îles; La terre inquiète; Les Indes. Paris: Seuil, 1965.
Boises. Paris: Acoma, 1977.
Le sel noir; Le sang rivé; Boises. Paris: Gallimard, 1983.
Pays rêvé, pays réel. Paris: Seuil, 1985.

Fiction

La Lézarde. Paris: Seuil, 1958. Renaudot Prize. Reprinted 1984.
Le quatrième siècle. Paris: Seuil, 1964.
Malemort. Paris: Seuil, 1975.
La case du commandeur. Paris: Seuil, 1981.
Mahagony. Paris: Seuil, 1987.

Theater

Monsieur Toussaint. Paris: Seuil, 1961. Stage version. Paris: Seuil, 1986.

Bibliography

Essay

Soleil de la conscience. Paris: Seuil, 1956.
L'intention poétique. Paris: Seuil, 1969.
Le discours antillais. Paris: Seuil, 1981.

WORKS BY EDOUARD GLISSANT IN
ENGLISH TRANSLATION

Monsieur Toussaint: A Play. Trans. Joseph G. Foster and Barbara Franklin, introducton and notes by Juris Silenieks. Washington, D.C.: Three Continents Press, 1981.
The Ripening. Trans. [J.] Michael Dash. London and Kingston: Heinemann, 1985. Caribbean Writers Series, 34.

LITERARY CRITICISM IN ENGLISH
ON EDOUARD GLISSANT

Burton, Richard. " 'Comment peut-on être Martiniquais?' The Recent Work of Edouard Glissant." *The Modern Language Review* 79, no. 2 (April 1984): 301–12.
Case, Frederick Ivor. "The Novels of Edouard Glissant." *Black Images* 2, nos. 3–4 (Autumn-Winter 1973): 3–12.
Dash, J. Michael. "Introduction." *The Ripening* by Edouard Glissant. London and Kingston: Heinemann, 1985.
Ormerod, Beverley. "Beyond *Négritude;* Some Aspects of the Work of Edouard Glissant." *Contemporary Literature* 15, no. 3 (Summer 1974): 360–69.
———. "Discourse and Dispossession; Edouard Glissant's Image of Contemporary Martinique." *Caribbean Quarterly* 27, no. 4 (1981): 1–12.
Silenieks, Juris. "Glissant's Prophetic Vision of the Past." *African Literature Today,* no. 11 (1980): 161–68.

Introductions

From a "dead-end" situation

Martinique is not a Polynesian island. This is, however, the belief of so many people who, given its reputation, would love to go there for pleasure. I know someone, who has always been dedicated to the Caribbean cause, who would jokingly assert that West Indians (he meant French-speaking West Indians) have achieved the ultimate in subhumanity. A Martinican political figure imagined as a bitter joke that in the year 2100, tourists would be invited by satellite advertisement to visit this island and gain firsthand knowledge of "what a colony was like in past centuries." This bitter laughter disguises a widespread anxiety: an inability to escape the present impasse. Rather than fulminate against these assertions, it is worthwhile to examine what made their formulation possible. Let us place them alongside the following episode. This was obligingly said to a French psychiatrist who voiced his concern about the ravages of mental disorder in Martinique, by a prefect who was no less French: "That is not important. The essential thing is that material poverty has *visibly* diminished. You no longer see malnourished children on the roadside. The problems you now raise are almost irrelevant."

These anecdotes, which seem loosely linked with reality, nevertheless circumscribe the object of my study. It was a matter of tracking down every manifestation of the multiple processes, the confusion of indicators that have ultimately woven for a people, which had at its disposal so many trained officials and individuals, the web of nothingness in which it is ensnared today.

An "intellectual" effort, with its repetitive thrusts (repetition has a rhythm), its contradictory moments, its necessary imperfections, its demands for formulation (even a schematic one), very often obscured by its very purpose. For the attempt to approach a reality so often hidden from view cannot be organized in terms of a series of clarifications. We demand the right to obscurity. Through which our anxiety to have a full existence becomes part of the universal drama of cultural transformation: the creativity of marginalized peoples who today confront the ideal of transparent universality, imposed by the West,[1] with secretive and multiple manifestations of Diversity. Such a process is spectacular everywhere in the world where murders, shameless acts of genocide, tactics of terror, try to crush the precious resistance of various peoples. It is imperceptible when we are dealing with communities condemned as such to painless oblivion.

The discourse of such communities (those shadowy threads of meaning where their silence is voiced) must be studied if we wish to gain a profound insight into the drama of creolization taking place on a global scale. Even if we consider this silence and this emptiness as meaningless in the face of the terrible and definitive muteness of those peoples physically undermined and overwhelmed by famine and disease, terror and devastation—which well-heeled countries accommodate so easily.

(Yes. The anxious serenity of our existence, through so many obscure channels linked to the trembling world. In our detached stillness, something somewhere breaks free from someone's suffering or hurt and comes to rest in us. The salt of death on exhausted men, wandering across a desert that is certainly not freedom. The devastation of entire peoples. Those

---

1. The West is not in the West. It is a project, not a place.

who are sold. Children blinded by their incomprehensible agony. Victims of torture who see death lingering in the distance. The smell of oil on dusty skins. The growing layers of mud. We are at the outer edge and remain silent.

But all this commotion burns silently in our minds. The bloodstained swirl of the planet stuns us without our realizing it. We guess that in the world a number of people in the same state of trepidation might be suffering from this common condition.

In this way each discourse implies concurrence. It does not matter that our raw materials are not exhausted here, that the multinationals do not exploit us brutally, that pollution is still slight, that our people are not gunned down at every turn, and that we cannot imagine the terrible methods used here and there for profit and death—nevertheless, we are part of the disorientation of the world. A morbid unreason and a stubborn urgency make us part of a global process. The same H bomb is for everyone.

The discourse of various peoples brings a certain pace and rhythm to this stabbing pulsebeat. Creolization is, first, the unknown awareness of the creolized. Unreason can be stubborn and urgency morbid. We are shown for example the advantage of large groupings; and I still believe in the future of small countries. In such communities, the process of creolization is expressed in moments of identifiable irrationality, is structured in comprehensive attempts at liberation. An analysis of this discourse points to that which, in the immense devastation of the world, emerges gradually in barely perceptible traces and allows us to carry on. The issue we consider here does not provide us with the arms to fight an economic war, a total war, in which all peoples are involved today. But each critical approach to the kind of contact existing between peoples and cultures makes us suspect that one day men will perhaps call a halt, staggered by the singular wisdom of creolization that will be a part of them—and that they will then recognize our hesitant clairvoyance.)

Caribbean Discourse

From this discourse on a discourse

Our intention in this work was *to pull together all levels of experience*. This piling-up is the most suitable technique for exposing a reality that is itself being scattered. Its evolution is like a repetition of a few obsessions that *take root*, tied to realities that *keep slipping away*. The intellectual journey is destined to have a geographical itinerary, through which the "intention" within the Discourse explores its space and into which it is woven.

The Caribbean, the Other America. Banging away incessantly at the main ideas will perhaps lead to exposing the space they occupy in us. Repetition of these ideas does not clarify their expression; on the contrary, it perhaps leads to obscurity. We need those stubborn shadows where repetition leads to perpetual concealment, which is our form of resistance.

The summary of a journey, the account of an expedition into the universe of the Americas, this multiple discourse carries the stamp of an oral exposé, thus making a link with one of its most promising agonies. When the oral is confronted with the written, secret accumulated hurts suddenly find expression; the individual finds a way out of the confined circle. He makes contact, beyond every lived humiliation, a collective meaning, a universal poetics, in which each voice is important, in which each lived moment *finds an explanation*.

(Thus, Caribbean discourse cannot be readily seized. But does not the world, in its exploded oneness, demand that each person be drawn to the recognized inscrutability of the other? This is one aspect of our inscrutability).

To risk the Earth, dare to explore its forbidden or misunderstood impulses. Establish in so doing our own dwelling place. The history of all peoples is the ultimate point of our imaginative unconscious.

Introductions

From a presentation distant in space and time

From the persistent myth of the paradise islands to the deceptive appearance of overseas departments, it seemed that the French West Indies were destined to be always in an unstable relationship with their own reality. It is as if these countries were condemned to never make contact with their true nature, since they were paralyzed by being scattered geographically and also by one of the most pernicious forms of colonization: the one by means of which a community becomes *assimilated*.

Indeed, there are numerous opportunities that were lost by the French West Indians themselves. The cruel truth is that Guadeloupe and Martinique have undergone a long succession of periods of repression, following countless revolts since the eighteenth century more or less, and the result on each occasion has been a more visible abandonment of the *collective spirit*, of the common will that alone allows a people to survive as a people.

So, the geographical layout. It would seem that this scattering of islands in the Caribbean sea, which in effect constituted a natural barrier to penetration (although it could be established that the Arawaks and the Caribs ploughed through this sea before the arrival of Columbus), should no longer be of significance in a world opened by modern means of communication. But in fact colonization has divided into English, French, Dutch, Spanish territories a region where the majority of the population is African: making strangers out of people who are not. The thrust of negritude among Caribbean intellectuals was a response perhaps to the need, by relating to a common origin, to rediscover unity (equilibrium) beyond dispersion.

While the structures of economic domination were being developed between the metropole and its colony, a double conviction was reinforced in the French Caribbean: first that these countries cannot survive by themselves; then that their inhabitants are French in actual fact, in contrast to the other colonized peoples who remain African or Indochinese. The French Caribbean then provides officers and subofficers for the colonization of Africa, where they are considered as whites and, alas, behave in that manner. French policy deliberately favors the emergence of a group of lower-level officials, from which a psuedoelite is formed, and who are persuaded that they are part of the Great Motherland. The big planters (who are called *békés* by us) will eventually learn that this system is their best form of protection. Forever unwilling to involve themselves in the national development of Martinique, they will become the commission agents of the new system, with substantial profits and a real inability to make economic decisions. The entry of the French Caribbean islands in the sterile zone of a tertiary economy was inevitable.

What was missing was a national base that would have made possible a concerted resistance against depersonalization. So we saw, in Martinique and in Guadeloupe, a people of African descent for whom the word *African* or the word *Negro* generally represented an insult. While the Caribbean masses danced the *laghia,* so obviously inherited from the Africans, Caribbean judges sentenced in Africa those whom they were helping to colonize. When a people collectively denies its mission, the result can only be disequilibrium and arrogance.

But all peoples one day come of age. If French Caribbean people have not inherited an atavistic culture, they are not thereby condemned to an inexorable deculturation. On the contrary. The tendency to synthesis can only be an advantage, in a world destined to synthesis and to the "contact of civilizations." The essential point here is that Caribbean people should not entrust to others the job of defining their culture. And that this tendency to synthesis does not fall into the kind of humanism where idiots get trapped.

Until the war of liberation waged by Toussaint Louverture, the peoples of Martinique, Guadeloupe, and Saint-Domingue (which then became Haiti) struggled together in solidarity. This applied as much to the colonizers as to the slaves in revolt and the freedmen (generally mulattoes); movement, sometimes limited, is not necessarily less permanent. Solidarity as well. Such was the case for Delgrès, of Martinican origin, who fell with his Guadeloupean companions at Fort Matouba in Guadeloupe, and whose example was so dear to the heart of Dessalines, Toussaint's lieutenant.

Haiti free but cut off from the world (international assistance did not exist, nor did the socialist countries, nor the countries of the Third World, nor the United Nations) the process of exchange that could have *created* the Caribbean dried up. Slave revolts, crushed in the small islands, are reduced to a succession of Jacqueries without support or the possibility of entrenchment and expansion; without expression or consequence. After the "liberation" of 1848, the struggle for freedom gives way in the French Caribbean to the demand for citizenship. The colonizers launch their creations in the political arena. The middle class, greedy for honors and respectability, willingly adapts to this game that guarantees posts and titles. The game culminates in the law of departmentalization in 1946, which constitutes in this matter the summit of achievement. French Caribbean people are thus encouraged to deny themselves as a collectivity, in order to achieve an illusory individual equality. Assimilation made balkanization complete.

The alarmed observer then realizes that unbelievable cowardice is a characteristic of the French Caribbean elite. Imitation is the rule (imitation of the French model), and any departure is considered a crime. This is the period of the literature of island exoticism in which a whining sentimentality prevailed. Also originating from this period, without the slightest doubt, is the feeling "You are not really so black" (or "You are like us, not like the Negroes") that our elite have so often had thrown in their face and, let us be frank, have legitimized. (There has been progress in this. In 1979, it is permissible to say explicitly in Martinican French: "Deep down, you are no more Caribbean than I am," which signifies the ultimate weakening of the elite.)

Each time this people rose up against its fate there has resulted an implacable repression, each time followed by a thinning out and further entrapment. There is a long list of missed opportunities. The reason for this is that the elite have never been able to propose (as would have been their function) the possibility of resistance for the masses who were struggling in specific conditions (the smallness of the islands, isolation, cultural ambiguity) against the denial of their existence. In this regard, political mimicry that has led these countries astray (you find there exactly the same parties as in France, and they appear or disappear according to the fluctuations of internal French politics) was an inspired creation of the colonial structure.

Today the French Caribbean individual does not deny the African part of himself; he does not have, in reaction, to go to the extreme of celebrating it exclusively. He must *recognize* it. He understands that from all this history (even if we lived it like a nonhistory) *another reality* has come about. He is no longer forced to reject strategically the European elements in his composition, although they continue to be a source of alienation, since he knows that he can choose between them. He can see that alienation first and foremost resides in the impossibility of choice, in the arbitrary imposition of values, and, perhaps, in the concept of value itself. He can conceive that synthesis is not a process of bastardization as he used to be told, but a productive activity through which each element is enriched. He has *become* Caribbean.

The notion of Caribbean unity is a form of cultural self-discovery. It fixes us in the truth of our existence, it forms part of the struggle for self-liberation. It is a concept that cannot be managed for us by others: Caribbean unity cannot be guided by remote control.

Introductions

From tracks left yesterday and today, mixed together

This people, as you know, was deported from Africa to these islands for servile labor on the land. "Liberated" in 1848, they found themselves fettered in two ways: because of the impossibility of producing by and for themselves and because of the resulting impotence in *collectively* asserting their true selves. Consequently, Martinicans lead an agitated existence, violently and irrevocably severed from the motherland of Africa and painfully, inevitably, and improbably cut off from the dreamland of France.

Off the coast of Senegal, Gorée, the island before the open sea, the first step towards madness.

Then the sea, never seen from the depths of the ship's hold, punctuated by drowned bodies that sowed in its depths explosive seeds of absence.

The factory where you disembark, more patched together than rags, more sterile than a razed field. The choice of pillage.

Elections where your stomach hurts endlessly. An economy of frustration. The cave where your dependency becomes bloated.

Vaval, giant of the carnival, instinctively paraded: high above us. We burn him in this sea.

Béhanzin, "African King," mirror of exiles, through whom we denied ourselves. He continues to wander among our fellowmen.

The crab-filled swamps, the flatness of the plantations, the factories overgrown with grass: the land contracts, and the cactus, and the sold-out sands.

The machete, more twisted than knotted entrails.

Caribbean Discourse

From the landscape

Because it is a concentrated whole that offers an intelligible dimension. At the same time, the threshold of heat blocked by rain; deeper yet, those fissures that become visible when the landscape unfolds.

In the north of the country, the knotted mass of somber greens which the roads still do not penetrate. The maroons found refuge there. What you can oppose to the facts of history. The night in full daylight and the filtered shadows. The root of the vine and its violet flower. The dense network of ferns. The primordial mud, impenetrable and primal. Under the acomas that disappear from view, the stuffy, erect mahogany trees supported by blue beaches on a human scale. The North and the mountains are one. There were dumped those peoples from India who were part of the nineteenth-century trade (making the process of creolization complete) and whom we call Coolies, in Guadeloupe, Malabars. Today, the flat fields of pineapple cut arid grooves in this aloof and remote world. Yet this prickly flatness is dominated by the shadow of the great forests. The strikers of the Lorrain district, coolies and blacks, all Martinican, were trapped there in 1976: *they turned over with their machetes the field of leaves soaked in blood.*

In the Center, the literal undulations of the cane fields. The mountains are subdued and become hills. Ruins of factories lurk there as a witness to the old order of the plantations. Where the setting sun yawns, marking the difference between the northern mountains and the central plains, the ruins of the Dubuc Great House (Château Dubuc) where the slaves disembarked (an echo of the island of Gorée they left behind) and where slave prisons still lie hidden underground. What we call the Plain, into which the Lézarde River emptied and from which the crabs have disappeared. The delta has been chewed up by make-believe enterprises, by an airstrip. Falling away before us, tiers of banana trees, a curtain of dense green foam between us and the land. On the walls of a house in Lamentin star-shaped bullet holes still remain from which year we no longer know when three striking cane workers were slaughtered by the police.

Finally the South, with its scattering of goats. The agitation of the beaches, forgetful of all who climbed the coconut trees, once trying to reach out to Toussaint Louverture in the land of Haiti. The salt of the sea claimed them. The whites of their eyes are in the glare of our sun. We come to a halt, not certain what slows us down at that spot with a strange uneasiness. These beaches are up for grabs. The tourists say they own them. They are the ultimate frontier, visible evidence of our past wanderings and our present distress.

So history is spread out beneath this surface, from the mountains to the sea, from north to south, from the forest to the beaches. Maroon resistance and denial, entrenchment and endurance, the world beyond and dream.

(Our landscape is its own monument: its meaning can only be traced on the underside. It is all history.)

From the lack of speech and from Creole

When the experience of reading, then access to "knowledge," is *granted* to a fraction of a community with an oral tradition (and this is done by an elitist system of education), the resulting dislocation is limited in its effect. One part of this elite is "wild" about its brand new knowledge; the rest of the community retains for some time, and alongside this delirium, its sanity.

If this "learning" spreads, without being related to an autonomous process of acquiring appropriate techniques, the disequilibrium of the elite becomes the norm that itself becomes "widespread," through which the entire subjugated community consents passively to surrender itself, its potential development, its real culture.

And if such an operation is conducted against a community whose oral language bears the secret, unlikely, and elusive stamp of the written one (this is the case, as we shall see, with the Creole language in Martinique), dispossession is likely to be terminal. A close scrutiny of this dispossession is one way of fighting against collective self-destruction.

This project is even more necessary because in Martinique (a country where illusion has constantly been stronger than reality) we are led in our journey by the once-again-visible mirages of social and economic progress. It would seem that the discourse on discourse (the reexamination of self) has come too late and that as a community we have lost the meaning of our own voice.

Also, how ridiculous it is to describe in books, to approach through the written word, that which just evaporates all around us.

Would an awakening to orality and the explosion of Creole satisfy the deficiency? Is the revolution that would nurture them still possible? Is the land which will *understand* them still there around us?

The Known, the Uncertain

DISPOSSESSION

Landmarks
The chronological illusion

It is possible to reduce our chronology to a basic skeleton of "facts," in any combination. For instance:

1502	"Discovery" of Martinique by Columbus.
1635	Occupation by the first French colonizers.
	Beginning of the extermination of the Caribs.
	Beginning of the African slave trade.
1685	Proclamation of the *Code Noir* by Colbert.
1763	Louis XV surrenders Canada to the English and retains Guadeloupe, Martinique, and St. Domingue (Haiti).
1789–97	Occupation of Martinique by the British.
1848	Abolition of slavery.
1902	Eruption of Mt. Pelée. Destruction of St. Pierre.
1946	Departmentalization.
1975	Doctrine of "economic" assimilation.

Once this chronological table has been set up and completed, the whole history of Martinique remains to be unraveled. The whole Caribbean history of Martinique remains to be discovered.

Caribbean Discourse

Reversion and Diversion

I

There is a difference between the transplanting (by exile or dispersion) of a people who continue to survive elsewhere and the transfer (by the slave trade) of a population to another place where they change into something different, into a new set of possibilities. It is in this metamorphosis that we must try to detect one of the best kept secrets of creolization. Through it we can see that the mingling of experiences is at work, there for us to know and producing the process of being. We abandon the idea of fixed being. One of the most terrible implications of the ethnographic approach is the insistence on fixing the object of scrutiny in static time, thereby removing the tangled nature of lived experience and promoting the idea of uncontaminated survival. This is how those generalized projections of a series of events that obscure the network of real links become established.[1] The history of a transplanted population, but one which elsewhere becomes another people, allows us to resist generalization and the limitations it imposes. Relationship (at the same time link and linked, act and speech) is emphasized over what in appearance could be conceived as a governing principle, the so-called universal "controlling force."

The nature of the slave trade forces the population subjected to it to question in several ways any attempt at universal generalization. Western thought, although studying it as a historical phenomenon, persists in remaining silent about the potential of the slave trade for the process of creolization.

First of all, because to have to change to an unprecedented degree forces the transplanted population to desecrate, to view critically (with a kind of derision or approximation),

---

1. Naturally, generalization has allowed the establishment of systematic scientific laws, within which it is not irrelevant to observe Western science has been confined, in the realm of the objective and the "remote."

what, in the old order of things, was a permanent, ritualized truth of its existence. A population that undergoes transformation in a distant place is tempted to abandon pure collective faith. Then, because the method of transformation (domination by the Other) sometimes favors the practice of approximation or the tendency to derision, it introduces into the new relationship the insidious promise of being remade in the Other's image, the illusion of successful mimesis. Because of which a single universal impulse prevails in an inconsequential way. Finally, because domination (favored by dispersion and transplantation) produces the worst kind of change, which is that it provides, on its own, models of resistance to the stranglehold it has imposed, thus short-circuiting resistance while making it possible. With the consequence that meaningless know-how will encourage the illusion of universal transcendence. A relocated people struggles against all of this.

I feel that what makes this difference between a people that survives elsewhere, *that maintains its original nature,* and a population that is transformed elsewhere *into another people* (without, however, succumbing to the reductive pressures of the Other) and that thus enters the constantly shifting and variable process of creolization (of relationship, of relativity), is that the latter has not brought with it, not collectively continued, the methods of existence and survival, both material and spiritual, which it practiced before being uprooted. These methods leave only dim traces or survive in the form of spontaneous impulses. This is what distinguishes, besides the persecution of one and the enslavement of the other, the Jewish Diaspora from the African slave trade. And, if only because the relocated population does not find itself, at the point of arrival and of taking root, in conditions that would favor the invention or "free" adoption of new and appropriate techniques, this population enters for a more or less long period of time a stagnant and often intangible zone of general irresponsibility. This is probably what would distinguish in general (and not individual by individual) the Martinican from another example of relocation, the Brazilian. Such a disposition is even more significant because violent use of technology (the growing disparity between the levels of manipulation and control of reality) is becoming a primordial factor in human relations worldwide. Two of the most unfounded attitudes in this situation may be to overestimate the importance of technical support as the substratum of all human activity and, at the other extreme, to reduce all technical systems to the level of an alien or degrading ideology. Technical impotence drives the colonized to these extreme positions. Whatever we think of such options, we feel that the word *technical* must be understood in the sense of an organized method used by a group to deal with its surroundings. The slave trade, which partly provided the population of the Americas, discriminated among the new arrivals; technical innocence has favored in the francophone Lesser Antilles more than anywhere else in the black diaspora, a fascination with imitation and the tendency to approximation (that is, in fact, to the denigration of original values).

Therein lie not only distress and loss but also the opportunity to assert a considerable set of possibilities. For instance, the possibility of dealing with "values" no longer in absolute terms but as active agents of synthesis. (The abandonment of pure original values allows for an unprecedented potential for contact.) Also the possibility of criticizing more naturally a conception of universal anonymity and of banishing this illusion to the body of beliefs of the imitative elite.

II

The first impulse of a transplanted population which is not sure of maintaining the old order of values in the transplanted locale is that of reversion. Reversion is the obsession with a single origin: one must not alter the absolute state of being. To revert is to consecrate permanence, to negate contact. Reversion will be recommended by those who favor single origins. (However, the return of the Palestinians to their country is not a strategic maneuver; it is an immediate struggle. Expulsion and return are totally contemporary. This is not a compensatory impulse but vital urgency.) White Americans thought they had in the last century gotten rid of the problem of the blacks by financing the return of blacks to Africa and by the creation of the state of Liberia. Strange barbarism. Even if one is satisfied or happy that a part of the black population of the United States had by this means escaped the terrible fate of the slaves and the new freedmen, one cannot fail to recognize the level of frustration implied by such a process in the scenario for creolization. The primary characteristic of the latter, the contemporary manifestation of contact between peoples, is indeed the even obscure awareness that these peoples have of it. Previous contacts were not accompanied in the same way by a consciousness of this consciousness. In the contemporary situation a population that would activate the impulse towards return without having become a people would be destined to face bitter memories of *possibilities* forever lost (for example, the emancipation of blacks in *the United States itself*). The flight of the Jews out of the land of Egypt was collective; they had maintained their Judaism, they had not been transformed into *anything else*. What to make of the fate of those who return to Africa, helped and encouraged by the calculating philanthropy of their masters, but *who are no longer African?* The fulfilment of this impulse *at this point* (it is already too late for it) is not satisfactory. It is possible that the state formed in this way (a convenient palliative) would not become a nation. Might one hazard a guess, on the other hand, that the existence of the nation-state of Israel may ultimately *dry up* Judaism, by exhausting progressively the impulse towards return (the demand for true origins)?[2]

2. The analysis of any global discourse inevitably reveals the systematic development of well-known situations (proof for all to see), as for instance on the map of significant situations in the relations between one people and another.

A transplanted population that becomes a people (Haiti), that blends into another people (Peru), that becomes part of a multiple whole (Brazil), that maintains its identity without being able to be "fulfilled" (North America),

Caribbean Discourse

As we have seen, however, populations transplanted by the slave trade were not capable of maintaining for any length of time the impulse to revert. This impulse will decline, therefore, as the memory of the ancestral country fades. Wherever in the Americas technical know-how is maintained or renewed for a relocated population, whether oppressed or dominant, the impulse to revert will recede little by little with the need to come to terms with the new land. Where that coming to terms is not only difficult but made *inconceivable* (the population having become a people, but a powerless one) the obsession with imitation will appear. This obsession does not generate itself. Without saying that it is not natural (it is a kind of violence), one can establish that it is futile. Not only is imitation itself not workable but real obsession with it is intolerable. The mimetic impulse is a kind of insidious violence. A people that submits to it takes some time to realize its consequences collectively and critically, but is immediately afflicted by the resulting trauma. In Martinique, where the relocated population has evolved into a people, without, however, coming effectively to terms with the new land, the community has tried to exorcise the impossibility of return by what I call the practice of diversion.

---

that is a people wedged in an impossible situation (Martinique), that returns partially to its place of origin (Liberia), that maintains its identity while participating reluctantly in the emergence of a people (East Indians in the Caribbean).

A dispersed people that generates on its own the impulse to return (Israel), that is expelled from its land (Palestine), whose expulsion is "internal" (South African blacks).

A people that reconquers its land (Algeria), that disappears through genocide (Armenians), that is in distress (Melanesians), that is made artificial (Micronesians).

The infinite variety of "independent" African states (where official frontiers separate genuine ethnic groups), the convulsions of minorities in Europe (Bretons or Catalans, Corsicans or Ukrainians). The slow death of the aborigines of Australia.

People with a millenarian tradition and conquering ways (the British), with a universalizing will (the French), victims of separatism (Ireland), of emigration (Sicily), of division (Cyprus), of artificial wealth (Arab countries).

III

Diversion is not a systematic refusal to *see*. No, it is not a kind of self-inflicted blindness nor a conscious strategy of flight in the face of reality. Rather, we would say that it is formed, like a habit, from an interweaving of negative forces that go unchallenged. Diversion is not possible when a nation is already formed, that is each time that a general sense of responsibility—even when exploited for the profit of part of the group—has resolved, in a provisional but autonomous way, internal or class conflicts. There is no diversion when the community

---

People who quickly abandoned their "expansion" or maintained it only in a halfhearted way (Scandinavians; Italy), who have been invaded in their own land (Poland, Central Europe). Migrants themselves (Algerians, Portuguese, Caribbean people in France and England).

Conquered or exterminated peoples (American Indians), those who are neutralized (Andean Indians), who are pursued and massacred (Indians in the Amazon). The hunted down and drifting people (Tziganes or Gypsies).

Immigrant populations who constitute the dominant group (the United States), who retain their identity within the larger group (Quebec), who maintain their position by force (South African whites).

Organized and widely scattered emigrants (Syrians, Lebanese, Chinese).

Periodic migrants, resulting from the very contact between cultures (missionaries, the Peace Corps; their French equivalent, the *coopérants*), and whose impact is real.

Nations divided by language or religion (the Irish people, the Belgian or Lebanese nationals), that is, by economic confrontation between groups.

Stable federations (Switzerland).

Endemic instabilities (people of the Indochinese peninsula).

Old civilizations transformed through acculturation with the West (China, Japan, India). Those which are maintained through insularity (Madagascar).

Composite people but "cut off" (Australians) and even more resistant to other peoples.

Scattered peoples, condemned to "adaptation" (Lapps, Polynesians).

These graphic models are complicated by the tangle of superimposed ideologies, by language conflicts, by religious wars, by economic confrontations, by technical revolutions. The permutations of cultural contact change more quickly than any one theory could account for. No theory of cultural contact is conducive to generalization. Its operation is further intensified by the emergence of minorities that identify themselves as such and of which the most influential is undoubtedly the feminist movement.

confronts an enemy recognized as such. Diversion is the ultimate resort of a population whose domination by an Other is concealed: it then must search *elsewhere* for the principle of domination, which is not evident in the country itself: because the system of domination (which is not only exploitation, which is not only misery, which is not only underdevelopment, but actually the complete eradication of an economic entity) is not directly tangible. Diversion is the parallactic displacement of this strategy.

Its deception is not therefore systematic, just as the *other world* that is frequented can indeed be on the "inside." It is an "attitude of collective release" (Marcuse).

The Creole language is the first area of diversion, and only in Haiti has it managed to escape this peculiar outcome. I must admit that the controversy over the origin and the composition of the language (Is it a language? Is it a deformation of French Speech? etc.) bores me; I am no doubt wrong to feel this way. For me what is most apparent in the dynamics of Creole is the continuous process of undermining its innate capacity for transcending its French origins. Michel Benamou advanced the hypothesis (repeated in Martinique in an article by M. Roland Suvélor) of a systematic process of derision: the slave takes possession of the language imposed by his master, a simplified language, adopted to the demands of his labor (a black pidgin) and makes this simplication even more extreme. You wish to reduce me to a childish babble, I will make this babble systematic, we shall see if you can make sense of it. Creole would then become a language that, in its structures and its dynamics, would have fundamentally incorporated the derisive nature of its formation. It is the self-made man among all pidgins, the king of all "patois," who crowned himself. Linguists have noticed that traditional Creole syntax spontaneously imitates the speech of the child (the use of repetition, for example, *pretty pretty baby* for *very pretty child*). Taken to this extreme, the systematic use of childish speech is not naive. I can identify in it—at the level of the structures that the language creates for itself (and perhaps it is a little unusual to treat a language as a voluntary creation that generates itself)—what black Americans are supposed to have adopted as a linguistic *reaction* each time they were in the presence of whites: lisping, slurring, jibberish. Camouflage. That is the context that facilitates diversion. The Creole language was constituted around this strategy of trickery. Today, no black American needs to resort to such a scenario: I suppose that few whites would fall for it; in the same way the Creole language in Martinique has gone beyond the process of being structured by the need for camouflage. But it has been marked by it. It slips from pun to pun, from assonance to assonance, from misunderstanding to ambiguity, etc. This is perhaps why witticisms, with their careful and calculated element of surprise, are rare in this language, and always rather crude. The climax of Creole speech does not release an appreciative smile, but the laughter of participation. It is by its nature unsubtle, thus demonstrating its link with a persistent practice among storytellers almost everywhere: poetic toastmasters, *griots,* etc. Haitian Creole quickly evolved beyond the trickster strategy, for the simple historical reason that it became very early the productive and responsible language of the Haitian people.

I have found in *La vie des mots* by Arsène Darmesteter, a work of "linguistic philosophy" devoted to the evolution of meanings of words in the French language and in some aspects "pre-Saussurean," the following observation: "One can still find actual examples of the influence of popular humor as it deforms words whose meanings are fixed and recognized in certain expressions. One discovers with surprise words of learned origin, having in scientific language their full and complete significance, that are reduced in popular usage to ridiculous or degrading functions. . . . A crude irony seems to take pleasure in degrading these misunderstood words and to inflict the vengeance of popular ignorance on the language of the educated."[3] The author's surprise became horror in the

3. 1886; second edition published in Paris by Delagrave, 1918.

face of the same practices found in the *joal* speech of the Québecois, in which the process of systematic derision can be seen at work at the very heart of a language (French) to which they nevertheless lay claim. It is not surprising that *joal* should have symbolized a period of Quebecois resistance to domination by anglophone Canada, nor for that matter that this symbol tended to disappear as such when Quebec could envisage itself as a nation and participate in the process of nation-building.

The strategy of diversion *can therefore lead somewhere* when the obstacle for which the detour was made tends to develop into concrete "possibilities."[4]

I think that religious syncretism is also a possible product of the tactic of diversion. There is something excessive in the element of spectacle in this syncretism, whether in Brazilian rituals, in Voudou, or in the rites practiced in the Martinican countryside. The difference once again is that what was a trickster strategy became elsewhere (in Brazil, in Haiti) a popular belief with a "positive" potential, whereas it continues here (in Martinique) as a "negative" relic, which therefore constantly needs to revert to the strategy of diversion in order to function. The nature of popular belief in Martinique is that it still functions as if *the Other is listening.*[5]

We can find quite logically one of the most dramatic manifestations of the need for the strategy of diversion in a threatened community in the migration of French Caribbean people

4. In this work, *positive* or *positiveness* is taken to mean that which activates a process in a way that is continuous or discontinuous, "economical" or non"economical," with the thrust of a collective will, whether impulsive or deliberate. Consequently, the negative (or negativity) is not a stage in the dialectical process, but the loss, the absence that prevents a natural collectivity (that is, whose conditions for existing are given) from becoming an actual collectivity (that is, whose capacity to exist becomes stronger and more explicit).

5. See, in this regard, comments on the discourse of M. Evrard Suffrin, who founded in Lamentin, Martinique, the Dogma of Ham movement: section 74 of the Paris edition of *Le discours antillais* (Seuil, 1981), p. 381.

to France (which has often been described as an officially sanctioned slave trade in reverse) and in the psychic trauma that it has unleashed. It is very often only in France that migrant French Caribbean people discover they are *different*, become aware of their Caribbeanness; an awareness that is all the more disturbing and unliveable, since the individual so possessed by the feeling of identity cannot, however, manage to return to his origins (there he will find that the situation is intolerable, his colleagues irresponsible; they will find him too *assimilé*, too European in his ways, etc.), and he will have *to migrate again*. An extraordinary experience of the process of diversion. Here is a fine example of the concealment, in Martinique itself, of alienation: one must look for it *elsewhere* in order to be aware of it. Then the individual enters the anguished world, not of the unfortunate psyche, but really that of psychic torture.

(There is, of course, the glorious return of those who went "West" [towards the East] and tried to take root anew. This is not the desperate arrival of the past, after being snatched from the African homeland and the Middle Passage. It is, this time, as if one discovered finally the true land where roots can be reestablished. They say that Martinique is the land of ghosts. It cannot, however, represent return but only diversion.) To be unable therefore to manage to live in one's country, that is where the hurt is deepest.

Diversion *leads nowhere* when the original trickster strategy does not encounter any real potential for development.

(We cannot underestimate the universal malaise that drives Europeans, dissatisfied with their world, toward those "warm lands" that are deserted by unemployment as well as subjected to intolerable pressures of survival, to seek in the *Other's World* a temporary respite.)

Ultimately, Caribbean intellectuals have exploited this need for a trickster strategy *to find another place:* that is, in these circumstances, to link a possible solution of the insoluble to the resolution other peoples have achieved. The first and perhaps the most spectacular form of this tactic of diversion is the

Jamaican Marcus Garvey's African dream, conceived in the first "phase" that drove him in the United States to identify with the plight of black Americans. The universal identification with black suffering in the Caribbean ideology (or the poetics) of negritude also represents another manifestation of redirected energy resulting from diversion. The historical need for the creolized peoples of the small islands of the French Caribbean to lay claim to the "African element" of their past, which was for so long scorned, repressed, denied by the prevalent ideology, is sufficient in itself to justify the negritude movement in the Caribbean. This assertion of universal identification is, however, very quickly surpassed, so much so that Césaire's negritude poetry will come into contact with the liberation movement among African peoples and his *Notebook of a Return to the Native Land* will soon be more popular in Senegal than in Martinique. A peculiar fate. Therein lies the diversion: an ideal evolution, contact from above. We realize that, if M. Césaire is the best known Martinican at home, his works are, however, less used there than in Africa. The same fate awaited the Trinidadian Padmore, who inspired in Ghana the man who seized independence, Kwame Nkrumah. But Padmore never returned to his native land, he who was the spiritual father of Nkrumah's Pan-Africanism. These forms of diversion are then also camouflaged or sublimated variations of the return to Africa. The most obvious difference between the African and Caribbean versions of negritude is that the African one proceeds from the multiple reality of ancestral yet threatened cultures, while the Caribbean version precedes the free intervention of new cultures whose expression is subverted by the disorder of colonialism. An intense attempt at generalization was necessary for the two formulations to find common ground: this liberal generalization made it understood that negritude did not take into account particular circumstances. Conceived as a fundamental inspiration for the emancipation of Africa, it never actually played a part as such in the historic episodes of this liberation. On the contrary, it was rejected as such, first in the context of anglophone Africa (which rejected its generalizing nature), then by the radical fringes of the African struggle (perhaps under the influence of revolutionary ideologies).[6]

The most important example of the effect of diversion is the case of Frantz Fanon. A grand and intoxicating diversion. I once met a South American poet who never left behind the Spanish translation of *The Wretched of the Earth*. Any American student is amazed to learn that you come from the same country as Fanon. It so happens that years go by without his name (not to mention his work) being mentioned by the media, whether political or cultural, revolutionary or leftist, of Martinique. An avenue in Fort-de-France is named after him. That is about it.

It is difficult for a French Caribbean individual to be the brother, the friend, or quite simply the associate or fellow countryman of Fanon. Because, of all the French Caribbean intellectuals, he is the only one to have *acted on his ideas*, through his involvement in the Algerian struggle; this was so even if, after tragic and conclusive episodes of what one can rightly call his Algerian agony, the Martinican problem (for which, in the circumstances, he was not responsible, but which he would no doubt have confronted if he had lived) retains its complete ambiguity. It is clear that in this case *to act on one's ideas* does not only mean to fight, to make demands, to give free rein to the language of defiance, but to take full responsibility for *a complete break*. The radical break is the extreme edge of the process of diversion.

The poetic word of Césaire, the political act of Fanon, led us *somewhere*, authorizing by diversion the necessary return to the point where our problems lay in wait for us. This point

6. I have observed, each time there is a debate at an international forum on the question of negritude, that at least half of the African intellectuals present would attack this theory, regularly defended by the French representatives, undoubtedly because they find in it the ambiguous generosity of the "generalizing theories" they so like to defend. Thus, Césaire's *Notebook of a Return to the Native Land*, whose thrust is Caribbean, is closer to the Africans than is the theory of negritude, which is by nature more general.

is described in *Notebook of a Return to the Native Land* as well as in *Black Skin, White Masks:* by that I mean that neither Césaire nor Fanon are abstract thinkers. However the works that followed negritude and the revolutionary theory of *Wretched of the Earth* are universal. They follow the historical curve of the decline of decolonization in the world. They illustrate and establish the landscape of a zone shared elsewhere. We must return to the point from which we started. Diversion is not a useful ploy unless it is nourished by reversion: not a return to the longing for origins, to some immutable state of Being, but a return to the point of entanglement, from which we were forcefully turned away; that is where we must ultimately put to work the forces of creolization, or perish.[7]

In the Beginning

The document that we shall examine is well known by those who are interested in the history of Martinique. It is the proclamation made on 31 March 1848 by the delegate of the Republic of France to the slaves who were agricultural laborers in Martinique. France had been proclaimed a republic, and

7. For us Martinicans, this place already is the Caribbean: but we do not know it. At least, in a collective way. The practice of diversion can be measured in terms of this existence-without-knowing. Herein lies one of the objectives of our discourse: reconnect in a profound way with ourselves, so that the strategy of diversion would no longer be maintained as a tactic indispensable to existence but would be channeled into a form of self-expression.

The tangential movement from Diversion becomes, at the level of self-expression, the conquest of the unspoken or the unspeakable (that is of the two main forms of repression), starting with the moment when the strategy of diversion, no longer imposed on reality, survives in the subtleties of understanding, analysis, and creation. Our growing emergence in the Caribbean brings this process to light and authorizes it.

naturally there followed a disintegration of the colonial order. The matter of the abolition of slavery arises, Schoelcher begins work on it, but the events in Paris have a delayed repercussion in Martinique. There is mass agitation among the slaves; it is clear that the planters are increasing strategies to oppose the decree that is being drafted. It is necessary therefore to soothe the widespread agitation, to ensure or maintain public order, to establish the most favorable conditions for transition. Such is the aim of this proclamation.

Its repulsive, hypocritical, sanctimonious, and basically proslavery posture has been pointed out (for example by M. Aimé Césaire, in his introduction to the *Oeuvres* (Works) of Victor Schoelcher[1]). I feel we have never considered this text in its entirety, never clarified its implications or its consequences. It is certainly not a text that *created* the historical events that followed; it is nothing but their prefiguration expressed in a public form. But it is certain that therein lies the expression, for once in written form, of a political will whose strategic orientation will be increasingly difficult to evaluate. That is already a reason to take an interest in such a document.

There is another, more disturbing one. It is that herein can be found the thinly veiled declaration of our alienation, the outline of what the Martinican people will have to undergo, the prefiguration of what the colonizer will try to make of us, and what in part (at least for what we call our elite) we have become. Considered in this light, the document is a pivotal text that reveals clearly what is hidden behind "emancipation" of the slaves: with in this case, the added mockery that it constitutes one of our first historical proclamations, supplied by the other and to that extent more insidiously powerful.

Glad Tidings! This will be the principle of our political and collective existence. Herein lies the first formulation of the Other Land.

The steamer. To get there more quickly. The transatlantic

1. Paris: Presses Universitaires de France, 1954.

liner, the *Latécoère*, the Boeing: the infinite manifestations of the umbilical cord.

The army "associated" with social and political life—(the general).

The goodness of the father. He takes care of his children; it is up to them to be well-behaved, to deserve his attention.

The intrusion of sentiment in sociopolitical relations. The masters are good (there are some bad ones). Their names are recorded, and it seems that at least one of them, M. Perrinon, was a mulatto (a free colored). Perhaps the same one after whom a street in Fort-de-France is named? Just like M. Reizet, who left his name to a district in Pointe-à-Pitre?

The assertion of the principle that it is in France that things change: when the republic replaces the monarchy, suddenly your lot improves. It was all the fault of Louis-Philippe.

The notion of buying back one's freedom, which legitimates the principle of an indemnification. (History repeats itself.) You were therefore the *rightful* property of your masters?[2]

The equivalence between the status of him who brings the glad tidings and the importance of the latter. The higher placed the delegate, the more the news is true and beneficial.

The habit that decisions are taken elsewhere. The law *arrives*. (Paris "makes" the law.)

The granting of freedom. It is rare that a colonizing country should so develop a theory of "Liberation."

The outline of the process of delays and stages: "Until the law becomes official, remain what you are, slaves."

Freedom is not one's due, it is the right to work for one's masters ("for oneself"). That is how it is deserved.

The sweetness of life in the Tropics, in comparison with the harsh reality of France.

---

2. This profitable and massive compensation, in the passage from slavery capitalism to "modern" capitalism, does remind us in principle of the disguised subventions that allow the *békés*, having abandoned today all productive projects, to recycle themselves in the tertiary sector.

The Known, the Uncertain

The Frenchman is more responsible: he works harder; and he is less happy.

The formation of an elite ("it is not everyone's right to govern"). The white man is destined to govern, naturally.

The appearance of the mayor of the "commune" as a substitute for the master. The beginning of a make-believe elite.

The value of the republic, its virtue. Its law determines what is real.

The mayor as representative of this republic. The shape of elections.

The mayor as intermediary between inhabitants and the higher authorities of Fort-de-France. "Clientelism" takes shape.

Distance placed between Martinique and Guadeloupe.

Martinicans are smarter than their Guadeloupean "comrades." They more easily grasp what is important.

The concept of being idle and free. To reject the system is a sin.

The priest linked to the mayor. Religion used to control future freedom.

Marriage to bring stability to the social whole.

There is the humbleness of birth, but one must not complain about it.

Patience. All is not going well today, but those responsible are working at it and tomorrow all will be well.

The idea of official visits. The chief delegate must *see*.

The chief delegate must go back to France and take those measures (the law) that will *provide* something (freedom, work, assistance . . .).

The understanding black.

The grateful black.

The black dancer and musician, serenading the delegate.

The emotion of the chief delegate before expressions of gratitude.

Once more marriage, *which will make everyone work*.

These are the strategic thrusts of alienation in 1848: the

town hall, the presbytery, the almshouse, the estate hospital, the master's greathouse, the workshops, the cabin of the overseer.

I do not know a more complete text dealing with the forms of our dispossession. From the economic point of view, it analyzes perfectly the movement from slave labor to psuedo-salaried labor in Martinique. From the political point of view, it outlines precisely the conditions for our "liberation." We know that the slaves of 1848 did not fall for these pretty words, and that the proclamation of the end of March did not forestall the revolts in May, which led to the promulgation of the decree of abolition *before* it arrived properly signed. The question to be debated is the long-term effect of such a strategy. It matters little, for example, that the delegate of the republic should have invented or embellished the episode of the blacks dancing with gratitude. If *in 1848* the majority of the slaves no doubt sneered at these documents that they heard proclaimed by a few agents of the state, how can we not admit that our people have been affected by this insidious strategy? We have all listened to M. Husson, and little by little stopped sneering.

So we will understand that many popular revolts in our country have not resulted in radical changes. The slaves fought in 1848, but the "liberation" that was then proclaimed did not operate on a collective scale. M. Husson was a genius, as miserable as his plan, but how effective it has been.

(Schoelcher writes: "Citizen Husson is a Martinican Creole, his family and his interests are there; he found himself between blacks and whites; so he could ascertain the impact of each word uttered." [3] But citizen Husson is here the *delegate of the republic:* protecting his interests, he knows how to confront the obtuse planters around him with *the first hint of a colonization that is as corrosive as it is oppressive.* Before collectively agreeing to these measures, the *békés* would have to

3. Cited in the anthology *Esclavage et Colonisation* (Paris: PUF, 1948), p. 162.

be crushed—from 1880 to 1946—by French capitalism. By this date, they would understand that M. Husson was working in their interest.

L O U I S   T H O M A S   H U S S O N
Provisional Director of the Interior for the French Republic

T O   T H E   F I E L D   S L A V E S
My Friends,

You have all heard the good news that has just come from France. It is true: it is General Rostoland and myself who brought it. We took the steamer in order to get here very quickly.

Freedom will come! Good luck, my children, you deserve it. It is the good masters who requested it for you: M. Pécoul, M. Bence, M. Froidefond des Farges, M. Lepelletier St. Rémy, M. Perrinon, M. de Jabrun and M. Reizet of Guadeloupe. All the masters who were in Paris gathered together and instructed these gentlemen to ask for your freedom from the Government, which agreed. Louis-Philippe is no longer King! He was the one who prevented your freedom, because he wanted each one of you to buy it back himself, and the republic, on the contrary, will buy it back for all of you at the same time.

But the republic needs time to gather the funds for the purchase and to pass the law of abolition. So, nothing has changed, for the present. You remain slaves until the law is official. Then Governor Rostoland will send me to tell you: "Freedom has come, long live the republic!"

Until then you must work according to the regulations in the law for the benefit of your masters. You must prove that you understand that freedom is not the right to wander aimlessly, but the right to work for oneself. In France, all free men work harder than you who are slaves, and they are far less happy than you, for over there, life is more difficult than here.

My friends, obey the orders of your masters in order to demonstrate that you know that not everyone is capable of being in charge. If you think you have something to complain about, confide in your masters in particular, and if you are not heard and you still think you are right, go to the mayor of your district for him to give you guidance.

The republic has given this responsibility to the mayor.

Otherwise, if the higher authorities residing in Fort-de-France (that is the new name for Fort-Royal) are constantly disturbed by your complaints, they will not have time to draft the law and the moment of freedom will be delayed.

Remember what happened in Guadeloupe!

From the time of your forefathers, the republic existed in France; it proclaimed freedom without compensating the masters, without organizing work.

It thought that the slaves would have understood that they were meant to work and abstain from disorder.

The English took possession of Martinique, and your grandfathers were no longer free.

In Guadeloupe, which escaped our enemies, everyone was free, but the former slaves abandoned their work and became more miserable every day.

After seven years of freedom, they forced the republic to reimpose slavery. That is why your friends in Guadeloupe are slaves to this day!

The Known, the Uncertain

I am convinced, my friends, that you will demonstrate more intelligence and that you will not be receptive to evil gossip: you will listen only to those who are honest.

Pay no heed, especially, to those free idlers. Do not forget that those who feared that you would be unwilling to work once you were free, used to say: "See how the freed slaves have become idle!"

Your enemies are those who are lazy! Have only one thing to say to them: "Go to work and let us deserve our freedom. . . ."

The priest is there to tell you you must work and marry to gain the rewards of the other world. Ask for his advice when something does not seem right to you. Remember, it was religion that first preached freedom when the whites themselves were not free.

Christ was born in a manger to teach the people from the countryside that they must not complain about their humble birth. He allowed them to crucify him (the form of punishment for the slaves in Judea) so that those who are unfortunate should see in his priests only friends destined to guide them.

So, my friends, have patience and confidence! If I am writing to you, it is because I do not have the time to come and see you all. In fact, I have just visited St. Pierre, Le Prêcheur, Macouba, Basse-Pointe, and I am in a hurry to return home and work on the law that will grant your freedom.

Today my mind is at ease, for I have seen your comrades; they are good men who know what freedom means. You are like them, I am sure. I would have liked you to be with me at M. de Courcy's residence. When I announced at his workshop that they were all going to be free, they all shouted: "Thank you M. Director! Long live work! Long live Sir! Long live Madame! And that evening, they serenaded their mistress. During the dinner, they sent me eleven married men, who introduced their wives to me and asked me, in the name of the workers, to thank the republic.

My friends! That was wonderful! That proves that the workshop had understood that in society married people are the most honorable and the most worthy of guaranteeing to the republic that henceforth the slaves will get married in order to be able to feed and care for an old father, a mother, a wife and children, brothers and sisters, an entire family, because in this way everyone will have to work when everyone is free.

Farewell, my good friends, I will come to see you one after the other.

When you wish to show your joy, shout:

Long live Work!
Long live Marriage!

Until the time when I come to say to you: "The law is official. Long live freedom!"

THIS CIRCULAR WILL BE SENT TO ALL THE MAYORS OF THE COMMUNES TO BE POSTED ON THE DOORS OF THE TOWN HALL, THE PRESBYTERY, AND THE ALMS HOUSE, THEY WILL BE RESPON SIBLE FOR SENDING COPIES TO ALL THE LANDOWNERS IN THE COMMUNE, WHO WILL BE ASKED TO DISPLAY THEM IN THE MOST VISIBLE PLACES ON THEIR PROP ERTY, SUCH AS THE HOSPITAL, BUILDINGS ON THE PLANTA

The Known, the Uncertain

T·ION, THE FOREMAN'S CABIN,
AND THEIR OWN DWELLING.

St.-Pierre, 31 March 1848
Signed: HUSSON

What has changed since then?
The good news still comes from elsewhere. Today it deals
with the publication of the figures for *official aid.*
The Boeings, steamers of the skies, are used *more, more
quickly, more often.*
The army is no longer repressive: it pacifies; it educates.
Good feelings are everywhere. "Ah! My good friends. That
would be wonderful." M. Dijoud in 1979, on the question of
racist incidents in high schools, declares: "We are all French.
The French must love each other." Which would have made
any audience in France (government or opposition) collapse
with laughter.
It is only in France that things change: "If the left wins,
there will be no more welfare"; "if the left wins, antonomy
will (finally) be possible."
The notion of delays and stages, an expression of political
pragmatism. There are delays on the left and delays on the
right.
(We are happy to have found responsible Frenchmen to
take care of us. Anything else is unrealistic.)
Elections as the solution to problems. "The Majority."
The distance, the rivalry, maintained between Guadeloupe
and Martinique.
Economic pressure (Social Security laws) favoring the development of "stabilizing" nuclear families.
We recognize that the role of the church has changed in the
last ten years. The calmest, and perhaps the most radical,
controversial speeches that I have heard these days (1979)
have been delivered by priests. There is evidence of a clear
South-American influence on the Martinican clergy. And

whatever you feel about religious alienation or fanticism, you cannot ignore the energy, the fraternal organizations, the activity in poor districts (more or less outside of the traditional scope of political activity) of the churches introduced into Martinique—Adventists, Protestants, Jehovah's Witnesses, etc.—even if you fear the fire-and-brimstone, escapist message of these sects and even if you know that the establishment of most of these churches is financed initially from the United States.[4]

The encouragement of delegation, of representation without power.

The folksingers "serenading" the prefect, in the luxury hotels or on passing ships.

The uninterrupted flow of visitors: ministers, delegations, commissions of inquiry, chairmen, executives, union secretaries, political leaders (to each his own), ad infinitum.

"I cannot stay any longer, I must return to Paris to act on what I managed to see and learn here. But I will not abandon you. In my own capacity I will continue to work for you" (minister's speech).

The expansive pronouncement: tomorrow things will be better.

The understanding black.

The grateful black.

The amiable black. The visitors marvel.

Nearly all the examples of derision are present embryonically in this text.

Today these are the strategic places of alienation: the town hall, the Social Security office, school administration offices, the school, public assistance, parking garages, supermarkets, associations, political and administrative meetings, sports arenas, credit organizations. As can be seen, there is social

---

4. Some American universities, for example, the University of Indiana (Bloomington), have created courses in Creole language in which future missionaries to Haiti and the other francophone Caribbean islands enroll.

progress. The plantation greathouse and the foreman's cabin are replaced by boards, offices, agencies.

To put the final touch to the quality of "historical document" in M. Husson's text, the poster was displayed in a *bilingual* form. In French on the left and in Creole on the right. Yes. A bilingual proclamation. How not to be amazed? Something "fundamental," like the treaty dividing the Carolingian empire. And if one can imagine that the Creole text was read aloud to the inhabitants of Martinique, who were no more literate in that language than in French, then imagine as well some civil servant commissioned to do the Creole "translation," cursing this extra, absolutely absurd task, and setting to work on this crazy black pidgin that will later fill us with wonder. M. Husson's text once again is an inspired prefiguration. It fixes such an undoubtedly feeble transcription of Creole speech that one is led to believe that this speech is simply a low form of patois. That is the ultimate historical effect of the document, which makes this perfect deformation of form the crowning achievement of the will to dislocate *in the most profound way.*

This proclamation ought to have been studied in Martinican schools, criticized by political parties, analyzed by cultural authorities. This text from the "past" is disturbingly contemporary. We can only tear ourselves away from derision by staring directly into it.[5]

Dispossession

I

No community would tolerate the notion of "dispossession," and that is a discouraging point with which to begin a scru-

5. On 15 July 1848, the general commissioner to French Guiana, M. André-Aimé Pariset, makes a similar proclamation. His text uses the same

tiny of the real. But not to do so is becoming dangerous, when dispossession is camouflaged and no one is aware of its corrosive presence.[1]

It all begins naturally with the first African snatched from the Gold Coast. Our new world was the trader's ocean. The land on the other side (our land) thus became for us an intolerable experience. But the traded population became a people on this land. Then came the real dispossession, with the first saucepan or the first plowshare, paid for by a planter with spices, with indigo, or with tobacco. In this barter the country went astray.

The Martinican planter, unlike his counterpart in the plantation of Louisiana or the Northeast of Brazil, cannot claim for himself any of the means of production that would favor his independence from the commercial system whose local "representative" he is.

He is dependent on the slave ship for supplies of ebony flesh. He is not the one who fixes the price or the quantities supplied. He does not have liquid cash (the principle of the barter is based on the value of a pound of sugar), he does not own a merchant fleet, he does not affect the fluctuations of the market for colonial products in the distribution zone. What is left for him? Plunder. No possibility of accumulation, reserves, technology. He exploits on a day-to-day basis.

The wars of independence in the New World (United States,

---

arguments, but in a much more "serious" tone, more bureaucratic and less "emotional," more "ideological." He was a career civil servant. He did not have the decisive brevity, the genius for derision, the affected miming of M. Husson.

1. The best example is the work of lucid French militants who, solidly rooted in the Caribbean, psychiatrists, psychologists, and educators, prove to you, while waiting to publish their findings in highly regarded professional journals, that you have a defeatist attitude to the Caribbean cause, or that your reflections are purely formal. Fraternal colonization is as disruptive as the paternalist kind. The mimetic trap is everywhere.

Mexico, Cuba, Brazil, Latin America) erupted in those places where the planters could escape the barter economy, by control of a currency, a fleet, a market. The war of independence in Haiti is in another category: the concentration of African peoples, the longstanding tradition of *marronnage*, the power of Voudou beliefs, population density, are here decisive factors. These enabling conditions were absent in Guadeloupe and Martinique.

The barter system is reinforced by the mechanism of state monopolies, from the time of Colbert onward. Which means that the Martinican economy (production and consumption) in its fullest range is totally absorbed into the French economy, without any alternative. The organization of the plantation system will provide the opportunity for a mild reaction, quickly suppressed by the policy of French beet-sugar producers ever since the middle of the nineteenth century. The barter economy will change subtly into pseudoproduction (pseudo, because it is nonautonomous) then into false production; finally it will be transformed into a system of exchange (exchange of public credit for private benefit in the area of tertiary production).

When these facts are brought to light, you are accused of some kind of sympathy for the *béké* cause. M. Jack Corzani, in his *Histoire de la littérature antillaise* (History of French Caribbean literature), suggests therefore that I would tend to favor a "sympathetic approach" to them. (A scene from the novel *Le quatrième siècle* (The fourth century), between an unorthodox planter and a runaway slave, gave rise to this ambiguity. And it is true that, given this novel's perspective, the two characters are marginalized in relation to the day-to-day evolution of the country. The overall meaning of this scene is, however, *that it is not enough to marginalize oneself in order to cause change.*) This is a terrible mistake. What I wish to show is, first, that the *békés* were never seen by the mass of slaves, who then became agricultural workers, as *the real enemy:* had it been so, from such a confrontation between these two social groups would have resulted an independent will that would have founded, in whatever way, the nation of Martinique. The colonizers were clever enough to conceal the true and total domination (invisible) under the no less real (and visible) exploitation by the *békés*. The principle of departmentalization in 1946 is precisely that incorporation into the French nation will guarantee protection against *béké* exploitation. But the *békés*, now impotent, will be, as is expected, salvaged and promoted by the system to the non-dangerous, nonproductive zone of the tertiary sector, which promises bountiful benefits but prevents the emergence of the nation. Furthermore, never has a policy of production been developed or carried out by this exploitative sector. Ultimately, no responsibility has been taken by them for technical improvement. Which creates a number of inadequacies.

The "economic" status of Martinique will be fixed according to this progression: *barter—psuedoproduction—exchange.*

Technical stagnation, resulting from the impossibility of long-term forecasting, here overlaps with the degeneration (on the popular level) of techniques of survival. It is true that basic techniques for the processing of sugar cane have changed little over the past two centuries. This technical entropy, reinforced by the dispossession of the lower strata, produces a paralysis of cultural creativity. Technical automatism, mental automatism.

The habit of collective nonresponsibility in economic production is encouraged by decisions made by the central authority that, while really preventing the appearance of production of a national nature, encourages through subventions and intermittent aid the maintenance of what I call pseudoproduction.

Three effects follow naturally:

1. *The lack of solidarity between sectors of the economy.*
   Under the pressure of equalization created by an external administration, indifference is the natural reaction of a

The Known, the Uncertain

Fort-de-France civil servant or a fisherman from St.-Luce to the crisis in banana production in Lorrain or to the bankruptcy of small cane farmers. Solidarities cannot exist at this level. There is no Martinican economy in the real sense.

2. *The futility of sectoral planning.* Periodically supplied for the sole purpose of proving that there is desire for change, the real effect of planning by economic sector is to maintain the equilibrium of a structure that is not expected to be productive. To maintain equilibrium, is, in fact, not to develop. Sectoral plans are by nature two-pronged. Bring profits to the tertiary sector, inject noncreative "aid" into the system of pseudoproduction.

3. *The weakness of resistance from different sectors.* These sectors are all the more easy to dominate because they can almost never activate a dynamic reaction within the whole of Martinican society.[2] It is striking to note that following the period 1939–45, in which Martinicans were unanimous in confronting a situation of characteristic aggression, in which Martinicans had to invent among themselves a complete system of self–defense, the solidarity of the people was tremendous; even if we must lament the fact that this solidarity was used as a force to "wrest free" the policy of assimilation in 1946 towards which everything (the logic of our nonhistory, the self-

2. A typical example of this can be seen in the serious conflicts that opposed (1977–79) the dockworkers of Fort-de-France to the small-scale banana farmers. Each time the dockworkers are on strike against their employers, the small farmers demonstrate, sometimes under police protection, against this strike that threatens their interests. No one is aware that the Draconian conditions (for fruit quality) imposed on the farmers and the conditions inflicted on the dockworkers stem from *the same policy,* whose inner workings need to be dismantled. The system (its police, authorities) appears within the country's economic activities as an important arbiter between sectorized and disunited zones. (Here one can consider the significance of the word *solidarity:* no new beginning is possible as long as individual problems are not considered in the context of the whole.)

interest of the middle classes, the objectives of reemergent French capitalism) was disturbingly pushing our country.

Martinican economists have been regularly caught in the trap of this learned and camouflaged notion of sectors. All their analyses of profitability, for instance, come up against the same obstacle, that of the Martinican input, which no one really knows how to consider.

At present the original principle of barter that created the system of exploitation has yielded to the principle of transfer that is at the center of the system of exchange. It is a matter of the same dispossession in a different form. Between the two, real productivity developed in the eighteenth and nineteenth centuries, with the plantation system: it never developed into an organized collective activity. The very notion of production (as a group effort) was consequently lost from view. We therefore did not move directly from the nonautonomous production of the past to the negated productivity of today; we knew that intermediary phase that I describe thus: a malproductivity.

If we therefore had to summarize in a schematic form, once more, the process of dispossession, we would do it perhaps according to the table illustrating the process of dispossession.

At each of the turning points in such a process, we can see the system become hesitant. First of all, when the passage from primitive colonialism to the plantation system makes precarious a centrifugal exploitation (it is Richlieu who leaves the big planters in charge of their productive processes) and a centripetal one (it is Colbert who equalizes all of that under the standard of central financing). Then, when there is rivalry between planters and beet-sugar farmers: continental sugar or tropical sugar? The question will be decided in favor of the former. Then, when pseudoproduction changes to a system of exchange (in the years 1960–70), the last moment of hesitation: to continue a predatory system in a production process for which, after the victory of the beet-sugar farmers, there is no longer any justification, or to equalize the whole in a total conversion to the tertiary sector that will make Martinique

The Known, the Uncertain

The Process of Dispossession

Economic Principle	Type of Production	Currency	Social Characteristics
barter (1st phase)	unorganized predatory economy (fragmented production)	the pound of sugar as currency	hesitation between "centrifugal" and "centripetal" growth
barter (2d phase)	predatory economy; plantation system (monoproduction)	"local" currency dependent on "national" currency	massive contribution to the French economy
pseudoproduction	pseudoeconomy; declining production artificially maintained (malproduction)	"local" currency absorbed by "national" currency	victory of French beet-sugar farmers
exchange	negated economy; intermittent attempts to rehabilitate (nonproduction)	disappearance of "local" currency	assimilation; exchange of public funds for private benefit and reexport

into a consumer colony? Naturally, it is the second option that will prevail, and it is not unjustified to draw a parallel between this victory and that of the ideas of Giscard d'Estaing in France.

These hesitations do not originate among Martinicans (*béké* planters, the middle class, or agricultural workers), but from French capitalists. They depend on an economic evolution and a balance of forces *in France itself,* and that is where the solutions are drawn up. We feel only their repercussions where we are, and in particular the political fallout, the logic of whose operation in Martinique is not clearly seen without the preceding analysis. It is in this process that the principle of overdetermination can be located, the source of which remains constantly "invisible" in the country itself.

II

The consequences in the economic "system" are established from the outset—Martinican history has seen only a few adjustments to this order of things:

1. The total absence of direct or self-generated investment.
2. The fear of surplus, linked to the inability to control an external market or to organize an internal one.[3]
3. The absence of accumulated capital, technical capacity, creative projects.
4. The habit of not producing, a consequence of the need to satisfy predatory impulses. The resulting repercussions will be influential in their turn:
   a. A corresponding absence of accumulation in collective cultural acquisition.
   b. The pulverization of the cultural domain tied to the plantation system.
   c. The absence of an independent creativity for resolving the conflicts between social strata.
   d. The appearance of the repeated pattern of revolt, then stagnation, without any idea of how to break free.

These forms of dispossession culminate, then, in the present system. French merchant capitalism found it unthinkable to continue to subsidize, for the simple purpose of social stability, an economy that was destined to be unprofitable. Especially since no section of the population seems capable of posing a sustained threat to this stability. The last hesitation has then been taken care of. The investment in public funds of

---

3. M. Gilbert Bazabas, a Martinican economist, has pointed to this obsessive inadequacy, related to productive and distributive fragmentation.

a small part of the surplus realized in France and worldwide by the French capitalist economy allows the creation in Martinique of an extended social stratum of those who sell services (functionaries), to which is added a migrant group of technicians in the tertiary sector coming from France, the development of passive consumerism (the finished products imported into Martinique being exchanged "directly" for services), the realization of significant private gain in this tertiary sector. Public subventions will therefore be less and less concerned with the production of finished goods (except to favor "transfer" to the tertiary sector) and more and more with the infrastructure and commercial equipment (roads, buildings, port, airport, consumer services, distribution circuits, credit organizations, etc.) and security (army, police force).

These equalizing subventions, this hypertrophy in the tertiary sector, produce a higher standard of living at the production level, and consequently inflict isolation on what remains of the productive social strata and confirm the isolation of sectors of productivity (sectorization). The result of this is, on the collective level, artificial social strata whose dynamic is neutralized *from the outside* and an institutionalizing of hollow entities: a nonfunctional elitism; on the individual level, the development of a dependent mentality, what can be called "the dependence of grey matter" in the "assimilated" sector of Martinican society. The process of total dislocation (the destruction of all productive capacity) aggravates the impulse towards imitation, imposes in an irresistible way an identification with the proposed model of existence (the French one), of reflection, and unleashes an irrational reluctance to question this model, whose "transmission" appears as the only guarantee of "social status."

III

It is perhaps not a spectacular thing for mankind to trace this process of dispossession. But its analysis usefully clarifies the inner workings, the hidden forms, of cultural contact, the contact that makes it possible. A few of us reckon (in Martinique) that no other community, perhaps, in the world is as alienated as our own, as threatened with extinction. The pressure to imitate is, perhaps, the most extreme form of violence that anyone can inflict on a people; even more so when it assumes the agreement (and even, the pleasure) of the mimetic society. This dialectic, in fact, suppresses this form of violence under the guise of pleasure. This form of suppression is important to track down.[4] The reductive power of imitation is even more terrible in that part of the world that is called, so symbolically, Micronesia. I have noted and summarized with horror, in the study of M. J.-P. Dumas, the obvious instances where the situation of these Pacific islands under American domination and that of the French islands in the Caribbean overlap[5]:

4. The present provides us with the example of an equally radical violence: that of the fierce reaction, in Iran, against imitation. For the ayatollahs Islam means anti-West. (But is not Islam, a cultural phenomenon from the Mediterranean, a part of the West? Like Judeo-Christian thought, it admits to a creator. I argued this position to the amused surprise of the Algerian novelist Rachid Boudjedra.) The extreme reaction against imitation originates within the same impulse that imposed the rape of imitation. On the contrary, the most secure protection against self-destructive imitation is the process of Creolization. (In this sense, and contrary to the official ideology with which Martinicans are bombarded every day, cultural cross-fertilization and imitation are *diametrically opposed*.) It is not irrelevant to note that violent reactions against imitation were intensified where an important reserve of economic resources made them possible. Total economic dislocation is the first condition of the growth of imitativeness. The surest method of combating the latter for a people is to regain the complete control of its system of production. One cannot begin cross-fertilization (to become relative, to reject origins) unless one is not lost in pseudoproduction. That is the vicious circle in which we are caught. Because seizing control of a system of production does not solve class oppression within the system. Because the complete control of an economy takes one away from the cross-cultural process (of relativity). These are the underlying contradictions of the nationalist position.

These contradictions are swept away when economic *intensity* moves to resolve them. They are aggravated when dispossession has crushed the consensus of the community.

5. Published in *Les Temps Modernes*, no. 383 (1978). M. Jean-Pierre Dumas's study does not tackle the "cultural" aspect of the Micronesian

The Known, the Uncertain

The recorded history of Micronesia is the history of its colonization. — The government control is in the Department of the Interior in Washington. — There is an increasingly important part played by Micronesians in positions of responsibility within the administration. One of the features of Micronesia is an excessive bureaucracy. — The money comes entirely from the United States. — The Micronesian Congress has a considerable power of recommendation. — The American High Commissioner has the power of veto over all the laws passed by this Congress. — Washington is especially interested in the overall size of the budget and is careful that it is not exceeded. — It is the executive, in Micronesia, that has the final authority. — The American administration is not without ambiguities or contradictions. — The role of Micronesia in American military strategy. — The Micronesians first proposed the status of free association with the United States. They can only invoke the status of independence as a last resort. — A large number of Micronesians have expressed their fear of independence. — This attitude can be explained by the amount of American aid that artificially sustains the economy of the "Territory." — The islands compete with each other, each one waiting for the lion's share of the aid. — Micronesia is wealth without development. — Anything can be grown in these islands. — It is more common to buy tuna fish than fresh fish. — It is extremely difficult to find local bananas, local vegetables, citrus fruit, alcohol from coconuts; on the

problem: preservation of language, persistence of traditions, intensity of popular resistance, psychic dislocation and forms of mental trauma, etc. The article is an objective presentation of facts; a "cultural" study could have forced to the surface interpretations on which the author does not venture an opinion within the context he has outlined.

other hand, it is easy to find in the four supermarkets of the town of Saipan frozen vegetables,
grapefruit and oranges from California, beer,
Coca-Cola, whisky, etc. — Massive external aid
maintains underdevelopment. — It has played a
role in the certain enrichment of the population,
but in the equally real impoverishment of the "Territory." — The salaries are on the average twice
as high in the public sector (administration) as in
the private sector. — Whence the lack of interest
among Micronesians in the business of real production, and their dependence in this regard on
American consumption patterns. — This inflow of
public-sector money has had the effect, on a limited work force, of suppressing all activity in the
traditional productive sector. — Why continue to
work hard in agriculture and fishing if one can
easily obtain money in the public sector? — The
Micronesian children no longer wish to eat bread-
fruit nor even local chicken but Kentucky Fried
Chicken. — Salaries are used to purchase imported consumer goods. — The population has
become accustomed to living above their means
and unwilling to adjust downward. The price
paid is evidently dependence. — Investment is essentially directed toward infrastructure. — The
American investment budget is totally devoted to
nonproductive investment. — The private sector
invests with the help of Japanese money in the
sector that turns the quickest profit: tourism. —
Saturation point has been reached, and the big
hotels are empty more often than full. — In short,
external aid has had the following effects: providing high salaries in the nonproductive sector; getting the population accustomed to a high level of
gratuitous spending on social services (education,
health); making the state the only employer in the
country; orienting investments toward infrastruc-

ture, to the detriment of productive investments. — In short, we are dealing with a consumer society with no real production. If the essence of underdevelopment is dependence, Micronesia is a completely dependent country, even more insidiously so since it is accompanied by a relatively high standard of living. — The desired result has been successfully obtained: the populations concerned cannot, whether they like it or not, do without the American presence for money, goods, culture, education, health. Domination is complete. — The local American administration, no worse than any other, cares more about managing, educating, than developing. — It is no longer a matter of nineteenth century colonization with its pure and simple exploitation of the country, but of something more subtle. But the "Micronesian experiment" shows that there can be no real "development" within dependence. — Neocolonialism can indeed exist with: a considerable democracy, an important amount of money poured into the country, and a real promotion of the native peoples. — Dependence is the product of a system and not of isolated individuals. — The value of Micronesia for the United States is not economic but strategic. — The potential of the ocean that surrounds these islands can be great in terms of maritime and mining resources. — But are the Micronesians themselves against dependence? Nothing is less certain. — It seems that no one wants to return to a *coconut economy*. — In a referendum: "Do you wish to be independent and face the consequences?," it is unlikely that the majority of Micronesians will vote "yes."—So?

The reductive force of imitation is deeply rooted. One could not hope to discover the "dynamics" of the situation in Martinique without going *there* to investigate. A visible difference between the Micronesian and the Caribbean situations is that the French system has produced an abstract and refined conception of this new form of colonialism: the urgency to persuade, to extract consent from the subjugated people, to subtly scorn (whereas the Anglo-Saxon visibly scorns) is both the symbolic and the major hidden reality of such a policy, which could have been applied only to small countries.[6]

COMPLEMENTARY NOTE

on the "stripped migrant" and technical awareness

I persist, in spite of sarcasm and hesitation, in exploring the full implications related to the diverse experiences of migrants in the Caribbean and Latin America. The enslaved African is the "stripped migrant." He could not bring his tools, the images of his gods, his daily implements, nor could he send news to his neighbors, or hope to bring his family over, or reconstitute his former family in the place of deportation. Naturally, the ancestral spirit had not left him; he had not lost the meaning of a former experience. But he will have to fight for centuries in order to recognize its legitimacy. The other migrant, also stripped to essentials, retained all of that; but he

6. M. Aimé Césaire comes to this conclusion (in the euphoria, admittedly, of 1948) in his introduction to the (Selected Works) *Oeuvres choisies* of Victor Schoelcher: "He brought political freedom to blacks in the French Caribbean . . . created a startling contradiction that cannot but explode the old order of things: *that which makes the modern colonized man at the same time a full citizen and a complete proletarian.* From this time on, on the edge of the Caribbean sea as well, the motor of History is about to roar into life."

It is difficult today to identify with these declarations.

Because we know that here political freedom has been only a constant lure. That the Martinican is neither a full citizen (he is not from the city) nor a complete proletarian (but a "dispersed" proletarian). That History is that which has been opposed unrelentingly to the converging histories of the Caribbean, and that since the "liberation" of 1848 what has indeed increased is the snoring of the sleep of assimilation, interrupted by tragic explosions of popular impulses, never enough to resolve the dilemma.

will be—Italian or Spanish from Latin America, Lebanese or Chinese confined to the tertiary sector—incapable of transforming into a _technological discourse_ the technical methods that he kept as part of his heritage. This privilege will be reserved in the "new world" for the WASP descendents of those who came on the _Mayflower_. The only other technological "entity," that of Aztec or Mayan peoples, will be swept away by the conquest. Over the entire American continent, whatever the degree of technical evolution of the people, Western technological systems prevail and their control is restricted to the dominant classes of the United States and Canada. The question is whether one should urgently consider a true integration, beyond piecemeal technical progress, of the "spirit" of this technology; or, if necessary, be prepared from now on to adapt this spirit to the emergent cultures of the Caribbean and Latin America. Without which domination will flourish. A concerted effort of this kind can combat, in small communities helplessly given over to the colonizing force of assimilation, total dependence (what I can then call technical ignorance) created from the combination of two factors: the lack of an endogenous technology (conceived as a collective approach to experience and action) and the necessary adoption of technical progress, imported from elsewhere.

Land

I remember the lingering fragrances that lay thick in my childhood world. I feel that then all the surrounding land was rich with these perfumes that never left you: the ethereal smell of magnolias, the essence of tuberoses, the discreet stubbornness of dahlias, the dreamy penetration of gladioli. All these flowers have disappeared, or almost. There barely remains along the roads, as far as smells go, the sudden sugary blanket of hog plums in whose wake you can get lost, or, in some places along the Route de la Trace, the delicate smell of wild lilies beckon. The land has lost its smells. Like almost everywhere else in the world.

The flowers that grow today are cultivated for export. Sculptured, spotless, striking in precision and quality. But they are heavy also, full, lasting. You can keep them for two weeks in a vase. Arum or anthurium, bunches of which adorn our airport. The porcelain rose, which is so durable. The heliconia, its amazing shaft multiplying infinitely. The King of Kings, or the red ginger lily, whose very heart is festooned with dark red. These flowers delight us. But they have no fragrance. They are nothing but shape and color.

I am struck by the fate of flowers. The shapeless yielding to the shapely. As if the land had rejected its "essence" to concentrate everything in appearance. It can be seen but not smelt. Also these thoughts on flowers are not a matter of lamenting a vanished idyll in the past. But it is true that the fragile and fragrant flower demanded in the past daily care from the community that acted on its own. The flower without fragrance endures today, is maintained in form only. Perhaps that is the emblem of our wait? We dream of what we will cultivate in the future, and we wonder vaguely what the new hybrid that is already being prepared for us will look like, since in any case we will not rediscover them as they were, the magnolias of former times.

Sardonic Interludes

The question of the selection of bananas (the legitimate and inflexible demand of French importers for high quality fruit leaving Martinique) tempts us to make reference to the over-ripe pears and the half-rotten grapes that Martinican consumers are prepared to buy (which is their lookout) on the shelves of Fort-de-France shops.

* * *

Not a single visitor who does not assure you that he has succumbed to the beauty of the land and the charm of the inhabitants. Martinicans are charming by profession.

* * *

Betting on cockfights, canoe or boat races, soccer matches, drag races of cars or motorbikes improvised at night on the five kilometers of "highway," or from commune to commune (with stakes that amount to a million old francs): the traditional circuit of underdevelopment.

* * *

In beautiful rounded white letters on a clean blackboard at the reopening of school: *it is forbidden to speak Creole in class or on the playground.*

* * *

HISTORY SIGNS ON

The former opening montage that signed on the television news broadcast of ORTF-Martinique (1970) could be seen as both an abridged history and an analysis of structures. It presented us with, in the amazing shorthand possible in montage, the Arc de Triomphe attached in all kinds of ways (boat, train, and airplane) to a field of pineapples, to a cane cutter (who wiped the sweat from his brow and raised his head, no doubt to see the said airplane go by), to a young Martinican woman, apparently "in the shadow *of these* pineapples in flower," finally to a rocky coast.

An abridged history, because here expressed in images is the true Martinican journey, even if one can imagine that between the pineapples and the rocks objectivity ought to have suggested the image of one of those heroes on horseback, whip in hand, who created our country.

A structural analysis as well, since here is symbolized (but we are told that a structure is never a symbol) the mechanics of the broadcasts from ORTF-Martinique, the clear majority of which originate quite simply (sent by this airplane, after a period of reflection or planning) in French television.[1]

Let this not lead to bitterness but to the admiring observation that form was suited here to content, and that it was great integrity that induced those in charge to announce their true intentions. However, it should have been necessary, after the broadcast (since no doubt the film materials, once used, are returned to their owners), for the montage to be shown again in the opposite direction at the end of this program, and for the rocky point, with all that preceded it (and which now would follow it), to then be propelled (pulled by an airplane flying backwards) as far as the original Arc de Triomphe.

The second montage (1973) had the advantage over the former one of a systematic use of mixing, no doubt to show that integration had been achieved: the Croix-Mission took turns with the place de la Concorde and the Bord-de-Mer with the Boul'Mich. It is quite true that on "grand occasions" news from elsewhere is sent here by satellite. But, how transparent, this montage (filled with highways, beaches, goods on the wharf, and in which you could see a lonely and tired fisherman, no doubt taking the place of the former cane cutter) came to an end with the image of a majestic cruise ship. So the news of

1. Alas! the intense folklorization, the absence of a sense of direction, imitation, and the failure of the imagination result in the fact that the rare broadcasts filmed locally are almost as destructive as the unremitting pressure of the imported programs.

the world, which arrives in the country only through the channel of the head office (everyone knowing that Martinique is incapable of having independent media), could have—in case the circuit that feeds us images is broken temporarily (by strikes, shortage of airplanes, problems with the satellite, punitive measures, expurgation, etc.)—been brought to us nevertheless by our waves of tourists, armed with their *paper from the ship*.

The present logo of FR3 goes even further. Here we have left behind the symbolic language of images to enter into "abstract" equations. As is done for every French province, news is from now on introduced by the geometric sketch of a hexagon. We are within the hexagon. No need to say more. And as a postscript the word *Martinique* is inscribed sometimes below the initials FR3. But it is nothing more than a part of the design.

* * *

(On the walls:)

PATENT YOUR IDEAS

*

(Advertisement for a brand of paint:)

WHAT IS GOOD FOR EUROPE
IS GOOD FOR THE FRENCH CARIBBEAN

*

(On the walls:)

BLACK ART IS EXPOSED
AT THE PARIS TRADE FAIR

*

(On a poster:)

TO REMAIN
FRENCH
VOTE FOR VALCIN

*

Here every visitor is an expert.

He arrives, amazed by his reception, pronounces a few words that he manages to improvise based on the rudiments of his discipline—after which each of his satisfied listeners is convinced that he has lived through a great Learning Experience.

*

(From the "local" newspaper—no need to give the date:)
HORSE RACING IN LAMENTIN
Last Meet of the Winter Season

*

(From the "local" newspaper—no need to give the date:)
HORSE RACING IN LAMENTIN
First Meet "of Spring"

*

Not one of these texts and observations, collected or compiled in 1973, is today irrelevant in meaning or implication.

In this way we get from 31 March 1973—when the news broadcast announces (an April Fools' Day hoax) that the French Caribbean tends (because of continental drift) to get closer to Europe, while the rest of the Americas drift away (which provokes the comment, under the headline "In a Dream Time," in a newspaper the following day: "We must acknowledge: it was a joke. . . . In the middle of the dry season, when we feel remote from everything, when the mind wanders, when Mt. Pelée fiercely comes to mind, the wave of a wand can tear us away from our nightmares. . . . The blessed day when our island, having cast off its ties with the Americas, would be fastened to the Metropolis, without an aerial bridge, without any kind of bridge, all dock duties abolished, things would look different for us")—to 27 September 1980, when FR3 makes the very solemn announcement: "It snowed on the mountains of Réunion!"

The Known, the Uncertain

*

So one still hears at this time Martinican students speak without a second thought about "spring break" and "summer vacation." That is how they are officially described.[2]

*

At the window in an administrative office, on 21 March 1978, a pleasant sixty-year-old greets me heartily: "So, M. Glissant, it is spring!"

*

(4 January 1979, directly from Paris and destined for the DOM, on the subject of an international meeting in Guadeloupe, the presenter on FR3 offers this detail: "Guadeloupean winter is very mild, between 20 and 25 degrees celcius." This was not meant to be funny or humorous.)

*

One can—it is amazing—hear a Martinican planter interviewed on television talk of "we Europeans."

*

You can be sure that he who is surprised by such bewildering practices, and either laughs or despairs because of them, is an intellectual with a complex.

*

(How to escape noticing that a community that has in this way become accustomed to this use of words, which so clearly as far as it is concerned, do not correspond to any reality, except that of fantasy, little by little gets lost in the unreal, and

2. There are even funnier examples of this. For example, candidates in an official examination (for entry into the police force, May 1979) sat their tests at 3:00 A.M., in order to coincide with the time of the exam in France. Imagine the candidate, driven to this examination by unemployment and

consequently irresponsible, use of words?) We are amazed that what was yesterday a staggering discrepancy—that is, the unconscious sense of an inadequacy, of a cause for anxiety— is today banal and neutralized: forever sunk in the standardized values of a standardized life. The study I made of verbal delirium in 1973 would today serve above all to categorize the neutralized language of this standardized life.

*

One can reckon on the rise of a more overt violence: not only verbal (the verbal incongruity having been sanitized in a void of nothingness) but state controlled: "Either you are French or, if not, watch yourself." But this violence is itself at the same time unreal, since we have been so worn out by attrition and standardization. (In official political life, the "violent" ones yield to the insidious, which is something new to us.)

*

More than ever the elites are preparing, each in its own way, to "control" something. Or, what amounts to the same thing, to "educate" the people. The thirst for power (for one would not know what to do with it) is even more acute, since it is our impotence that always increases. State control is thereby further strengthened.

*

We can expect in the future a winter resort at the peak of Mt. Pelée. That is the dream. To assimilate in our tactic of diversion white winter here reconstituted as fantasy.

*

At the foot of Mt. Pelée. A primary school in St.-Pierre. A tramp pleasantly but unexpectedly appears in one of the

---

who gets there by sticking close to the walls of the sleeping town, because of the risk of being arrested by a police patrol. Teachers who are candidates for the important CAPES examination are asked to arrive at 5:00 A.M., etc.

classes. He is dirty, untidy, perhaps drunk. But he is white. A little girl gets up and instinctively informs the teacher: "Miss, the School Inspector."

Land

Is there any trace, any vestige of African beliefs in what we feel about death? The tradition of the wake, where we drink and tell tales, where we make jokes, where we imitate the dead person and laugh at his weaknesses while in the house the family keeps vigil, yet careful that nothing runs out for the people outside enjoying themselves—does this tradition contain African survivals? It is certainly unsettling not to believe in a beyond that is, as it were, yours. It is perhaps more "normal" to take leave of the dead, whom we send to another world, if this "other world" comes to you reinforced by tradition, thereby making the link between birth and death.

Just as the Martinican seems to be simply passing through his world, a happy zombi, so our dead seem to us to be hardly more than confirmed zombis. Naturally, I am speaking of cultural significance and not individual sentiment. Does the adoption of a Christian paradise satisfy such a longing? Remember that the first generations of slaves brought here wished for death "in order to return to Africa." The beyond was the same as the lost country.

The time has perhaps come for human communities to reject a beyond. This collective rejection is decisive and "meaningful" only when it results from *a movement within the community*. Death too can be demystified.

We feel this in Martinique. Our collective attitude toward death is at the same time morbid (we are, for example, fascinated by road accidents), mocking (we avoid the emptiness of death by laughter), and a deep complicity (we see through it our former world, our lost land). Even today, a burial is for us a "national event," and one of the most listened-to broadcasts on the radio is the one that gives the death announcements, intended for those who wish to pay their final respects to their loved ones. I heard a young black American minister preach, very dynamic and "new look." It was an Adventist ceremony and the nonbelievers in the congregation appreciated as enlightened novices his approach to the world beyond. Someone on this occasion confided to me: "Really I would willingly become an Adventist, since their burial ceremonies are much more moving."

The Quarrel with History

Reading the paper "The West Indian Writer and His Quarrel with History"[1] by Edward Baugh allows me to put forward the following observations.

If it is ridiculous to claim that a people "has no history," one can argue that, in certain contemporary situations, while one of the results of global expansion is the presence (and the weight) of an increasingly global historical consciousness, a people can have to confront the problem posed by this consciousness that it feels is "vital," but that it is unable to "bring to light": because the lived circumstances of this daily reality do not form part of a continuum, which means that its relation with its surroundings (what we would call its nature) is in a discontinuous relation to its accumulation of experiences (what we would call its culture). In such a context, history as far as it is a discipline and claims to clarify the reality lived by this people, will suffer from a serious epistemological deficiency: it will not know how to make the link. The problem faced by collective consciousness makes a creative approach necessary, in that the rigid demands made by the historical approach can constitute, if they are not restrained, a paralyzing handicap. Methodologies passively assimilated, far from reinforcing a global consciousness or permitting the historical process to be established beyond the ruptures experienced, will simply contribute to worsening the problem.

The French Caribbean is the site of a history characterized by ruptures and that began with a brutal dislocation, the slave trade. Our historical consciousness could not be deposited

1. Paper presented at the Carifesta colloquium (Kingston, Jamaica, 1976). The cultural and literary problematics in the anglophone Caribbean is concerned with these concepts primarily. The historian as poet (for example, Brathwaite), the novelist as historian (for example, Naipaul), history and the project of writing (for example, Lamming): the recurrence of the theme is constant. The meeting points between Caribbean literatures (anglophone, francophone, hispanophone, Creole) do not result from a decision on the part of those who produce this writing: they are still hidden traces of the same historic movement, of an adherence to the culture.

gradually and continuously like sediment, as it were, as happened with those peoples who have frequently produced a totalitarian philosophy of history, for instance European peoples, but came together in the context of shock, contraction, painful negation, and explosive forces. This dislocation of the continuum, and the inability of the collective consciousness to absorb it all, characterize what I call a nonhistory.

The negative effect of this nonhistory is therefore the erasing of the collective memory. When in 1802 Colonel Delgrès blew himself up with his three hundred men using the stock of gunpowder at Fort Matouba in Guadeloupe, so as not to surrender to six thousand French soldiers who were encircling him, the noise of this explosion did not resound immediately in the consciousness of Martinicans and Guadeloupeans. It happened that Delgrès was defeated all over again by the sly trickery of the dominant ideology, which succeeded for a while in twisting the meaning of his heroic act and removing it from popular memory. Consequently, the French government's March 1848 proclamation to the slaves in Martinique asserted that Guadeloupeans had *themselves demanded* the reimposition of slavery in 1802. And when the Caribbean hero, Toussaint or Martí, was victorious, this was localized within their respective countries. The ideological blockade functioned just like the economic blockades against Haiti in the past, and against Cuba in the present. If Bolivar found help and comfort in Haiti, if therefore for a while the notion of a common Caribbean history was real, this period was short-lived. Today, however, we are hearing the blast from Matouba. In order to repossess their historical space, the French Caribbean countries needed to break through the dead tissue that colonial ideology had deposited along their borders.

Therefore, because of their colonial origin, these peoples for a long time could only oppose the latter (and especially in the Lesser Antilles) in sporadic bursts of a resistance that persisted, and not in the inexhaustible confrontation that the African countries, for example, could manage. The ancestral community of language, religion, government, traditional values—in brief, a worldview—allowed these peoples, each in its own way, to offer continuous, open resistance. The patience and the self-confidence created by such a cultural hinterland was not available to us for a long time.

What resulted was that the French Caribbean people did not relate even a mythical chronology of this land to their knowledge of this country, and so nature and culture have not formed a dialectical whole that informs a people's consciousness. So much so that obscured history was often reduced for us to a chronology of natural events, retaining only their "explosive" emotional meanings. We would say: "the year of the great earthquake," or: "the year of the hurricane that flattened M. Celeste's house," or: "the year of the fire on Main Street." And that is precisely the recourse open to any community without a collective consciousness and detached from an awareness of itself. No doubt the same chronology can be observed in peasant communities in certain industrialized countries.

One cannot condemn this practice of a "natural" chronology as pure alienation. A study of the folk imagination, made fashionable because of the excesses of industrial and administrative dehumanization, demonstrates that the process is more rational than it was first thought to be. But nature once severed from its meaning is as impoverished (for man) and impotent as being subjected to history. The creative link between nature and culture is vital to the formation of a community.

Today we hear the blast from Matouba, but also the volley of shots fired at Moncada. Our history comes to life with a stunning unexpectedness. The emergence of this common experience broken in time (of this concealed parallel in histories) that shapes the Caribbean at this time surprises us before we have even thought about this parallel. That means also that our history emerges at the edge of what we can tolerate, this emergence must be related immediately to the complicated web of events in our past. The past, to which we were subjected, which has not yet emerged as history for us, is, however, obsessively present. The duty of the writer is to explore this obsession, to show its relevance in a continuous fashion to the immediate present.[2] This exploration is therefore related neither to a schematic chronology nor to a nostalgic lament. It leads to the identification of a painful notion of time and its full projection forward into the future, without the help of those plateaus in time from which the West has benefited, without the help of that collective density that is the primary value of an ancestral cultural heartland. That is what I call *a prophetic vision of the past.*[3]

"History [with a capital *H*] ends where the histories of those peoples once reputed to be without history come together." History is a highly functional fantasy of the West, originating at precisely the time when it alone "made" the history of the World. If Hegel relegated African peoples to the ahistorical, Amerindian peoples to the prehistorical, in order to reserve History for European peoples exclusively, it appears that it is not because these African or American peoples "have entered History" that we can conclude today that such a hierarchical conception of "the march of History" is no longer relevant. Reality has, for example, forced Marxist thought to concede that it is not in the most technically advanced countries, nor in the most organized proletariat, that the revolution will first be successful. Marxism has thus used objective reality and its own viewpoint to criticize the concept of a linear and hierarchical History. It is this hierarchical process that we deny in our own emergent historical consciousness, in its ruptures, its sudden emergence, its resistance to exploration.

Because the collective memory was too often wiped out, the Caribbean writer must "dig deep" into this memory, following the latent signs that he has picked up in the everyday world.

2. The time has come to ask oneself whether the writer is (in this process) the one who hoards the written or initiates the spoken? If the process of historicization does not call into question the status of the written? If the written record is "adequate" for the archives of collective memory?
3. Preface to the first edition of *Monsieur Toussaint* (Paris: Seuil, 1961).

The Known, the Uncertain

Because the Caribbean consciousness was broken up by sterile barriers, the writer must be able to give expression to all those occasions when these barriers were partially broken. Because the Caribbean notion of time was fixed in the void of an imposed nonhistory, the writer must contribute to reconstituting its tormented chronology: that is, to reveal the creative energy of a dialectic reestablished between nature and culture in the Caribbean.

As far as we are concerned, history as a consciousness at work and history as lived experience are therefore not the business of historians exclusively. Literature for us will not be divided into genres but will implicate all the perspectives of the human sciences. These inherited cateogries must not in this matter be an obstacle to a daring new methodology, where it responds to the needs of our situation. The quarrel with History is perhaps for Derek Walcott[4] the affirmation of the urgency of a revaluation of the conventions of analytical thought.

A reality that was long concealed from itself and that took shape in some way along with the consciousness that the people had of it, has as much to do with the problematics of investigation as with a historical organization of things. It is this "literary" implication that orients the thrust of historical thought, from which none of us can claim to be exempt.[5]

NOTE I
Concerning history as neurosis

Would it be ridiculous to consider our lived history as a steadily advancing neurosis? To see the Slave Trade as a traumatic shock, our relocation (in the new land) as a repressive phase,

---

4. The works of the St. Lucian poet, Derek Walcott, have provided for the Jamaican poet, Edward Baugh, the main argument for the text I examine here: "History is irrelevant in the Caribbean."
5. The chronological delusion and the simplification of a clear "periodization" are the "cultural" shields against the emergence of a historical

slavery as the period of latency, "emancipation" in 1848 as reactivation, our everyday fantasies as symptoms, and even our horror of "returning to those things of the past" as a possible manifestation of the neurotic's fear of his past? Would it not be useful and revealing to investigate such a parallel? What is repressed in our history persuades us, furthermore, that this is more than an intellectual game. Which psychiatrist could state the problematics of such a parallel? None. History has its dimension of the unexplorable, at the edge of which we wander, our eyes wide open.

NOTE 2

Concerning transversality

However, our diverse histories in the Caribbean have produced today another revelation: that of their subterranean convergence. They, thereby, bring to light an unsuspected, because it is so obvious, dimension of human behavior: transversality. The implosion of Caribbean history (of the converging histories of our peoples) relieves us of the linear, hierarchical vision of a single History that would run its unique course. It is not this History that has roared around the edge of the Caribbean, but actually a question of the subterranean convergence of our histories. The depths are not only the abyss of neurosis but primarily the site of multiple converging paths.

The poet and historian Brathwaite, in his recapitulation in the magazine *Savacou* of the work done in the Caribbean on our history (our present-day and obviously overlapping histories), summarizes the third and last section of his study with the single phrase: "The unity is submarine."

To my mind, this expression can only evoke all those Africans weighed down with ball and chain and thrown overboard whenever a slave ship was pursued by enemy vessels

---

longing. The more this pseudoperiodization appears "objective," the more one feels that this longing—so subjective, obsessive, unclear—has been suppressed.

and felt too weak to put up a fight. *They sowed in the depths the seeds of an invisible presence.* And so transversality, and not the universal transcendence of the sublime, has come to light. It took us a long time to learn this. We are the roots of a cross-cultural relationship.

Submarine roots: that is floating free, not fixed in one position in some primordial spot, but extending in all directions in our world through its network of branches.

We, thereby, live, we have the good fortune of living, this shared process of cultural mutation, this convergence that frees us from uniformity.

Carifesta 1976

The 1976 Caribbean Festival was organized in Jamaica around Caribbean heroes: this time, Toussaint Louverture, José Martí, Juarez, Bolivar, Marcus Garvey. A popular gathering at this time consecrated in a spectacular and massive way what had been until then nothing but a dream of intellectuals. In this way, Carifesta conveyed to a collective consciousness the impulses of a few.

A scurrilous publication in Martinique criticized the "separatist intellectuals" of this country in 1979 for encouraging a "Toussaint complex," that is, for trying to compensate by the adoption of other people's heroes for the absence in Martinique itself of a great popular hero. And it is true that this absence contributes to a community's affliction with a paralyzing *sense of powerlessness.* The same publication, in the same article, made every effort to celebrate the role of Victor Schoelcher in the liberation of Martinican slaves in 1848. What was the writer of the article then doing if not looking for a victorious and tutelary hero? The fact is that the debate surrounding Schoelcher is a false one; the real issue is not the importance of his role, which was undeniable and effective, but primarily the context of his activities (the movement from a slave economy to a market economy; the growing influence of French beet-sugar farmers, whose advertisements in Paris declare at this time: "My sugar is not tainted with black blood"; the concerned intervention of English abolitionists) and the use then made of these activities: Schoelcherism, which was for a long time a veritable ideology. Beyond the figure of Schoelcher, one cannot but observe that the form, the atmosphere, the trend of the "liberation" of 1848 carry within themselves the seeds of assimilation; Schoelcherism is the symbolic form of this movement. It is not a question—we shall see this elsewhere—of knowing whether this liberation was seized in a bloody fashion by the slaves in revolt. Martinican history is packed with futile revolts. It would be funny in this regard to provoke a *war of dates*: 27 April (declaration of the Abolition plan), 22 May (slave revolt), thus splitting hairs on chronology and proclamations. The problem is a deeper mystification, contained in the principle and the progress of Abolition: the suppression of the specific nature of the Martinican people.

The absence of an outstanding popular figure (of a hero) does not result from the logic of defeat. A self-confident people has the ability to transform into a mythical victory what may have been a real defeat; so the *Song of Roland* transformed into heroic symbolism the error in strategy and the rout of Charlemagne at Roncevaux. One can go so far as to argue that the defeats of heroes are necessary to the solidarity of communities.

The legitimacy of adopting Caribbean heroes everywhere in the Caribbean, including Martinique, is still to be shown. It could not be more obvious. Toussaint Louverture is a maroon, of the same kind, I was going to say the same race, as the most significant and misunderstood of the runaway slaves of Fonds-Massacre in Martinique. It is a question of *the same historical phenomenon*. And it is because the Martinican people have not mythified the defeats of the runaway slaves, but purely and simply acnowledged them, that we have today a debate about Toussaint. Here the *historical phenomenon* must be recognized.

The Known, the Uncertain

On this day, in the Kingston stadium, thousands of Caribbean people coming from everywhere acclaimed the names I mentioned earlier. Whether they won or not, these men, who had made the true history of the Caribbean, were born once and for all in the collective consciousness. Now, is Martinique a cyst in a zone of Caribbean civilization? Is Toussaint Louverture another's hero, and Schoelcher our "true" one? That Martinican intellectuals are still debating such issues reveals, in a disturbing way, the intensity of the disorientation inflicted on them. Could they recognize in Frantz Fanon one of the figures who have awakened (in the deepest sense of the word) the peoples of the contemporary world? They could not. Other people's heroes are not ours; our heroes, of necessity, are primarily those of other people.

History and Literature

I

It is not the literary side of things that has caused me anguish, as one would have expected of any writer concerned with devoting his attention to self-expression; it is rather the historical side, in the excessive or inadequate reflection on lived reality, with which, like any man today, and like any Martinican, I cannot help feeling involved. For history is destined to be pleasure or distress *on its own terms*. After being folktale, story, or speech, after being record, statistic, and verification, after being a universal, systematic, and imposed whole, history insofar as it is the "reflection" of a collective consciousness today is concerned with the obscure areas of lived reality. At every stage in this evolution, each conception of the historic was accompanied by a particular form of rhetoric. It is this link that I would like to trace, in order to show how History (whether we see it as expression or lived reality) and Literature form part of the same problematics: the account, or the frame of reference, of the collective relationships of men with their environment, in a space that keeps changing and in a time that constantly is being altered.

The critic Pierre Brodin analyzes a work by the American novelist Joan Didion, *A Book of Common Prayer*. Here is his description of the heroine of the book: "Child of the American West, she had inherited from her parents a faith in certain family values, the virtues of land cleared for cultivation and well irrigated, abundant harvests, thrift, industry, judicial system, progress, learning, the ever-ascending evolution of Mankind. But she was untouched by History, innocent of politics. She knew that there was always something happening in the world, but she believed it would all end well." [1] This example is revealing: it concerns the complacent kind of person who believes that history is simply a sequence of events, to which therefore there will always be an *outcome;* and it comes close to asserting that people who are happy have no history. But today, and the critic's comment suggests this, these beliefs are identified as a kind of weakness. We can be the victims of History when we submit passively to it—never managing to escape its harrowing power. History (like Literature) is capable of quarrying deep within us, as a consciousness or the emergence of a consciousness, as a neurosis (symptom of loss) and a contraction of the self.

In our situation, historical consciousness can be (or be lived primarily as) the repertoire of responses of an individual-within-a-country to an Other-Elsewhere that would appear in terms of difference or transcendence. One cannot be a historian unwittingly, or work on language, and yet isolate oneself from the drama of the relationship that the poet Segalen clearly identified when he tried to contrast the diversity of the world to the spread of a dominant sameness. My aim will be also to show that in History as in Literature Western thought

1. Pierre E. Brodin in a review of Joan Didion's *A Book of Common Prayer* in *Liberté* (Montreal) 19, no. 114 (November–December 1977): 103–9.

The Known, the Uncertain

(since it is the one that prevails here) has practiced this form of domination, and that it has not managed (in spite of persistent advantages) to resist the liberating force of diversity.

Before coming to the intent behind the project of a literature or a history of the Caribbean, I feel it necessary to consider a few of the sustained links between History and Literature.

First of all, that the earliest link between a view of history and the urge to write can be traced back to myth.

Myth disguises while conferring meaning, obscures and brings to light, mystifies as well as clarifies and intensifies *that* which emerges, fixed in time and space, between men and their world. It explores the known-unknown.

Myth is the first state of a still-naive historical conscious-ness, and the raw material for the project of a literature.

We should note that, given the formative process of a his-torical consciousness, myth anticipates history as much as it inevitably repeats the accidents that it has glorified; that means it is in turn a producer of history. This is why on the eve of the battle of Marathon the Greek warriors sang of the exploits of Achilles before Troy, just as on the eve of the victorious con-frontation of Bonaparte's armies in 1802, the Haitians cele-brated the exploits of the maroon Mackandal, as they were idealized in their imagination. (This is an example of how myth "clarifies.")

However, in general the revelations of myth are obscure, are not immediately apparent. Which is what I mean when I say it both obscures and clarifies. As the first form of literary ex-pression, myth *coils* meaning around the image itself: which means that it is as distant from pure realism as it is from scru-pulous and in-depth analysis. (A long time passed before a systematic explanation of the story of Oedipus could be ad-vanced.) We can derive from this an initial point of contact, which could be described in the following manner: In the evo-lution over time of Western thought, history and literature first come together in the realm of myth, but the first as a pre-

Caribbean Discourse

monition of the past, and the second as memory of the future. Both obscure yet functional.[2]

It is not surprising that myth has "fed" religious anxieties. First of all, because religious thought (feeling) was the most appropriate early manifestation of the plunge into the depths, precisely where myth was content to obscure what it revealed. Then, because primitive religious thought ordained a genesis and an ordering of the world, which elaborated a conceptual framework. Genesis, which is the fundamental explanation, and ordering, which is the ritualized narrative, anticipate what the West would ascribe to Literature (that it is almost divine creation: the Word made Flesh)—the notion of Genesis—and what would be the realm of historical consciousness (a selective evolution)—that of Ordering.

Thus, in our own area of concern, the official history of

2. I do not know if it is the need to *delay* all revelation (while it is being fulfilled) that determines that in myth (as in tragedy, which for the Greeks originated in myth) the achievement of collective harmony assumes the ritual sacrifice of a hero, at the very least his apparent failure. This sacrifice is the veil behind which revelation is fulfilled: it is a distracting image that conceals the meaning of the mythic or tragic act, while consecrating it. (Thus, the veil of Christ's face would be the last sign of the Mystery of Christ's Passion.) M. René Girard has developed in his work a theory of the "sacrificial victim" as the basis for history (*Violence and the Sacred* [Baltimore: Johns Hopkins University Press, 1977]; *Things Hidden since the Foundation of the World* [London: Athlone Press, 1977]). Herman Gunkel writes—in a volume in the *Bibliothèque d'ethnologie historique* series, translated from the German by Pierre Gilbert as *Une théorie de la légende: Herman Gunkel et les légendes de la Bible* (Paris: Flammarion, 1979)—on the subject of his exegesis of the Old Testament and in particular of the Book of Genesis: "Myths—let us not shrink from the word—are *stories about Gods*, as opposed to legends, in which the actors are men." Monotheism permits in the Old Testament only the appearance of "faded" myths, in a state of degeneration in relation to older versions (Oriental, for example). In preference to these definitions, which allow Gunkel to construct a hierarchy myth-legend-history in the genesis of the Old Testament, I would perhaps take the approach that proposes legend as the popular and poetic expression of a collective consciousness and myth as the product (often clever, informed in an unstructured way) of ideas responsive to or on the level of a collective impulse.

The Known, the Uncertain

Martinique (totally fashioned according to Western ideology, naturally) has been conceived in terms of the list of discoverers and governors of this country, without taking into account the sovereign beauties—since there were no male sovereigns—that it has produced. (Those are indeed the key chapters of our official history. The Martinican elite can see "power" only in the shape of the female thigh. Empress, queen, courtesan: History is for them nothing but a submission to pleasure, where the male is dominant; the male is the Other. This notion of history as pleasure is about making oneself available.)

But the encounter between genesis and ordering in almost all the early myths, including those of African and Oriental traditions, is sufficient evidence that the magic of the word and the hallowing of time and place are combined to offer a clarification of a basic relationship, the one that links the opposing notions of culture and nature. The control of nature, and of one's nature, by culture was the ideal of the Western mind, just as to broaden one's culture to the cosmic dimensions of one's nature, and all nature, was perhaps the dream of the Oriental mind. From this dichotomy have come the different notions of being-in-the-world of which we are aware. For the Western mind, it is a matter of learning the natural Genesis, the primordial slime, the Eternal Garden, and embarking— even at the risk of condemnation (like the myth of Adam and Eve, and the real experience of Socrates, which are both about taking the risk)—on a journey to an ordering-knowledge. History and Literature agree (with the rare episodes of a blending of the two that quickly came to an end, as with the pre-Socratic philosophers) to separate man from the world, to subject nature to culture. The linear nature of narrative and the linear form of chronology take shape in this context. Man, the chosen one, knows himself and knows the world, not because he is part of it, but because he establishes a sequence and measures it according to his own time scale, which is determined by his *affiliation*.

Such notions reinforce each other. In the case of History, after the methodological beginnings of the eighteenth century, which are surely achievements in scientific thought as well, a tremendous belief will begin to grow in the objectivity of the historian. In the case of Literature, a no less great bias, at the same time, will unleash the ravages of "imitation," and it is the belief in the powers of realism, which, for instance, the blind imitators of Balzac will struggle in vain to apply. The surface effects of literary realism are the precise equivalent of the historian's claim to pure objectivity. And at the same time the ambiguities emerge. To the pair realism-objectivity, one could legitimately oppose another pair: romanticism-subjectivity. As opposed to the claim of describing *the whole of the real,* one might prefer the attempt to completely reconstruct (or to recreate) in depth one part of this reality. Whatever the case, man, not as agent but as will, had been placed at the center of the literary and historical drama; the work often went no further than appearances, no deeper than the expression of this wish.

To dig underneath, to reveal the inner workings, that is the aim of the kind of history recently called sociological, and one must admit that this was the ambition behind the attempt of modern Western poets who, with Rimbaud, Lautréamont, and Baudelaire, became engaged in bringing to light (after the German romantics) what was concealed *under the surface.* In these new conceptions of history and of literature it would be believed that man is not at the center of things. The perspective of genesis-ordering then yields to an exploration of the depths, and man is not the privileged subject of his knowledge; he gradually becomes its object. The power of myth wanes: he is explained and put in his place. He is no longer the mind probing the known-unknown. Psychoanalysis, economic theory, the social sciences in general have a destructively clarifying effect on the functional power of myth. Humanism (the notion of man as privileged) will thus begin to be defeated and, what interests us now, Western man will have gradually and with great pain ceased to have faith in himself as being at the center of things.

But another area of ambiguity was discovered in the mean-

The Known, the Uncertain

time within this process. It is that before embarking on the course of *revelation*, History and Literature had attempted to put together a total system. For many, Shakespeare was behind the first manifestation of this trend.

We know the importance of the parallel, in the works of Shakespeare, between the great tragedies and the tragedies of history. The problems of succession to the English throne, just like those of the succession to the Danish throne, pose the universal and metaphysical question of *legitimacy*. What is this legitimacy in Shakespeare, if not the sanction of the balance between nature and culture, through which man would abandon the old ordering alchemy of the Middle Ages and enter into the sphere of diversification that will be called the modern age? A grandiose perspective, which gives a sense of the reach of Shakespeare's work, with, alas, one overlooked area: in this totalizing equilibrium a hierarchy was established, from Caliban to Prospero; and it is not difficult to see that Caliban-nature is contrasted *from below* with Prospero-culture. In *The Tempest* the legitimacy of Prospero is thus linked to his superiority, and epitomizes the legitimacy of the West. The ambiguity is therefore that Literature and History were at the same time proposed in the West as *instruments of this Totality* (moving from primitive linearity to a global system), but that in this proposed Totality was inserted the unprecedented ambition of creating man in the image of the Western ideal, with degrees in the elevation from Caliban to Prospero.

At this stage, History is written with a capital *H*. It is a totality that excludes other histories that do not fit into that of the West. Perhaps therein lies the link between Bossuet (Providence) and Marx (the class struggle): this ethnocentric principle unites the mechanics of the Historical process (the Christian God, the proletariat of industrialized nations) with the soul of the West.[3] The hierarchical system instituted by Hegel

3. One is struck by the geographical progression along which Marx "orients" his theory of models: Asiatic (remote), then ancient (that is, Mediterranean), then feudal (that is, "European"), then capitalist, in the heart of the

(ahistory, prehistory, History) corresponds clearly with the literary ideology of his time. Literature attains a metaexistence, the all-powerfulness of a sacred sign, which will allow people with writing to think it justified to dominate and rule peoples with an oral civilization. And the last Western attempt to conceptualize a History, that of Toynbee, will organise the Total System based on a discriminatory sequence (great civilizations, great states, great religions) indispensable in such a project.

It is against this double hegemony of a History with a capital *H* and a Literature consecrated by the absolute power of the written sign that the peoples who until now inhabited the hidden side of the earth fought, at the same time they were fighting for food and freedom.

Only technical hegemony (that is, the acquired capacity to subjugate nature and consequently to intoxicate any possible culture with the knowledge created from this subjugation and which is suited to it) still permits the West, which has known the anxieties resulting from a challenged legitimacy, to continue to exercise its sovereignty which is no longer by right but by circumstance. As it abandons right for circumstance, the West dismantles its vision of History (with a capital *H*) and its conception of a sacred Literature.

The thrust of this argument drives us to say that the present intellectual reaction (in the face of the new world situation) clearly constitutes a revealing transformation of the relationship between history and literature; that the methodological and fundamental distinction between diachrony and synchrony could also be seen as a *trick;* that, no longer capable of dominating the History of the world, the West chose this method of refining the idea that histories would no longer weigh so heavily on consciousness and self-expression.

---

industrial cities of Europe. This presents the march towards History (towards its fulfillment) on which all *converges.* The histories of various peoples and their resolutions have overturned this process. History has *fragmented* into histories.

The Known, the Uncertain

It is, however, simpler to consider this transformation, not as a trick, but as a kind of logical eventuality. In the face of a now shattered notion of History, the whole of which no one can claim to master nor even conceive, it was normal that the Western mind should advance a diversified Literature, which is scattered in all directions but whose meaning no one could claim to have mastered.

Now, to follow the logic of these ideas to its conclusion, we should let the weight of lived experience "slip in." Literature is not only fragmented, it is henceforth shared. In it lie histories and the voice of peoples. We must reflect on a new relationship between history and literature. We need to live it differently.[4]

INTERMEDIARY NOTE
Concerning Borges: Inquiries

In order to get to know who Borges is (in this way daring to conduct another inquiry into his significance), to go beyond the obvious information given in his biography (Argentinian, contemporary, omniscient, etc.), to go through time and space, investigate relationships, secrets, revelations. The fact is that the isolation he imposes on himself, which makes him as close to and as distant from his nearest neighbor as a sage from an-

---

4. Two "American" writers have dramatically approached this lived reality. Saint-John Perse, because of the inability to *inscribe* himself on his place of birth (the Caribbean), *distances* himself by wandering (his is a poetics of *departure*). He eventually finds haven in an idea, that of the West; and, incapable of living histories, he chooses to glorify History.

Borges from Argentina, having left neither his country nor his city, but ill at ease with some of his compatriots, reconstructs a *historical pattern* in which abstract (and often hidden) connections are more important than the absurdities of the here and now. He attempts a refutation of time, he fixes History at its origin. These are two literary imaginations who have faced the often ordinary hazards of cultural diversity, and chosen to transcend them through a *universal absolute*. But this transcendence "from above" demands the *dramatization* of an irretrievable solitude. If all writing were seen as implying a form of dramatization, Saint-John Perse and Borges represent for us the "terminal" image of the writer (as Hegel was for a time that of the philosopher).

cient China, favors his intention to be above all a spirit "growing" in all directions, in search of other spirits. Borges abolishes frontiers in time and space.

It seems that there is nothing that he does not know, that he has not studied or imagined. In him could be identified a taste for knowledge that ranges free and makes connections rather than the kind that stubbornly quarries the same bedrock. But he does not investigate other literatures, neither French nor Spanish nor Saxon; he reconstructs them into a single one that is the Literature of Borges. When one has accepted Borges's capacity for appropriation (and why should we not? "All books are written by the same mind"), one sees that authors like this are capable of mental relocation, so much so that in each case we come upon those (uncertain) areas on the other side of reason where Borges's logic gives excessive emphasis to the unspeakable. Where does Literature end and the unknown begin? Borges has, he says, devoted his life "to literature and, sometimes, to the perplexities of metaphysics": he has in this way tried, by transcending himself and the world, to make contact with fellow spirits whom he sought beyond time and space. But "it is our misfortune that the world is real, and my misfortune that I am Borges." It is our good fortune that he writes as a witness of his failure. If we resist "metaphysical perplexities," literary pleasure is left.

This bloodless perspective (of the erudite savant, of the librarian) shapes one of the most daring forms of worldview. From scribe to mandarin to honest transcriber (a rare breed) to gentleman to refined researcher, what an unremitting, subterranean continuity. If reality persists, it is as pure appearance; and if substance is absent, the vortex increases. To extend a total vision, in all its variations, is to ascribe an even greater unity to it. It is therefore possible that Borges has dreamed of being, "after the Words of Shakespeare and Swift," the third echo of this famous declaration: "I am who I am." A single being within a single enigma.

But it is because he suffers this sense of belonging to his own world that Borges, in spite of his origins, has a universal impact.

· · · · ·

III

The relationship between history and literature is concealed today in what I call the *longing for the ideal of history*. The passion for or the preoccupation with history does not manifest itself in the writer as a need for a reserve of information to which he has easy access, not as a reassuring framework, but rather as the obsession with finding the *primordial source* toward which one struggles through revelations that have the peculiarity (like myth in the past) of obscuring as well as disclosing.

This primordial source is at the same time the explanation of origins, the echo of Genesis, that which reorients the evolution of the collective drama. But myth could plunge into the depths of the lived experience; it is then impossible for the present literary work to take its place. Too intensely personal, it often departs from lived experience in order to give it meaning. While doing this, however, myth's capacity to explore and reveal continues to haunt; the *longing for history* is the symptom of this obsession. If it manifests itself almost always by or through a failure (the novel's protagonist does not fulfil his mission, for example, or fulfils it and dies in the process), it is perhaps in accordance with another of the laws that govern myth (and consequently tragedy): the need to secure (to ensure) revelation by the hero's "sacrifice" of atonement, because of whose death the community reunites.[5]

In Faulkner's *Absalom! Absalom!* the *longing for history* is generally concerned with the true origins (the birth) of the Sutpen family, and in particular with the origins of the character called Bon. For, if the latter is black, his claim to possess Julie Sutpen will end in tragedy; but we will discover that he is perhaps *also* the brother (the mulatto half brother) of the

5. "The hero assumes the power of the group, and the final harmony is provoked by his demise" (*L'intention poétique* [The Poetic Intention], 1969). This constant feature in Western tragedy distinguishes it from the drama, with no collective intrigue.

latter. The original act of incest has a later repercussion. We clearly see that it is a question of a yearning (the knowledge of origins, of the origin) whose fulfilment would be deadly. Also, this journey to the beginning of time will twist in a spiral *toward* a point on this side that is quite the opposite of the luminous spiral ascent suggested in the case of Joan Didion's heroine. (Indeed, how to decide whether what *one* suspects (or learns) first, what *one* fears the most, will be that Bon is the brother, or that he is black, or that he is both brother and black?) This repercussion along the spiral can only create vertigo. Literature *continues* thereby one of the aspects of myth: its *coiled nature*. But the coiled pattern of myth led to a linear line of descent, the fundamental order, whereas, for instance, the coiled structure of *Absalom! Absalom!* is linked to an impossible quest. Linearity gets lost. The longed-for history and its nonfulfilment are knotted up in an inextricable tangle of relationships, alliances and progeny, whose principle is one of dizzying repetition. Do we have to recall that the prevalent principle of establishing family relationships in Martinique, ". . . Médésir, who is the nephew of Madame Ada whose mother Mrs. Fifine had two other descendants with M. Philemon and the older of the two fathered two sons with the cousin of Félicité Macali who was the adopted god-daughter of Mrs. Ada who. . . ." is the same principle that governs the tangle of relationships in Faulkner? It is a case of perversion of the original line of descent (that fundamental order): here man has lost his way and simply turns in circles.[6] How could he fix himself in the center of things while his legitimacy seems uncertain? A community can so doubt itself, get lost in the swirl of time.

Knowing what happened (why—that is, for what "valid" reason—the whites exterminated the Indians and reduced the

6. In *Sally Hemings*, a novel in which Barbara Chase-Riboud reconstructs the life of the slave who was Thomas Jefferson's concubine (New York: Viking Press, 1979), the author has the heroine and her brother say: "So strange to have blood in your veins and not know where it comes from . . ."

blacks to slavery, and whether they will be held accountable) is the question that *one* (yes, that Faulkner) cannot afford not to ask. A question that will require no *active* reply. The important thing is, not the reply, but the question. The ritual death of Bon, the final catastrophe, the tragedy of Thomas Sutpen (who "so suitably" comes from Haiti) do not discriminate between the antagonistic protagonists; they have no *legitimacy*. The latter is reserved in Faulkner for those who are "pure" (those not of mixed blood) blacks or Indians, whose pure suffering encompasses everyone else's and redeems the original sin. The yearning for history is in the harking back to a history so often relived, the negation of history as encounter and transcendence, but the assumption of history as passion.[7]

We know the idea behind *The Lost Steps* by Alejo Carpentier, according to which going upstream towards the source of the river is also to go back through time to a primordial period, across accretions or accumulations of time and space. The longing for history in this case is, not legitimacy of the Faulkner variety, but innocence; it is however the same harrowing absence. Yes, history is desire; and what it desires, as we see here, sometimes is misleading. For Carpentier's hero is obsessed because he once touched paradise (he "knew genesis") and this vision (this obsession) is the lure that pulls him

---

"Yes. Not like the Bible, where you can say he was the son of . . . who was the son of . . . who was the son of . . . That's what you mean?"

"Yes, she said, yes, that's what I mean. If I could know that the son of the son of my son would have some knowledge of me, would have something . . . a portrait of me . . ."

There we can grasp the difference that stretches between the West's appropriation of history by establishing a line of descent and the longing for this ideal, "destined to remain a longing."

7. A southern novelist, Shelby Foote, constructs one of his books, *Jordan County* (1954), as a series of stories that range from the present to the past, the last one treating the circumstances of the first contacts between whites and Indians, and providing the key to the violence to come, the course of which had been followed since the first story. That is the way back to a primordial past: Shelby Foote gives a direct response to the question that Faulkner turned into a swirl of time.

once more towards an impossible return. A lure? Yes. Just as consciousness perverted the known-unknown, so myth once had the function of revealing as it became more obscure. "Knowledge" is more than difficult, untenable: it cannot be gained. The hero will have to return to the demands of the "here and now" (which is, not the known, but the done), so renouncing the notion, the beginning of history. These kinds of failure matter. Failure leaves a trail that permits others to go forward. The literary work, so transcending myth, today initiates a cross-cultural poetics.

If we reconstruct now the journey of the hero of *One Hundred Years of Solitude* by García Márquez, we see that it is circularity that deeply penetrates the notion of history. It is the last gesture of Aureliano that will reveal the first word of his history, and will immediately cancel it out. The revelation is the known-unknown, the search for which will leave him exhausted. The death of everything is in the knowledge of origins, and history is a painful way of fulfilling what has been said. The desired ideal of history is therefore in this case self-sustaining and is involved in devouring itself. The difficulty of knowing history (*one's* history) provokes the deepest isolation. As opposed to the spiral *ascent* of the North American heroine, here we have a *return* down the spiral, infectiously tragic and decisively obscure, which not only a chosen hero but a people will want to use to repossess the beginning of their time. This infectious return is what makes Faulkner a kindred spirit in the quest for "the Other America."

And we should notice how in this world the primordial forest is in each case patiently defiant. Sutpen clears it in vain. Aureliano crosses it (he sees therein the essential hub of time caught on the tree tops), the narrator of *The Lost Steps* "goes down" through it and down through time as well. The forest is defiant and compliant, it is primitive warmth. Conquering it is the *objective*, to be conquered by it is the true subject. This is not the Eternal Garden, it is energy fixed in time and space, but which conceals its site and its chronology. The forest is the last vestige of myth in its present literary manifestation. In its

The Known, the Uncertain

impenetrable nature history feeds our desire. The forest of the maroon was thus the first obstacle the slave opposed to the *transparency* of the planter. There is no clear path, no *way forward,* in this density. You turn in obscure circles until you find the primordial tree. The formulation of history's yearned-for ideal, so tied up with its difficulty, introduces us to the dilemma of peoples today still oppressed by dominant cultures.[8]

IV

It so happens, as in Africa sometimes, that myth can be conveyed through a tale. (Epic narratives also recount myths and reinforce collective memory.) This overlapping must not make us forget the differences that separate both genres. Myth is not symbolic; its structure is not "clear"; its intention is not evident from the outset. On the other hand, by being activated in the real world, its application is assured: in the West for instance, *the line of descent,* which gives insight into History. Therefore, the two successive "zones" in which myth operates produce at the level of formulation an "obscurity" that must be opposed; at the level of its repercussion a "clarification" that creates history.

The tale operates in the opposite fashion. The tale is transparent in its structures as in its intention: its symbolic value is clear. It is not an exploration of the known-unknown, it is a stylized reading of the real. But the extent of its application is uncertain; it does not enter a community's history as a clear or decisive factor.

These opposing approaches lead to different notions of the world. Myth not only prefigures history and sometimes generates history but seems to prepare the way for History, through its generalizing tendency. The tale, on the other hand, deals

8. The longing for history, the torture of true origins, can produce caricature: a pretentious display of "antiquity." So Faulkner could see these medieval castles that American millionaires reconstructed stone by stone in the countryside of Virginia and Texas. In our countries the lower middle class did their wretched imitation of *The Magnificent Ambersons.* All of this has been swept away by the rush of modernity.

only with stories that cannot be generalized; it can happen that the tale (in the Caribbean for instance) can react to a gap in history by simply acknowledging it. It is possible that the function of the tale is here to combat the sometimes paralyzing force of a yearning for history, to save us from the belief that History is the first and most basic dimension of human experience, a belief inherited from the West or imposed by it.

Likewise, myth consecrates the word and prepares the way for writing; on this level, the folktale proceeds by means of a sacrilegious approach. So what is attacked is from the outset the sacred status of the written word. The Caribbean folktale focuses on an experience suppressed by decree or the law. It is antidecree and antilaw, that is to say, antiwriting.

V

The fragmented nature of the Caribbean folktale is such that no chronology can emerge, that time cannot be conceived as a basic dimension of human experience. Its most used measure of time is the change from day to night. During the night, Brer Rabbit will set the traps in which Brer Tiger will be dramatically caught when day comes. Thus night is the forerunner of the day. Obscurity leads transparency. The rhythm of night and day is the only measure of time for the slave, the peasant, the agricultural worker. In a great number of folktales heard during childhood, the storyteller tells about receiving at the end of the story a kick in his bottom that hurled him into his audience.[9] This final ritual in the tale does not only attest to its lucidity (the storyteller is not important, the story told is not sacred), but also to a discontinuous conception of time. As opposed to myth, the tale does not hallow cultural accretion and does not activate it.

Let us say again without fear of repetition.

Myth, which is mysterious, opens up the full range of the unknown; the tale, which is straightforward, sees this as inadequate.

9. See in this regard the Breton tales published by Jakez Hellias.

The Known, the Uncertain

The tale has crossed this primordial forest; but it does not emerge with a line of action, it increases the darkness in the tortured consciousness. The Caribbean folktale zeroes in on our absence of history: it is the site of the deactivated word. Yet it says it all. Where myth explores the known-unknown and emerges with an absolute view of history through a systematic process, the tale animates ordinary symbols in order to proceed to approximations, by going back and forth. The Caribbean tale outlines a landscape that is not possessed: it is anti-History.

Its characteristics are formed in such an approach.

The sudden changes in tone, the continuous breaks in the narrative and its "asides," the accumulation of which creates a nonuniform whole.

The abrupt psychological twists, that is the absence of any psychological description as such. "Psychology" is an indication of the passage of time.

The economy of its "morality": its shrewdest maneuver consists of repeating each time the same situation and to be careful not to propose exemplary "solutions." The art of Diversion.

The taste for excess, that is, in the first place the total freedom with regard to the paralyzing fear of repetition. The art of repetition is refreshingly inventive. It is a pleasure to re-examine the text. Onomatopeia or, even deeper, the repeated chant swirls in the dizzying rush of reality.

The relative nature of the "sacrificial victim," who is not treated solemnly. The victim—Brer Tiger, for instance—is nothing but a joke. There are certainly in his relationship with Brer Rabbit the echo of the adventures of Ysengrin the Wolf and Reynard the Fox. The difference is that here no heroic verse-chronicle functions as the other ("respectable") dimension of the real.

This last characteristic permits us to understand the way in which we have intimate contact with our overlapping tales without ever yielding to the temptation to identify a sublimated History.

The tale has given us a sense of the collective, while implying that we still have to possess the latter.

VI

This collectivity that is the subject of the narrative, what is
basically spoken, forces us to draw up its relationship to the
individual: In what way does a community influence the individuals who make it up? Or vice versa?

When the collectivity does not yet permit the individual to
stand out, we are faced with what Western thought (for which
the dignity of the individual is the yardstick) calls primitive
societies.

Each time the individual opposes the group in order to re-
fashion it and to give it a new dynamism, we witness (in "History") revolutions in thought, whether by Socrates or Jesus
Christ, which is a good indication of the rhythm of each
beginning.

It can so happen that the unnatural and triumphant group
oppresses the individual and restricts his emergence. Then it is
a case of unnatural communities, of which Fascist systems and
excessive nationalism provide examples.

Another case of the deviant collectivity is found in the
pseudocollectivities in which the group has suppressed the individual: it is not a question of Fascist aberration, it is the idea
of a pure collectivity as the ultimate objective, which obscures
the group as a reality.

But we have here the embattled, nonexistent group that
consequently makes the emergence of the individual impossible. The question we need to ask in Martinique will not be,
for instance: "Who am I?"—a question that from the outset is
meaningless—but rather: "Who are we?"

There is not even embryonic evidence of a unanimous in-
clination towards the tragic. We will not repeat the "miracle
of Greece." The fact is that all tragedy, in the Western sense, is
discriminatory. It reconstructs the legitimacy of a culture's
emergence, it does not offer the infinite variations of cultural
synthesis.

VII

I had grappled with this idea of the new tragedy, and I was surprised by how hard it was to pin down. I had envisaged a tragedy of the cross-cultural imagination, and one that, among other things, would not necessitate a ritual sacrifice of the community's hero. A tragedy of so many of Us, of so many of Me, implied in a single individual, or shared by all. But I would need the unifying force of History, another trap, and the myth of a new line of descent.

The rejection of the tragic is equally for the West the clear sign of the rejection of an outmoded kind of unanimity. But tragic victimization is not able to satisfy us either. We have suffered from the lack of the tragic in our history: for instance, by not making the maroon our tutelary hero. But we could not possibly seek reassurance in the notion of a unifying force that is the objective of the austerities of tragedy. Our folktales are perhaps also antitragic: their disruption of history and the rejection of any form of transcendental legitimacy.

With us history and literature, their capitalization removed and told in our gestures, come together once again to establish, beyond some historical ideal, the novel of the relationship of individual to collectivity, of individual to the Other, of We to Us. The cross-cultural imagination is the framework for this new episode. I am told that this collective novel cannot be written, that I will always lack certain concrete realities. But it is a fine risk to take.

Landmarks

Missed Opportunities

Marronnage: Stripped of its original meaning (cultural opposition), it is lived by the community as a deviation deserving punishment. The group is thus deprived of a hero who could act as a catalyst for the group.

Emancipation in 1848: The struggle of the slaves is deformed by the dominant ideology. Schoelcherism is the manifestation of this deviation. The document of emancipation ensures a new restriction to self-expression.

Inculcated ideals: French citizenship (the ideal of citizenship in a distant country, France) alternates with the ideal of return to a distant country (Africa), short-circuiting the real country). The republican ideal ("the legitimacy of the republic"). The lay school, which was compulsory. France forever.

Departmentalization in 1946: The most concrete form of fear and self-denial, marking the extreme edge of alienation, the limit of self-expression as well. At the same time, other former colonies rejected the Other, setting out on the tough journey towards national identity and independence. (Which does not mean that the problems of neocolonialism were solved.)

Today colonial domination no longer needs the support of a heroic ideology (the ideal of the "Motherland, etc.). It is content to control through a passive consumerism and demonstrate its inevitability. It allows the principle of mixing what is called "a French background" and "local peculiarities." There are no more opportunities to be missed.

Partitions and Periods

To persist in categorizing Martinican history according to the French historical model (centuries, wars, reigns, crises, etc.) is to align the first so closely with the second that in fact by this means you ultimately camouflage the main feature of such a history of Martinique: its overdetermination. The overemphasis on links with periods of French history is a trap created by an assimilationist way of thinking, spread through Martinican "historians," who do not bother to dig any deeper. They deny the very thing they are giving an account of, since the more natural its depiction, the more one avoids the basic deformation that it assumes. It is not a simple matter of the effect of colonial domination. If that were the case, we would really be right to consider the history of the French Caribbean islands as just a desperate vestige of the colonial adventure. It is a matter of something on which no one has seriously reflected: the French colonizer, because he is fully aware of the fact that he has managed to put into effect (we shall see how) his particular brand of assimilation; the colonized Martinican because he is upset to see himself look so good in this mirror. It is a case of what I call successful colonization. What is the use of making ritual and almost magical reference to the forms of decolonization in the world: national army, total revolution, liberation front, if the questioning of this success is not undertaken? Then these are simply a kind of verbal impulse whose only function is to satisfy those so afflicted by other people's ways of proceeding and capable of rationalizing by ideological means what then appears to be a collective impasse. This question of the periodization of Martinican history must be more profoundly reconsidered.

If therefore one abandons the absurd catalogue of official history (the Third Republic, the interwar period, etc.) and one tries to see what really happened in this country, I feel that we will easily come to an agreement on the "periods" of Martinican history:

The slave trade, settlement.
The world of the slaves.
The plantation system.
The appearance of the elite, urban life.
The triumph of beet sugar over cane sugar.
Legitimized-legitimizing assimilation.
The threat of oblivion.

This poses no particular difficulty, as far as methodology is concerned. Researchers will even be in agreement on the approximate dates (approximation as primarily part of the hypothesis) and the "contents" of these periods.

Caribbean Discourse

1. *The slave trade, the original settlement* (1640–85). Extermination of the Caribs. Introduction of sugar cane. First process of refinement. Cultural diversity. Discontinuous slave trade. Barter economy. The traded slaves aspiring to "return to Africa."

2. *The world of the slaves* (1685–1840). Promulgation of the *Code Noir*. Systematic slave trade. Establishment of plantation system. Progressive development of the monoculture of sugar cane. Revolts with no witnesses. Links between the islands.

3. *The plantation system* (1800–1930). This period overlaps with the preceding one. Appearance in France of beet sugar. "Emancipation" in 1848. Internal Balkanization (the effects of the plantations themselves) and external (the isolation of the islands within the Caribbean). Aborted attempts at resistance from the *békés*.

4. *The appearance of the elite, urban life* (1865–1902). This period is therefore included in the preceding one! Industralization and beet sugar. Development of a representative "class" (mulattoes, then the middle class). Parliamentary representation. With the town of Saint Pierre disappears one of the last possibilities for an "independent resolution of class conflict." Development of "republican" ideologies.

5. *Victory of beet sugar* (1902–50). Disappearance of the *békés* as producers. Rise of a nonfunctional representative elite, development of towns and the craft trade. The 1946 law of assimilation. Elite schools. French West Indians as minor officials in Africa.

6. *Assimilation* (1950–65). Predatory economy as the system grinds to a halt. Pseudoproduction. Disappearance of the craft trade. Development of infrastructure. Widespread schooling for the basic education needed for migration to France. Official doctrine of political assimilation. But also an awareness of the ideas of decolonization.

---

7. *Oblivion?* Official doctrine of economic "assimilation." Triumph of the system of exchange (public funds for private benefit) and pseudoproduction. *Békés* and mulattoes put together as privileged functionaries in the tertiary sector. Ports and airports. But also unbearable tension and apparently with no "resolution."

It is then that the Martinican "historian," separated from his precise lists of governors and treaties and clauses, bursts into mocking laughter. I agree with him that the contents of this periodization do not allow us to exclaim that we have discovered another America. We have, however, turned around the view of our history: an "internal" perspective this time. We are now able to demonstrate the principle: on no occasion has the resolution of class conflict been "internal" here but on the contrary always externally manipulated.

There is therefore a real discontinuity beneath the apparent continuity of our history. The apparent continuity is the periodization of French history, the succession of governors, the apparent simplicity of class conflict, the episodes, carefully studied by our "historians," of our invariably aborted revolts. The real discontinuity is that in the emergence of each of the periods that we have defined, the decisive catalyst of change is not secreted by the circumstances but externally determined in relation to another history. It then becomes easy to remove this artificial dependency by asserting, in a progressive or reactionary way, the "common history" shared by Martinique and France.

It is the external nature of the elements determining change that makes me speak, on the matter of historical division, of partitions and not of periods. A historical partition is simply what one is subjected to; a period assumes an all-encompassing momentum within a community, when it is as much a product of its history as working within its history. The notion of historical partition is therefore a functional methodology. A partition becomes a period for the outside observer only when the community reconstructs for itself a common ideal that makes the past part of a coherent whole. For us, the repossession of the meaning of our history begins with the awareness of the real discontinuity that we no longer passively live through. The phenomenon of "successful colonization" is a working hypothesis, not the established statement on our destiny.

History, Time, Identity

A new contradiction now comes to light. Histories of peoples colonized by the West have never since then been uniform. Their apparent simplicity, at least since the intervention of the West, and even more so in the case of "composite" peoples like the Caribbean people, conceals the complex sequences where external and internal forces lead to alienation and get lost in obscurity.

The peoples have reacted to this camouflage. Their persistence in considering time in terms of a natural experience (we study time as the product of the link between nature and culture, and the phenomenon that among our peoples emphasizes the "natural" nature of time) reflects very clearly a general instinctive response against the ambition of imposing a "single" historical time, that of the West.

But at the same time, our elite has consented to this imposition. They have progressively contaminated the thinking of everyone by this belief in a single history and in the strength (the power) of those who create it or claim to be in charge. Contradiction is created by these two approaches: the lived rejection of a too "cultured" notion of history and the belief in the idea of history as force and power coming from an (external) culture.

(We should note the way in which the conception of natural time is linked to the appreciation of subjective space: for all the communities that are not caught in the urgent need to discover, to go beyond, to outshine the other. Ask a Martinican peasant or native, I suppose, the way: the directions he will provide will have nothing to do with the precise and objective

The Known, the Uncertain

nature of the location that is at stake. He will play with it. You will also find that he will not attempt to impose on you any set notion of time. He will offer a version *parallel to* your own.)

Herein lies the explanation of why the quest for identity becomes for certain peoples uncertain and ambiguous: there is a contradiction between a lived experience through which the community instinctively rejects the intrusive exclusiveness of a single History and an official way of thinking through which it passively consents in the ideology "represented" by its elite. Ambiguity is not always the sign of some shortcoming.

But the contradiction—not being clarified within the collective consciousness, where historical memory has not been able to play its cumulative role—feeds a morbidly irrational mechanism, which allows us to accept the implied logic that suggests that from historical evolution to social evolution our community has "progressed" towards the consumerism that threatens it today.

One of the most disturbing consequences of colonization could well be this notion of a single History, and therefore of power, which has been imposed on others by the West. The struggles for power and the wild assertion of power in South America in the nineteenth century and in Africa today (after decolonization) are the result of this. We begin to realize that as much as the stages of the class struggle or the growth of nations, the profound transformation of mentalities in this regard creates the possibility of changing the world order.

The struggle against a single History for the cross-fertilization of histories means repossessing both a true sense of one's time and identity: proposing in an unprecedented way a revaluation of power.

COMPLEMENTARY NOTE

The table that follows tries to suggest an outline of the economic and literary production process. It could not possibly account for the infinite variety of coincidences, happy or disturbing, that have emerged in this process.

The Process of Literary Production

Periods	Economic process	Situation of social strata	External relation
1640– 1765	Clearing the land Fragmented economy	Big whites and small whites	Persistence of African past
1765– 1902	Plantation economy Real production in a monoculture Inability of *békés* to escape the barter system	Racial manicheism (blacks and whites) according to the dichotomy of the plantation Towns and the mulattoes	Hardy traces of African survivals; natural expression of Martinican identity
1902–46	Reduction of the *békés'* importance as producers	Process of forming the elite Sophisticated racism: the color spectrum	Denial of the African element; French literary fashions imported late
1946–60	Balance between exploitation and exchange	Growth in the civil servant sector	Influence of African and world decolonization
1960–80	Nonproduction System of exchange, tertiary sector	*Békés* and middle class submit to system that favors them	Deculturation by the media; contacts with the Caribbean
Prospective	Oblivion or organization of a Martinican economy	Hierarchy of dependents or independent resolution of conflicts	Isolation as "French" or integration in the Caribbean

The Known, the Uncertain

The Process of Literary Production (continued)

Oral expression	Written work	Cultural resistance
Formation of Creole language	Missionary writing	Attempts to maintain the African past
Creole oral literature (following patterns of life)	Béké literature denying the real country "Exotic" elite literature	Oral Dispersed Indecisive
Decline of oral literature	High point of an imitative elite literature	Elite descriptive writing
Folklorization of oral popular culture	End of an imitative literature	Elite protest literature (negritude) Militant literature (Fanon)
Reactions in defense of Creole	Spread of literary production	Elite products of cross-culture imagination (Caribbeanness) Written Creole literature
Neutralization or reanimation of popular content	Sterilization or creative explosion	Disappearance of a community or birth of a nation

Cross-Cultural Poetics

NATIONAL LITERATURES

Sameness and Diversity

I

We are aware of the fact that the changes of our present history are the unseen moments of a massive transformation in civilization, which is the passage from the all-encompassing world of cultural Sameness, effectively imposed by the West, to a pattern of fragmented Diversity, achieved in a no less creative way by the peoples who have today seized their rightful place in the world.

The tug of Sameness, which is neither uniformity nor sterility, interrupts the efforts of the human spirit to transcend that universal humanism that incorporates all (national) peculiarities. The dialectical process of opposition and transcendence has, in Western history, *singled out* the national ideal as a special target, which had to be negated and then crushed. In this situation, the individual, in his capacity as the ultimate instrument of transcendence, has managed to assert in a subversive way his right to defy this particular process, while being a part of it. But, in order to feed its claim to universality, the ideal of Sameness required (had need of) the flesh of the world. The other is a source of temptation. Not yet the Other as possible basis for agreement, but the other matter to be consumed. So the peoples of the world were exposed to the predatory impulses of the West, before discovering that they were the object of emotional sublimation by the West.

Diversity, which is neither chaos nor sterility, means the human spirit's striving for a cross-cultural relationship, without universalist transcendence. Diversity needs the presence of peoples, no longer as objects to be swallowed up, but with the intention of creating a new relationship. Sameness requires fixed Being, Diversity establishes Becoming. Just as Sameness began with expansionist plunder in the West, Diversity came to light through the political and armed resistance of peoples. As Sameness rises *within* the fascination with the individual, Diversity is spread *through* the dynamism of communities. As the Other is a source of temptation of Sameness, Wholeness is the demand of Diversity. You cannot become Trinidadian or Quebecois, if you are not; but it is from now on true that if Trinidad and Quebec did not exist as accepted components of Diversity, something would be missing from the body of world culture—that today we would feel that loss. In other words, if it was necessary for Sameness to be revealed in the solitude of individual Being, it is now imperative that Diversity should "pass" through whole communities and peoples. Sameness is sublimated difference; Diversity is accepted difference.[1]

If we do not count the fundamental effects of this passage (from Sameness to Diversity) that are seen in political struggles, economic survival, and if we do not compute the essential episodes (in the annihilation of peoples, migrations, deportations, perhaps the most serious aberration that is assimilation), and if we insist on the global view, we will see that the ideal of Sameness, product of the Western imagination, has known a progressive enrichment, a place in harmony with the

1. We reconsidered the issue in 1979 in the light of contemporary events: for instance, "the right to be different" could not be located in biological segregation—see M. Louis Pauwels and the "new right" in France—which would end up immediately in a hierarchy of cultural essences. Diversity leads to cultural contact: that is the modern tendency among cultures, in their wanderings, their "structural" need for an unreserved equality.

world, to the extent that it has managed to "slip by" almost without having to *declare itself*, from the Platonic ideal to the lunar rocket. National conflicts have been the internal repercussions of the West's striving for a single goal, that of imposing the whole of its own values on the world, as if they were universal. This is also how the very specific slogan of the French bourgeoisie in 1789, "Liberty, Equality, Fraternity," has tended for a long time to be considered in an absolute way as one of the cornerstones of universal humanism. The irony was that it, in fact, meant that. This is how the positivism of Auguste Comte, in fact, became a religion in South America among an alienated elite.

What is called almost everywhere the acceleration of history, which is a consequence of the saturation of Sameness, like a liquid overflowing its vessel, has everywhere released the pent-up force of Diversity. This acceleration, swept along by political struggles, has suddenly allowed peoples who yesterday inhabited the hidden side of the earth (just as there was for a long time a hidden side of the moon) to assert themselves in the face of a total world culture. If they do not assert themselves, they deprive the world of a part of itself. This self-assertion can take a tragic form (Vietnam wars, crushing of the Palestinians, massacres in South Africa), but also manifests itself in politico-cultural expression: salvaging of traditional African tales, politically committed poetry, oral literature ("oraliture") from Haiti, shaky union of Caribbean intellectuals, quiet revolution in Quebec. (Without taking into account the intolerable aberrations: African "empires," South American "regimes," self-inflicted genocide in Asia, which could be considered the—inevitable?—negative side of such a worldwide movement.) I define national literature as the urge for each group to assert itself: that is, the need not to disappear from the world scene and on the contrary to share in its diversification.

Let us take the literary work's widest impact; we can agree that it serves two functions: the first is that of demythification, of desecration, of intellectual analysis, whose purpose is to dismantle the internal mechanism of a given system, to expose the hidden workings, to demystify. It also has a hallowing purpose in reuniting the community around its myths, its beliefs, its imagination or its ideology. Let us say, in a parody of Hegel and his discussion of the epic and the conscience of the community, that the function of hallowing would be the product of a still-naive collective consciousness, and that the function of desecration is the effect of a politicized way of thinking. The main difficulty facing national literatures today, as they are defined here, is that they must combine mythification and demystification, this primal innocence with a learned craftiness. And that, for example, in Quebec the barbed sneers of Jacques Godbout are as necessary as the inspired flights of Gaston Miron. The fact is that these literatures do not have the time to develop harmoniously from the collective lyricism of Homer to the mordant scrutiny of Beckett. They must include all at once struggle, aggressiveness, belonging, lucidity, distrust of self, absolute love, contours of the landscape, emptiness of the cities, victories, and confrontations. That is what I call our irruption into modernity.

But another transition is taking place today, against which we can do nothing. The transition from the written to the oral.[2] I am not far from believing that the written is the universalizing influence of Sameness, whereas the oral would be the organized manifestation of Diversity. Today we see the revenge of so many oral societies who, because of their very orality—that is, their not being inscribed in the realm of transcendence—have suffered the assault of Sameness without being able to defend themselves.[3] Today the oral can be pre-

---

2. At the time when we Martinicans experience the often alienating transition from orality to writing.

3. This justified revenge cannot conceal the growing distance that, in fact, separates rich and poor countries. Any theory of this transition (from Sameness to Diversity, from written to oral) would be naive if it concealed in even a small way the terrible power of alienation and domination inflicted by the rich countries and their ultimate representative: the multinationals. It is silly to say this; it would be even more so to forget it.

served and be transmitted from one people to another. It appears that the written could increasingly perform the function of an archive and that writing would be reserved as an esoteric and magical art for a few. This is evident in the infectious spread of texts in bookshops, which are not products of writing, but of the cleverly oriented realm of pseudoinformation. The creative writer must not despair in the face of this phenomenon. For the only way, to my mind, of maintaining a place for writing (if this can be done)—that is, to remove it from being an estoric practice or a banal reserve of information—would be to nourish it with the oral. If writing does not henceforth resist the temptation to transcendence, by, for instance, learning from oral practice and fashioning a theory from the latter if necessary, I think it will disappear as a cultural imperative from future societies. As Sameness will be exhausted by the surprising dynamism of Diversity, so writing will be confined to the closed and sacred world of literary activity. There the dream of Mallarmé (which is therefore also that of M. Folch-Ribas) will find fulfilment, the old dream of the ideal of Sameness, that all would end up as a Book (with a capital B). But that will not be the book of the world.

A national literature poses all these questions. It must signal the self-assertion of new peoples, which one calls their rootedness, and which is today their struggle. That is its hallowing function, epic or tragic. It must express—and if this is not done (only if it is not done) it remains regionalist, that is moribund and folkloric—the relationship of one culture to another in the spirit of Diversity, and its contribution to the totalizing process. Such is its analytical and political function which does not operate without calling into question its own existence.

We see that if Western literatures no longer need a hallowed presence in the world, a useless activity after these serious charges against Western history, an activity that would be qualified as a kind of mediocre nationalism, they have *on the other hand* to reflect on their new relationship with the world, which will be used, not to underline their dominant place in

Caribbean Discourse

the process of Sameness, but their shared role in cultural diversity. This is what was understood by those French writers who, in the caricatured manner of Loti, the tragic manner of Segalen, the Catholic manner of Claudel, the esthetic manner of Malraux, sensed that after so much wandering through the West, it now finally was necessary to undertake the understanding of the East.[4] Today Diversity brings new countries into the open. When I look at literary activity in France at present, I am struck by its inability to understand this phenomenon, this new basis of cultural relationship in the world: that is, ultimately by its lack of generosity.[5] And I am not far from thinking that we are faced (in France) with a culture now on the outskirts of the world.

But the process of Diversity is persistent. It is surfacing everywhere. Western literatures will discover the process of belonging and will become again a part of the world, symbolic of many nations—that is, a cluster of narratives.

II

I have argued elsewhere that a national language is the one in which a people produces. We can furthermore observe that the mother tongues of peoples recently discovering their place in the sun are, because of their historic situation, oral languages.

These two ideas allow us to throw light on the dense mass of new national literatures.

Where a cultural hinterland predated the intrusion of a transcendental Sameness, and where an independent process of production had been initiated, the problem is relatively "simple": it will be necessary to repossess the national language and culture by submitting them to the creative criticism of political thought. This is, I suppose, what can take place in

4. Paul Claudel's book *La Connaissance de l'Est* was translated into English as *The East I Know* (New Haven: Yale University Press, 1914). *(Trans.)*

5. The naivete of the pronouncements of certain French representatives in international cultural conferences is staggering. Their ethnocentricity is not subtle and is impervious to even the probings of irony.

Cross-Cultural Poetics

Algeria. It is not necessary to create national solidarity; critical thought can demystify a social order, multilingualism (if it continues) is no longer a source of alienation.

Where a cultural hinterland did not predate the intrusion of transcendental Sameness, where a system of production allowed an "internalizing," without deep dislocation, of the imported language, the cultural and political conflicts that arise are clear and straightforward. That is the case in Cuba, I think, where the Spanish language is truly the national language of Cuba. The solidarity of the nation is faced with no obstacle; monolingualism is not reductive.

Where alienation from the system of production works against a community that nevertheless can resort to a dense hinterland (whether this cultural density predated colonial intrusion, as in countries of black Africa, or it was constituted *after the fact,* as in Haiti), the community does not disintegrate. Cultural contact is made (and perhaps its natural resources will dry up, thus creating the vulnerability of poor nations), but its language holds firm (even if multilingualism is present), and its struggle never ceases. It is capable of making its threatened language a weapon in the struggle, as the Puerto Ricans use Spanish against English.

Where the absence of a preexisting cultural hinterland does not allow a people to take cover in a cultural underground and where an autonomous system of production has no longer been maintained, the tragedy begins. The maternal oral language is repressed or crushed by the official language, even and especially when the latter tends to become the natural language. That is a case of what I call a "cornered" community.[6]

No people tolerates for a very long time both cruel and in-

6. Communities supported by their cultural hinterland and often by subsistence economies cannot be suppressed (the Kurds, in spite of being scattered through five countries), except by extermination and dispersion (the Armenians). Elsewhere, ancestral cultures have been eradicated by oblivion on the economic level, where survival (subsistence economy) has not been "organized" as a form of large-scale resistance (certain communities of Oceania).

sidious alienation from its cultural hinterland and a systematic reduction of its productive capacity. That is one of the basic axioms of the cross-cultural process. National literature becomes in this case the exposure of this double threat. For, in the absence of national production and general cultural suppression, a people turns on itself; at this point it lives (submits to) its convulsions without being able to bring them to light on a collective basis. In such a situation the sacred is inconceivable; and sacrilege is degrading. Its collective spiritual energies turn, for instance, to superstitious practices and its critical capacity to an obsession with gossip. This is what can be observed, I know, in Martinique, where the process of being assimilated by an external (French) culture results in one of the most threatened instances, perhaps the most exemplary one, of integration into the ideal of Diversity.

On the edge of the political struggle, the writer tries to expose the inner mechanism of this insertion, even if his practice threatens to introduce temporarily a form of despair which is not resignation. Exhausting this despair, *of which no one is aware anymore on a daily basis,* means reopening the wound and escaping the numbing power of Sameness. Therein does not lie pessimism, but the ultimate resource of whoever writes and wishes to fight on his own terrain.

Techniques

We say that a national literature emerges when a community whose collective existence is called into question tries to put together the reasons for its existence.

The literary activity that is part of such a collective consciousness in search of itself is not only a glorification of the community but also a reflection on (and concern with) the specific question of expression. This form of discourse is not satisfied with mere expression, but articulates at the same time why it uses that form of expression and not another.

Cross-Cultural Poetics

Just as a community can constitute an independent state and nevertheless experience a profound form of cultural alienation, so an individual can proclaim that he wishes to regain his identity and yet suffer from a terminal inadequacy even in the way in which his cry is expressed.

Cultural alienation therefore can exist at a deeper level than conscious articulation. In this regard depersonalization affects the structures of "literary" creativity that are put into practice but not thought through.

One of the primary difficulties faced by a writer is concerned with the way in which he deals with reality. Now realism, the theory and technique of literal or "total" representation, is not inscribed in the cultural reflex of African or American peoples. I am often irritated by reading books that give an account of the miserable reality of our countries, and it is because I then have the impression of being faced with a substitute, a wretched one, for Balzac or for Zola. Western realism is not a "flat" or shallow technique but becomes so when it is uncritically adopted by our writers. The misery of our lands is not only present, obvious. It contains a historical dimension (of not obvious history) that realism alone cannot account for. This is why the works I speak about often sink into a simplistic folklorization that undermines their investigative potential. Jacques Stephen Alexis understood this need not to use without modification the techniques of realism when he developed a theory of *marvelous realism* in Haitian literature, and García Márquez has illustrated this transcending of realism in the baroque narrative of *One Hundred Years of Solitude*.

An immediate consequence of this approach can be found in the *function of landscape*. The relationship with the land, one that is even more threatened because the community is alienated from the land, becomes so fundamental in this discourse that landscape in the work stops being merely decorative or supportive and emerges as a full character. Describing the landscape is not enough. The individual, the community, the land are inextricable in the process of creating history.

Landscape is a character in this process. Its deepest meanings need to be understood.

These observations are linked to the problem of the rhythmic structure of the literary work. The pattern of the seasons has perhaps shaped, in the works of Western literature, a balanced rhythm between neutral zones of narrative that are periodically crossed by explosive flashes that arouse the emotions and bring "revelation." A conclusive illustration of this technique is the European sonnet, with its final thrust that both summarizes and transcends the clear meaning of the poem. It appears that the forms of expression in black cultures do not follow this clever shifting from neutral to strong moments in the structure of a work. The unvarying season (the absence of a seasonal rhythm) leads to a monotony, a plainsong whose obsessive rhythm creates a new economy of the expressive forms. To aim for spectacular moments, or twists in the narrative, for "brainwaves," is perhaps for our writers to perpetrate at the technical level an unconscious and unjustified submissiveness to literary traditions alien to their own. Technical vigilance is here not a question of splitting hairs.

Also—and how often have I repeated this in my own discourse—time in our poetry and novels[1] does not produce the impressive harmony that Proust has for instance put together. Many of us have never fully understood our historical times; we have simply experienced them. That is the case of Caribbean communities which only today have access to a collective memory. Our quest for the dimension of time will therefore be neither harmonious nor linear. Its advance will be marked by a polyphony of dramatic shocks, at the level of the conscious as well as the unconscious, between incongruous phenomena or "episodes" so disparate that no link can be dis-

1. Again it must be admitted that these activities (the poem and the novel) are seen by us as exclusively intellectual (or for a few intellectuals) *in that they remain separate from the poetics of the group.* These are simply signs of a possible orientation and which will no doubt be transformed when the group comes into its own. Neither poem nor novel are for that matter our genres. Something else will perhaps emerge.

cerned. Majestic harmony does not prevail here, but (as long as for us the history to be discovered will not have encountered the past so far misunderstood) an anxious and chaotic quest.

We realize that literature in these conditions cannot be an object of pleasure or reassurance. Now this raises the question of *the one for whom the work is written.* A generous tendency in our works tempts us to place ourselves from the outset "within reach" of those who suffer social or cultural alienation. A justifiable tendency insofar as we have a concrete effect on the symptoms of this alienation. But an almost elementary statement of our needs, if it is valuable in our daily struggle, can also prevent us from seeing the deeper structures of oppression which must nevertheless be brought to light. This act of exposure, paradoxically, is not performed each time in an open and clear way. Western thought has led us to believe that a work must always put itself constantly *at our disposal,* and I know a number of our folktales, the power of whose impact on their audience has nothing to do with the clarity of their meaning. It can happen that the work is not written *for someone,* but to dismantle the complex mechanism of frustration and the infinite forms of oppression.[2] Demanding that in such a situation they should be immediately understandable is the same as making the mistake of so many visitors who, after spending two days in Martinique, claim they can explain to Martinicans the problems in their country and the solutions that need to be implemented.[3]

2. In order to exorcise the chaos of lived experience. There too the techniques of expression are not innocent. An exploration of the chaos of memory (obscured, alienated, or reduced to a range of natural references) cannot be done in the "clarity" of a linear narrative. The production of texts must also produce history, not in its capacity to facilitate some happening, but in its ability to raise a concealed world to the level of consciousness. Exploration is not analytical but creative. The exposé is quivering with creativity, obscure because of its incongruous contents whose coming together is not immediately apparent.

3. A work can go directly towards its objective, which in this situation is to clarify, at least to simplify *in order to be better understood.* This no

Finally, we should perhaps not forget that we have a role to play in the complex reuniting of writing and speech; in so doing, make our contribution to the expression of a new man, liberated from the absolute demands of writing and in touch with a new audience of the spoken word.

(But it is here that we must locate one of the "limitations" of literature. In a discussion in 1979 with the Haitian historian Leslie Manigat, we noticed the way in which the Rastafarian movement in the Caribbean [dirt and drugs, pride in refusing to work, the radical nature of their fierce rejection] corresponded to the negritude movement in that their actions legitimized the latter. Leslie Manigat opposed what he called at this time the inevitable "invasion of barbarians" to the intellectual dream of the learned, who will always feel ill at ease [even hostile] in the face of these extremist adherents to their theory. The barbarian invasion is, however, necessary; it is through this that values can regain their equilibrium: the true reaffirmation of equal stature for the components of a culture. But can the traditional intellectual who has produced his theory of negritude accept the Rasta who applies it in a concrete way? One can also see in this phenomenon one of the symptoms of the transition from written to oral. Reggae in the realm of the "audio-visual" corresponds to "poetry." Anglo-

---

doubt explains the impact of *Roots* by Alex Haley, whose aim was to bring to light an obliterated historical continuum. The simplicity of the technical means used, which are related to the enlarged televised version, is important to us. Whatever our reservations about this simplification (I think, for example, that the persuasive but overly calm picture of the journey by slave ship does not convey the anxious, diabolical nature of such an experience *where no individual remains himself*) or about the tendencies of the work that are too close to the author's ideology (the entire story ends with the emergence of a well-established conformist family that has succeeded), one could not deny here the worth of the simple techniques used and the objective sought after and attained. Bookshops have been broken into by black Americans in order to get copies of *Roots*. *Stealing as a means of cultural transfer:* the extraordinary historical consequence of a book in the world for which it is responsible.

phone poets like Brathwaite [Barbados] or Walcott [St. Lucia] try, perhaps, to transcend [in *drum-poetry*] this opposition. Whereas I feel that Brathwaite revives thirty years later Aimé Césaire's discourse, he places it actually in a new context: the concrete and diverse realm of lived experience. Brathwaite's link is not as much with Césaire's poetics as with the broken rhythms of Nicolás Guillén or Léon Gontran Damas. The written becomes oral. Literature includes in this way a "reality" that seemed to restrain and limit it. A Caribbean discourse finds its expression as much in the explosion of the original cry, as in the patience of the landscape when it is recognized, as in the imposition of lived rhythms.)

Forms of Music

Music is such a constituent part (because of rhythm) of our historical and everyday existence that we run the risk as a community of underestimating its "discipline": the arduous work to achieve perfection. It is possible that "facility" could be one of the obstacles to orality, just as "formalism" can become a parallel one for writing. But this aspect of the question is negligible. There is, though, a musical history of Martinique that is interesting to trace.

Let us first attempt a comparison with the prestigious history of jazz. When the large plantations of the southern United States collapse, the blacks begin the move that will lead them first to New Orleans (bars, brothels, riverboats), then to the great sprawling cities: Chicago or New York, where they will become the proletariat and the lumpen proletariat and have to face the unrelenting industrial world of America. At each of the stages of this process that I outline here, black music is reborn. Gospel and blues, New Orleans and Chicago style, Count Basie's big band, bebop, free jazz. This music progressively records the history of the community, its confrontation with reality, the gaps into which it inserts itself, the walls which it too often comes up against. The universalization of jazz arises from the fact that at no point is it an abstract music, but the expression of a specific situation.

The Creole song in Martinique and the beguine in Guadeloupe are primarily manifestations of the world of the plantations. When the system collapses, nothing replaces it. Neither massive urbanization, nor industrialization. The Martinican people remain in a state of suspension in time, before the present system of exchange makes them into a dependent community. Musical creativity, cut off from the imperatives of reality, becomes folkloric (in the worst sense). It does not evolve towards newly adapted forms.

The universalization of the beguine was real (it is even possible that it exercised a profound and more durable influence on Europe, for instance, than do salsa and reggae today), but this music is soon worn out.

Cross-Cultural Poetics

In the 1930s, French Caribbean musicians, however, use a form and technique that often revealed a link with jazz musicians. The sounds from the lip position on the clarinet or the trombone show a striking resemblance in these two musical forms. Besides, even before this time, there is a convergence between Caribbean and South American music. Certain styles will evolve and grow stronger. Others, like the beguine, will experience the fate of outdated, unnecessary forms.

It is not fair to consider the "beguine," because of the folkloric use we now make of it, as the expression of alienation. The "beguine" is the true voice of Martinique, from the plantations to the intense activity of the town of St.-Pierre. But, from 1902 (from 1940 in Guadeloupe) it no longer develops, having no further link with a community that could use it to express its view of the world. It stops being a collective form of experience and, even if it continues to be popular, it is no longer on the level of everyday use.

In the years 1950–60, musical production in Martinique is reduced to a kind of automatic churning out of music, in clear response to the apathy created by the collapse of all productivity and creativity in the country. The ease with which the Martinican willingly accepts being folkloric in others' eyes comes from this emptiness.

Musical styles that emerge and become established are really the necessary creations of places where entire communities are struggling, not in a state of sustained oblivion, but in the face of a major, unrelenting threat: the slums of Kingston where reggae slowly takes shape, the ghettoes of New York where salsa bursts into life.

When Haitian music becomes all the rage in Martinique, soon to be followed by that of Dominica, the professionals react in a xenophobic manner. Soon, however, under the influence of political militants, a movement will emerge drawing on dances and songs from the countryside (in Martinique, the bèllè immediately appropriated by folkloric groups for tourist entertainment; in Guadeloupe, in a more durable way, the place of honor once more given to the gros-ka, the perfect peasant instrument). It is not certain that such initiatives would meet with success: what is needed is a consensus that is created either by a common activity or by a struggle conducted by everyone.

In the meantime, a phenomenon occurs in which Martinican musicians, finally abandoning their xenophobic attitudes, have their role to play. A fiercely anonymous Caribbean style is created under the combined influence of jazz, reggae, and salsa. This new hybrid spreads as far as the dance bands of Africa: on both sides of the Atlantic something happens, encouraged by tourists and the distribution of records. Naturally, at the level of night club music. However, it is not impossible that therein lies the possibility of a fruitful syncretism— if it does not turn out to be an anonymous vulgarization.

Thus, because it has been opened to the Caribbean, Martinican music has regained a capacity for renewal. Naturally, it will not manage in this way to replace the need for a functional context, which is what sustains any collective and popular form of musical expression. But it is possible that this exposure could permit the creativity and solidarity that will make rootlessness more tolerable, make the present void more negotiable.

But the solution for the French Caribbean is perhaps an escape into the future. You must "do things" in your country in order to be able to sing about it. If not, musical creativity is reduced to a numbing, neurotic practice that contains nothing but the capacity for disintegration that we spoke about at the beginning of this essay.

COMPLEMENTARY NOTE
on the drum

The following observation is perhaps not important. I have, however, been struck by the difference between drumming techniques in Africa and in the Caribbean. In Africa, the drum is a language that becomes structured speech: there are orchestras of drums in which each instrument has its voice. The

drum is part of a system. In the Caribbean it is more often isolated or used for accompaniment. Orchestrated drumming is
rare, and never as complete or self-contained. Compared with
the African instrument, the Caribbean drum gives me the impression of a tiny voice. Its rhythm is less variable. I do not
come to a conclusion of "decadence" in this matter; Caribbean rhythms have their personality. But perhaps we can note
the dysfunction of the instrument, which is no longer related
to a collective experience, reflected in the harmony of the
"orchestra."

Acceptance

This group of black American students with whom we had a
friendly discussion (April 1971) was not a homogeneous one
nor did it have a shared ideology. As students of Lincoln University (Pennsylvania) and of Howard University (Washington, D.C.), they represented quite a diverse social spread. It is
therefore the "average" opinion of the black American students that we tried to ascertain; it is all the more remarkable
to observe the disparity that can exist between this average
opinion and that of the Martinican. It seems that black American attitudes are radicalized by the situation, outside of political consciousness and even when the latter is absent (or not
apparent). This "circumstantial" radicalization is, in our eyes,
the most invaluable aspect of the black American experience.
When a historically oppressed community takes hold of the
right to accept or refuse those who come into contact (or
claim to) with it, it has achieved the only true freedom: based
on which, acceptance does not mean alienation.
    At the end of our discussion we asked them:
"Why did you come to Martinique?"
"We wanted to learn about the situation of the blacks in
Martinique, but we have not received much information."
"We know what our situation in the United States is like,

and we do not like to talk about it all the time. We would like to know what the situation is in all the Americas."

"One of the reasons for the confusion in our minds is the diverse aspects of and opinions on the question in Martinique. We speak with you, we speak with a representative of the French government. You say one thing; he says another. It is the same phenomenon as in the United States, for us and those who govern us."

"Does Martinique appear on first sight to be a black country?"

"No, we see that people have black skins, but as for the inside, that is another matter."

Chile

In the paintings of Zañartu, the mountains of the Andes are organized into a single peak, but one that has a multiple and obsessive presence. This craterless volcano can be divided at times: suddenly it becomes a man's silhouette, cut halfway down, his legs tied to an airless mass. That is where fire has its origin.

For some time we, who are his friends, have been awaiting Zañartu's patient shaping in a gnarled clay of the dislocations of worlds. Here is a sudden cry from Chili. All that touches this land has another meaning.

(We think of the Other America. Here we are forced to recognize what we have been so long *severed from:* the tremendous swirl of dead people through whom the hope of the peoples around us stubbornly endures.)

I remember (here in this land with the surging sea all around) the shadows cut into the night, disincarnate and wraithlike forms, the broken blossoms that have always haunted the canvases of Zañartu.

Perhaps a future continuously postponed; but a despair unceasingly defied. That is what the present state of this America rekindles in our hearts.

Cross-Cultural Poetics

*

The extermination of the Caribs has created a difference between the Caribbean and South America. The existence of the
Amerindian population shapes our vision of the Other America. It is not an exaggeration to say that up to today this silent
community brings a coherence to the continent, with the possible exception of the Brazilian subcontinent. All of this America is anyway the product of three legacies: the Amerindian,
the African, the Western. In the Caribbean, the Amerindian
legacy was taken care of by the Spanish. It can even happen
that this heritage (a pre-Columbian display) can be used to
conceal African survivals. Yet there is some continuity between
the archipelago and the continent. Civilizations of maize,
manioc, sweet potato, pepper, and tobacco, cultures created
since colonization and built around the plantation system,
lands destined to a functional syncretism, our lands share
three common spaces: the heights of the Andes, where the
Amerindian world passionately endures, the plains and plateaus in the middle, where the pace of creolization quickens,
the Caribbean sea, where the islands loom![1] I have said in the
introduction to this book that the Martinican landscape (the
mountains in the north, the plains in the middle, the sands to
the South) reproduces in miniature these spaces.

Evidence can also be found in our political experience. The
horrors of depersonalization and assimilation are shared in
Puerto Rico (associated with the United States) and Martinique (Department of France). The apparently fated development of "macoutism" and military regimes is as relevant to
Haiti as to the small states of Latin America, and we have
tried to explain why. "Macoutism" develops into varieties of

---

1. The ethnologist Darcy Ribeiro has developed a hypothesis that divides
the peoples of America into people who witness, people who are transplanted, and new peoples. Guillermo Bonfil Battalla explains this distribution (Carifesta 79, Cuba): the people who witness have always been there
(Aztecs of the Yucatán), the transplanted peoples have not changed (Argentina, Chili), the new peoples are born from cross-breeding (Brazil). Rex
Nettleford proposes—in *Caribbean Cultural Identity* . . . (Los Angeles:

Fascism, almost all on the same lines, in the large countries of America (Brazil, Argentina, Chili) which are very Europeanized and where capitalist structures are entrenched.

It was once thought that it was the Spanish language that linked most strongly Cuba, Puerto Rico, and the Dominican Republic with Latin America. But Haiti is a peasant-based culture just like Colombia. The African presence, so long suppressed, forms a fringe around the Caribbean, from Brazil to Panama in the west (the coast), and from Venezuela to Cuba in the east (the islands). It is not impossible that in this zone multilingualism will appear as necessary to survival and will *also* use languages that are threatened today, Creole and Amerindian ones.

*

Pieces of the puzzle are still missing.

A South American writer commented that if Bolivar is celebrated as a liberator, he had nevertheless chosen to ignore the question of the popular masses, who cannot be excluded from a resolution of the South American situation. Is this true?

I have, on the other hand, heard it said that the Spanish language will be "the" language of the revolution in Latin America. To which a Cuban replied that the Communists in the United States argued the same thing in the thirties, but in that case it was for English; and if they had been followed (but how?), the Cuban revolution surely would not have been what

Center for Afro-American Studies and UCLA Latin American Center Publications, 1978), p. 149—the following classification: Plantation America (the Caribbean, the eastern littoral of the Americas), Meso-America (Mexico, Peru, Guatemala), Euro-America (Argentina, Chili, and also the greater United States and Canada). The degree of similarity between the two systems of classification is remarkable: Meso-America and the people who witness, Euro-America and the transplanted peoples, Plantation America and the new peoples. This insistence on devising systems of classification is evidence of the present intensity of the cross-cultural process.

it was. No language should be chosen or promoted at the expense of another, once the other one is *spoken* by a people. So links, discontinuities, are established between problematics, questionings, places, memories decomposed and recomposed.

*

Two painters, who complement each other, are witnesses to the links. In Wifredo Lam the poetics of the American landscape (accumulation, expansion, power of history, the African connection, presence of totems) is *part of the design*. From the dense layers of the jungle to those clear spaces hardly touched by color, where so many mythical birds alight. Paintings of both rootedness in the earth and ascent upwards. Roberto Matta represents the intense conflicts that shape men's minds today. Paintings of multiplicity; I even dare to say: multilingualism. I feel in this a visible continuity between inside and outside, the dazzling convergence of here and elsewhere.

*

What does this other America mean to us? What do we mean to it? Before its dense and multiple presence, we seem to fade into insignificance. Would we simply be several drops left by this immense river after it had broken up and slowed down? Could we in fact be the other source, I mean the necessary stop where it gathers together its energy for the journey? In one way or another, the Caribbean is the outgrowth of America. The part that breaks free of the continent and yet is linked to the whole.

The Cuban Landscape

I am amazed by the persistence of official propaganda in presenting the resurgence of Caribbean history and its present direction as evidence of the influence of Soviet imperialism and the advance of international Communism. On the chessboard of world politics, those who call the moves, official or real, visible or hidden, are unable to understand such cultural phenomena, which are not part of the unremitting necessity of profit or international competition, although they must submit to it. The United States of America is determined to show its military strength in the region to head off "destabilization." There are also some funny moments. Returning from the great Caribbean festival (Carifesta) that was held in Cuba in 1979, my son of thirteen was stopped at the Lamentin airport in Martinique: the police claimed the right to seize books he had acquired in Havana (children's cartoons, a copy of the magazine *Casa de las Américas* dealing with the Caribbean) that anyone can receive in the mail.

But what is important about Carifesta is not that it took place in Cuba in 1979; it began in Guyana, continued in Jamaica, and will take place in Barbados in 1982. What is important about Carifesta is its cultural impact. The problem that Cubans will have to face is that of the permissible emergence of African cultures, which for so long have been suppressed in that country, even if they have had a great effect on how the country's culture manifested itself. It is not certain that Socialist programs are enough, if the will to be Caribbean—that is part of a plural culture—is not apparent. It is not a foregone conclusion either that these measures will fail.

This is the problem of Caliban, that island creature whom a prince from the continent wished to civilize. The theme of Caliban has touched Caribbean intellectuals in a surprising way: Fanon, Lamming, Césaire, Fernández Retamar. The fact is that Caliban, as the locus of encounters and conflicts, has become a symbol. Above and beyond Shakespeare's savage cannibal, a real dynamic is at play—not only in the Caribbean but in many places in the Third World—a dynamic constituted by encounters among these three necessities: the class struggle, the emergence or the construction of the nation, the quest for a collective identity. The facts of social and cultural

Cross-Cultural Poetics

life are only rarely combined and reinforced in harmony. It is claimed in Panama that the negritude movement promoted by Panamanians of Caribbean origin is in opposition to the will to reinforce the Panamanian nation. It is asserted in Trinidad that the resolution of political or economic problems is achieved or not achieved (depending on the ideology of the speaker) by the aggressive affirmation of either Indian or African identity.[1] It is argued in Cuba that the solution to problems of social inequality will mean the simultaneous removal of racism. All of that is the true Caribbean problematic. It is why Caliban deserves such a passionate scrutiny.

1. Rivalry that is almost always bloody between racial groups is one of the constants of the colonial heritage in the Third World. Transcending them is not yet within sight.

Natural Poetics, Forced Poetics

I define as a free or natural poetics any collective yearning for expression that is not opposed to itself either at the level of what it wishes to express or at the level of the language that it puts into practice.

(I call self-expression a shared attitude, in a given community, of confidence or mistrust in the language or languages it uses.)

I define forced or constrained poetics as any collective desire for expression that, when it manifests itself, is negated at the same time because of the *deficiency* that stifles it, not at the level of desire, which never ceases, but at the level of expression, which is never realized.

Natural poetics: Even if the destiny of a community should be a miserable one, or its existence threatened, these poetics are the direct result of activity within the social body. The most daring or the most artificial experiences, the most radical questioning of self-expression, extend, reform, clash with a given poetics. This is because there is no incompatibility here between desire and expression. The most violent challenge to an established order can emerge from a natural poetics, when there is a continuity between the challenged order and the disorder that negates it.

Forced poetics: The issue is not one of attempts at articulation (composite and "voluntary"), through which we test our capacity for self-expression. Forced poetics exist where a need for expression confronts an inability to achieve expression. It can happen that this confrontation is fixed in an opposition between the content to be expressed and the language suggests or imposed.

This is the case in the French Lesser Antilles where the mother tongue, Creole, and the official language, French, produce in the Caribbean mind an unsuspected source of anguish.

A French Caribbean individual who does not experience some inhibition in handling French, since our consciousness is haunted by the deep feeling of being different, would be like someone who swims motionless in the air without suspecting that he could with the same motion move in the water and perhaps discover the unknown. He must cut across one language in order to attain a form of expression that is perhaps not part of the internal logic of this language. A forced poetics is created from the awareness of the opposition between a language that one uses and a form of expression that one needs.

At the same time, Creole, which could have led to a natural poetics (because in it language and expression would correspond perfectly) is being exhausted. It is becoming more French in its daily use; it is becoming vulgarized in the transition from spoken to written. Creole has, however, always resisted this dual deformation. Forced poetics is the result of these deformations and this resistance.

Forced poetics therefore does not generally occur in a traditional culture, even if the latter is threatened. In any traditional culture, that is where the language, the means of expression, and what I call here the form of expression (the collective attitude toward the language used) coincide and reveal no deep *deficiency,* there is no need to resort to this ploy, to this counterpoetics, which I will try to analyze in relation to our Creole language and our use of the French language.

Forced poetics or counterpoetics is instituted by a community whose self-expression does not emerge spontaneously, or result from the autonomous activity of the social body. Self-expression, a casualty of this lack of autonomy, is itself marked by a kind of impotence, a sense of futility. This phenomenon is exacerbated because the communities to which I refer are always primarily oral. The transition from oral to written, until now considered in the context of Western civilization as an inevitable evolution, is still cause for concern. Creole, a not-yet-standardized language, reveals this problem in and through its traditional creativity. That is why I will try to discuss first of all the fundamental situation of Creole: that is, the basis of its orality.

Caribbean Discourse

The Situation of the Spoken

1. The written requires nonmovement: the body does not move with the flow of what is said. The body must remain still; therefore the hand wielding the pen (or using the typewriter) does not reflect the movement of the body, but is linked to (an appendage of) the page.

The oral, on the other hand, is inseparable from the movement of the body. There the spoken is inscribed not only in the posture of the body that makes it possible (squatting for a palaver for instance, or the rhythmic tapping of feet in a circle when we keep time to music), but also in the almost semaphoric signals through which the body implies or emphasizes what is said.[1] Utterance depends on posture, and perhaps is limited by it.

That which is expressed as a general hypothesis can now perhaps be reinforced by specific illustration. For instance, the alienated body of the slave, in the time of slavery, is in fact deprived, in an attempt at complete dispossession, of speech. Self-expression is not only forbidden, but impossible to envisage. Even in his reproductive function, the slave is not in control of himself. He reproduces, but it is for the master. All pleasure is silent:

1. I have always been fascinated by the well-known Italian story, probably invented by the French, of the notice posted in a bus: "Do not speak to the driver. He needs his hands for driving." The motionless body in the act of writing, moreover, favors a neurotic "internalization." The orality that accompanies the "rules of writing" is that of *speaking well* (in seventeenth-century French) which is fixed in a reductive monolingualism. Stendhal says about Italy in the nineteenth century (*De l'amour,* Chapter 49) that there one speaks rarely in order to "speak well"; and also that "Venetian, Neapolitan, Genoese, Piedmontese are almost totally different languages and only spoken by people for whom the printed word can exist only in a common language, the one spoken in Rome." Let us add, by contrast, that such a strategy would not be possible today for Creole. One could not simply decide, for example, to opt unanimously for the Haitian transcriptive model (probably the most elaborate one). The freedom to write is necessary for the Creole language, above and beyond the variations in dialect.

that is, thwarted, deformed, denied. In such a situation, expression is cautious, reticent, whispered, spun thread by thread in the dark.

When the body is freed (when day comes) it follows the explosive scream. Caribbean speech is always excited, it ignores silence, softness, sentiment. The body follows suit. It does not know pause, rest, smooth continuity. It is jerked along.

To move from the oral to the written is to immobilize the body, to take control (to possess it). The creature deprived of his body cannot attain the immobility where writing takes shape. He keeps moving; it can only scream. In this silent world, voice and body pursue desperately an impossible fulfilment.

Perhaps we will soon enter the world of the nonwritten, where the transition from oral to written, if it takes place, will no longer be seen as promotion or transcendence. For now, speech and body are shaped, in their orality, by the same obsession with past privation. The word in the Caribbean will only survive as such, in a written form, if this earlier loss finds expression.

2. From the outset (that is, from the moment Creole is forged as a medium of communication between slave and master), the spoken imposes on the slave its particular syntax. For Caribbean man, the word is first and foremost sound. Noise is essential to speech. Din is discourse. This must be understood.

It seems that meaning and pitch went together for the uprooted individual, in the unrelenting silence of the world of slavery. It was the intensity of the sound that dictated meaning: the pitch of the sound conferred significance. Ideas were bracketed. One person could make himself understood through the subtle associations of sound, in which the master, so capable of managing "basic Creole" in other situations, got hopelessly lost. Creole spoken by the *békés* was never shouted out loud. Since speech was forbidden, slaves camouflaged the word under the provocative intensity of the scream. No one could translate the meaning of what seemed to be nothing but a shout. It was taken to be nothing but the call of a wild animal.[2] This is how the dispossessed man organized his speech by weaving it into the apparently meaningless texture of extreme noise.

There developed from that point a specialized system of significant insignificance. Creole organizes speech as a blast of sound.

I do not know if this phenomenon is common in threatened languages, dying dialects, languages that suffer from nonproductivity. But it is a constant feature of the popular use of Martinican Creole. Not only in the delivery of folktales and songs, but even and often in daily speech. A requirement is thus introduced into spoken Creole: speed. Not so much speed as a jumbled rush. Perhaps the continuous stream of language that makes speech into one impenetrable block of sound. If it is pitch that confers meaning on a word, rushed and fused sounds shape the meaning of speech. Here again, the use is specific: the *béké* masters, who know Creole even better than the mulattoes, cannot, however, manage this "unstructured" use of language.

In the pace of Creole speech, one can locate the embryonic rhythm of the drum. It is not the semantic structure of the sentence that helps to punctuate it but the breathing of the speaker that dictates the rhythm: a perfect poetic concept and practice.

So the meaning of a sentence is sometimes hidden in the accelerated nonsense created by scrambled sounds. But this nonsense does convey real meaning to which the master's ear cannot have access. Creole is originally a kind of conspiracy that concealed itself by its public and open ex-

2. The Creole language will call for a noise, a disorder; thus aggravating the ambiguity.

pression. For example, even if Creole is whispered (for whispering is the shout modified to suit the dark), it is rarely murmured. The whisper is determined by external circumstances; the murmur is a *decision* by the speaker. The murmur allows access to a *confidential* meaning, not to this form of nonsense that could conceal and reveal at the same time a *hidden* meaning.

But if Creole has at its origin this kind of conspiracy to conceal meaning, it should be realized that this initiatic purpose would progressively disappear. Besides, it has to disappear so that the expression of this conspiracy should emerge as an openly accessible language. A language does not require initiation but apprenticeship: it must be accessible to all. All languages created for a secret purpose make the practice of a regular syntax irrelevant and replace it by a "substitute" syntax. So, to attain the status of a language, speech must rid itself of the secretiveness of its "substitute" syntax and open itself to the norms of an adequate stable syntax. In traditional societies this transition is a slow and measured one, from a secret code to a medium open to everyone, even the "outsider." So speech slowly becomes language. No forced poetics is involved, since this new language with its stable syntax is also a form of expression, its syntax agreed to.

The dilemma of Martinican Creole is that the stage of secret code has been passed, but language (as a new opening) has not been attained. The secretiveness of the community is no longer functional, the stage of an open community has not been reached.

3. As in any popular oral literature, the traditional Creole text, folktale or song, is striking in the graphic nature of its images. This is what learned people refer to when they speak of concrete languages subordinate to conceptual languages. By that they mean that there should be a radical transition to the conceptual level, which should be attained once having left (gone beyond) the inherent sensuality of the image.

Now imagery, in what we call expressions of popular wisdom, is deceptive, that is, it can be seen as first and foremost the indication of a conscious strategy. All languages that depend on images (so-called concrete languages) indicate that they have implicitly conceptualized the idea and quietly refused to explain it. Imagery in a language defined as concrete is the deliberate (although collectively unconscious) residue of a certain linguistic potential at a given time. In a process as complete, complex, perfected as its conceptual origins, imaginative expression is secreted in the obscure world of the group unconscious. The original idea is reputed to have been conceived by a god or a particular spirit, in the twilight about which Hegel, for example, speaks.

But the Creole language, in addition, is marked by French—that is, the obsession with the written—as an *internal* transcendence. In the historical circumstances that gave rise to Creole, we can locate a forced poetics that is both an awareness of the restrictive presence of French as a linguistic background and the deliberate attempt to reject French, that is, a conceptual system from which expression can be derived. Thus, imagery, that is, the "concrete" and all its metaphorical associations, is not, in the Creole language, an ordinary feature. It is a deliberate ploy. It is not an implicit slyness but a deliberate craftiness. There is something pathetic in the imaginative ploys of popular Creole maxims. Like a hallmark that imposes limitation.

One could imagine—this is, moreover, a movement that is emerging almost everywhere—a kind of revenge by oral languages over written ones, in the context of a global civilization of the nonwritten. Writing seems linked to the transcendental notion of the individual, which today is threatened by and giving way to a cross-cultural process. In such a context will perhaps appear global systems using imaginative strategies, not conceptual structures, languages that dazzle or shimmer instead of simply "reflecting." Whatever we think of such an eventuality, we must examine from this point on what conditions Creole must satisfy in order to have a place in this new order.

4. Creole was in the islands the language of the plantation system, which was responsible for the cultivation of sugar cane. The system has disappeared, but in Martinique it has not been replaced by another system of production; it degenerated into a circuit of exchange. Martinique is a land in which products manufactured elsewhere are consumed. It is therefore destined to become increasingly a land you pass through. In such a land, whose present organization ensures that nothing will be produced there again, the structure of the mother tongue, deprived of a dynamic hinterland, cannot be reinforced. Creole cannot become the language of shopping malls, nor of luxury hotels. Cane, bananas, pineapples are the last vestiges of the Creole world. With them this language will disappear, if it does not become functional in some other way.

Just as it stopped being a secret code without managing to become the norm and develop as an "open" language, the Creole language slowly stops using the ploy of imagery through which it actively functioned in the world of the plantations, without managing to evolve a more conceptual structure. That reveals a condition of stagnation that makes Creole into a profoundly threatened language.

The role of Creole in the world of the plantations was that of defiance. One could, based on this, define its new mode of structured evolution as "negative" or "reactive," different from the "natural" structural evolution of traditional languages. In this, the Creole language appears to be organically linked to the cross-cultural phenomenon worldwide. It is literally the result of contact between different cultures and did not preexist this contact. It is not a language of a single origin, it is a cross-cultural language.

As long as the system of production in the plantations, despite its unfairness to most of the population, was maintained as an "autonomous" activity, it allowed for a level of symbolic activity, as if to hold the group together, through which the *influential* group, that of the slaves, then the agricultural workers, imposed its form of expression: in their speech, belief, and custom, which are different from the writing, religion, law that are imposed by a *dominant* class.

The Creole folktale is the symbolic strategy through which, in the world of the plantations, the mass of Martinicans developed a forced poetics (which we will also call a counter-poetics) in which were manifested both an inability to liberate oneself totally and an insistence on attempting to do so.

If the plantation system had been replaced by another system of production, it is probable that the Creole language would have been "structured" at an earlier time, that it would have passed "naturally" from secret code to conventional syntax, and perhaps from the diversion of imagery to a conceptual fluency.

Instead of this, we see in Martinique, even today, that one of the extreme consequences of social irresponsibility is this form of verbal delirium that I call habitual, in order to distinguish it from pathological delirium, and which reveals that here no "natural" transition has managed to *extend* the language into a historical dimension. Verbal delirium as the outer edge of speech is one of the most frequent products of the counterpoetics practiced by Creole. Improvisations, drumbeats, acceleration, dense repetitions, slurred syllables, meaning the opposite of what is said, allegory and hidden meanings—there are in the forms of this customary verbal delirium an intense concentration of all the phases of the history of this dramatic language. We can also state, based on our observation of the destructively non-functional situation of Creole, that this language, in its day-to-day application, becomes increasingly a language of neurosis. Screamed speech becomes knotted into contorted speech, into the language of frustration. We can also ask ourselves whether the strategy of delirium has not contributed to maintaining Creole, in spite of the conditions that do not favor its continued existence. We know that delirious speech can be a survival technique.

But it is in the folktale itself, that echo of the plantation, that we can sense the pathetic lucidity of the Creole speaker. An analysis of the folktale reveals the extent to which the *inadequacies* with which the community is afflicted (absence of a hinterland, loss of technical responsibility, isolation from the Caribbean region, etc.) are fixed in terms of popular imagery. What is remarkable is that this process is always elliptical, quick, camouflaged by derision. That is what we shall see in the folktale. The latter really emanates from a forced poetics: it is a tense discourse that, woven around the inadequacies that afflict it, is committed, in order to deny more defiantly the criteria for transcendence into writing, to constantly refusing to perfect its expression. The Creole folktale includes the ritual of participation but carefully excludes the potential for consecration. It fixes expression in the realm of the derisively aggressive.

Creole and Landscape

1. I do not propose to examine the Creole folktale as a signifying system, nor to isolate its component structures. Synthesis of animal symbolism (African and European), survivals of transplanted tales, keen observation of the master's world by the slave, rejection of the work ethic, cycle of fear, hunger, and misery, containing hope that is invariably unfulfilled; much work has been done on the Creole folktale. My intention is more modest in its attempt to link it to its context.

What is striking is the emphatic emptiness of the landscape in the Creole folktale; in it landscape is reduced to symbolic space and becomes a pattern of succeeding spaces through which one journeys; the forest and its darkness, the savannah and its daylight, the hill and its fatigue. Really, places you pass through. The importance of walking is amazing. "I walked so much," the tale more or less says, "that I was exhausted and I ended up heel first." The route is reversible. There is, naturally, vegetation along these routes; animals mark the way. But it is important to realize that if the place is indicated, *it is never described*. The description of the landscape is not a feature of the folktale. Neither the joy nor the pleasure of describing are evident in it. This is because the landscape of the folktale is not meant to be inhabited. A place you pass through, it is not yet a country.

2. So this land is never possessed: it is never the subject of the most fundamental protest. There are two dominant characters in the Creole folktales: the King (symbolic of the European it has been said, or is it the *béké?*) and Brer Tiger (symbolic of the *béké* colonizer or simply the black foreman?); the latter, always ridiculed, is often outwitted by the character who is in control, Brer Rabbit (symbolic of the cleverness of the people).[3] But the right to the possession of land by the dominant figures is never questioned. The symbolism of the folktale never goes so far as to eradicate the colonial right to ownership, its moral never involves a final appeal to the suppression of this right. I do not see resignation in this, but a clear instance of the extreme strategy that I mentioned: the pathetic ob-

3. We must note that this symbolism is in itself ambiguous. The King, God, the Lion. Where, in fact, is the colonizer? Where is the administrator? Rabbit is the popular ideal, but he is hard on the poor; perhaps he is "mulatto," etc. The proposed ideal is from the outset shaped by a negation of popular "values." One can only escape by ceasing to be oneself, while trying to remain so. The character of Brer Rabbit is therefore *also* the projection of this individual ingenuity that is sanctioned by a collective absence. ("Bastardizing of the race. Here is the major phenomenon. Individual solutions replace collective ones. Solutions based on craftiness replace solutions based on force." [Aimé Césaire and René Ménil, "Introduction au folklore martiniquais," *Tropiques*, no. 4 [January 1942]: 10.)

session, in these themes—in a word, the inflexible maneuver—through which the Creole folktale indicates that it has *verified* the nature of the system and its structure.

In such a context, man (the animal who symbolizes him) has with things and trees, creatures and people, nothing like a sustained relationship. The extreme "breathlessness" of the Creole folktale leaves no room for quiet rest. No time to gaze at things. The relationship with one's surroundings is always dramatic and suspicious. The tale is breathless, but it is because it has chosen not to *waste* time. Just as it does not describe, it hardly concerns itself with appreciating the world. There are no soothing shadows or moments of sweet langor. You must run without stopping, from a past order that is rejected to an absurd present. The land that has been suffered is not yet the land that is offered, made accessible. National consciousness is budding in the tale, but it does not burst into bloom.

Another recurring feature is the criterion for assessing the "benefits" that man here recognizes as his own. Where it is a matter of the pleasure of living, or the joy of possessing, the Creole tale recognizes only two conditions, absence or excess. A pathetic lucidity. The benefits are ridiculously small or excessive. Excessive in quantity, when the tale makes up its list of food, for instance; excessive in quality when the tale works out the complicated nature of what is valuable or worth possessing. A "castle" is quickly described (ostentatious, luxurious, comfortable, prestigious) then it is said in one breath, and without any warning, that it has two hundred and ten toilets. Such extravagance is absurd, for "true wealth" is absent from the closed world of the plantation. Excess and absence complement each other in accentuating the same impossible ideal. The tale thus established its decor in an unreal world, either too much or nothing, which exceeds the real country and yet is a precise indication of its structure.

We also observe that there is in the tale no reference to daily techniques of work or creation. Here, the tool is experienced as "remote." The tool, normally man's instrument for dealing with nature, is an impossible reality. Thus, equipment and machinery that are featured in the tale are always associated with an owner whose prestige—that is, who is above the rest—is implicit. It is a matter of "the truck of M. This" or the "sugar mill of M. That." The tool is the other's property; technology remains alien. Man does not (cannot) undertake the transformation of his landscape. He does not even have the luxury of celebrating its beauty, which perhaps seems to him to be a mocking one.

Convergence

1. Where then to locate the will to "endure"? What is the effect of such a "forced" poetics or counterpoetics, which does not spring to life from a fertile past, but, on the contrary, builds its "wall of sticks" against fated destruction, negation, confinement?
   a. This counterpoetics therefore ensures the synthesis of culturally diverse, sometimes distinct, elements.
   b. At least a part of these elements does not predate the process of synthesis, which makes their combination all the more necessary but all the more threatened.
   c. This characteristic contains all the force (energy, drama) of such a forced poetics.
   d. This forced poetics will become worn out if it does not develop into a natural, free, open, cross-cultural poetics.

The thrust behind this counterpoetics is therefore primarily locked into a defensive strategy—that is, into an unconscious body of knowledge through which the popular consciousness asserts both its rootlessness and its density. We must, however, move from this unconscious awareness to a conscious knowledge of self.

Here we need perhaps some concluding observations, relating to the link between this situation and what is called today ethnopoetics.

Cross-Cultural Poetics

2. First of all, from the perspective of the conflict between Creole and French, in which one has thus far evolved at the expense of the other, we can state that the only possible strategy is to make them *opaque* to each other. To develop everywhere, in defiance of a universalizing and reductive humanism, the theory of specifically opaque structures. In the world of cross-cultural relationship, which takes over from the homogeneity of the single culture, to accept this opaqueness—that is, the irreducible density of the other—is to truly accomplish, through diversity, a human objective. Humanity is perhaps not the "image of man" but today the evergrowing network of recognized opaque structures.

Second, poetics could not be separated from the functional nature of language. It will not be enough to struggle to write or speak Creole in order to save this language. It will be necessary to transform the conditions of production and release thereby the potential for total, technical control by the Martinican of his country, so that the language may truly develop. In other words, all ethnopoetics, at one time or another must face up to the political situation.

Finally, the previous discussion adequately demonstrates that, if certain communities, oppressed by the historical weight of dominant ideologies, aim at converting their utterance into a scream, thereby rediscovering the innocence of a primitive community, for us it will be a question of transforming a scream (which we once uttered) into a speech that grows from it, thus discovering the expression, perhaps in an intellectual way, of a finally liberated poetics. I think that ethnopoetics can reconcile these very different procedures.

Counterpoetics carried out by Martinicans (in works written in French, the use of the Creole language, the refuge of verbal delirium) therefore records simultaneously both a need for collective expression and a present inability to attain true expression. This contradiction will probably disappear when the Martinican community is able to really speak for itself: that is, choose for itself. Ethnopoetics belongs to the future.

Cross-Cultural Poetics

The epic of the Zulu Emperor Chaka, as related by Thomas Mofolo,[1] seems to me to exemplify an African poetics. Evidence of parallels with Western epic forms is not lacking: depiction of a tyrannical tendency (ambition), involvement of the Zulu community in the hero's tragedy, the rise and fall of the hero. You could not consider the magical aspect (origin of the warrior, importance of medicine men, practices and rites) as a particularly African theme. All epics that relate how peoples advance make this appeal to divine intervention. The oral form is not peculiar either; after all, Homer's poems were meant to be sung, recited, or danced.

There are two specific features that make *Chaka* particularly interesting. It is an epic that, while enacting the "universal" themes of passion and man's destiny, is not concerned with the *origin* of a people or its early history. Such an epic does not include a creation myth. On the contrary, it is related to a much more dangerous moment in the experience of the people concerned, that of its forthcoming contact with conquerors coming from the North. One is struck by the similarity between the experiences of these great, fugitive African rulers, who created from a village or tribe huge empires and all ended up in prison, exile, or dependent. (Their experience is repeated as caricature in the ambitions of these pseudo-conquerors who appeared as a postcolonial phenomenon, former subordinates or officers in colonial armies, who cause so much ridicule or indignation in the West, which created them and gave them authority.) All the great African conquerors of

1. Thomas Mofolo, *Chaka* (London and Nairobi: Heinemann, 1981).

the eighteenth and nineteenth centuries were haunted in this way by the approach of the white man. It is to the latter that Chaka refers when he is assassinated by those close to him. It seems that his life, his actions, and his work are the ultimate barrier with which he tries to prevent their intrusion, and only he understands. African poets will also be haunted by this fate, and their poems will chronicle these experiences. We in Martinique were touched by this obsession when the King of Dahomey, Béhanzin, was deported here. The epic of these conquered heroes, which was also that of their peoples or tribes, sometimes of their beliefs, is not meant, when recounted, to reassure a community of its legitimacy in the world. They are not creation epics, great "books" about genesis, like the *Iliad* and the *Odyssey,* the Old Testament, the sagas, and the chansons de geste. They are the memories of cultural contact, which are put together collectively by a people before being dispersed by colonization. There is no evidence therefore of that "naive consciousness" that Hegel defines as the popular phase of the epic, but a strangled awareness that will remain an underlying element in the life of African peoples during the entire period of colonization.[2]

(In my reading of transcriptions of African epics [those of the Segou Empire among the Bambaras, for example, compiled and translated by African researchers and Lilyan Kesteloot], I am aware of a certain "suspension" of the narrative: as if, while composing his discourse, the poet seems *to be waiting for something* that he knows he cannot stop. The succession of kings does not give rise to [nor is it based on] a theory of legitimacy. The epic is disruptive. History comes to an abrupt end. Memory becomes secretive, it must be forced to the surface. The white man ultimately intrudes and forces it into the open. The secret fire of the communal palaver is dispersed in

2. A popular series brings back to life today these historical figures from Africa. Almost each volume insists on this encounter between the African chiefs and the inevitable colonizer, who appears as the very embodiment of their destiny. (In the series *Les Grandes Figures Africaines.*)

the wind. The foresight of the epic is to have always known that this contact with another culture *would come.* This anticipation of cultural contact has been interpreted by O. Mannoni as a dependency complex: "Wherever Europeans have founded colonies of the type we are considering, it can safely be said that their coming was unconsciously expected—even desired—by the future subject peoples."[3] Frantz Fanon denounced this interpretation—*Black Skin, White Masks.* European peoples, while being aggressive concerning the cross-cultural process, could not understand its poetics, which to them represented weakness and surrender.[4] M. Mannoni made this blindness the basis for his theory.)

The other characteristic derives from a basic feature of the epic narrative, which has disappeared almost completely from Western literature: I call it *the poetics of duration.* At no point does language in the African epic claim to delight, surprise, or dazzle. It does not harangue the listener; it appeals to him; it captivates him; it leads him through its dense accretions in which little by little its message is outlined. To my mind, the creation of distinct literary genres has facilitated the disappearance of such a poetics in Western literatures. The existence of the novel and its specific conventions has increasingly caused all exploration of time and all related techniques to be restricted to this genre. At the same time the poem became the realm of the *unsayable:* that which is dazzling is its conciseness, the brilliance of its revelations, the extreme edge of clairvoyance. A *poetics of the moment.* But to discriminate in this manner between the genres and to confine them to poetics so diametrically opposed neutralize these poetics in relation to

3. Dominique O. Mannoni, *Prospero and Caliban: The Psychology of Colonization* (New York: Praeger, and London: Methuen, 1956), p. 86.
4. The West continues to be today the most dynamic agent of cross-cultural contact, through the frightening technological capacity that enables it to control systems of communication all over the globe and to manage the wealth of the world. It is beginning, however, to realize its power, and to that extent to go further than M. Mannoni.

Cross-Cultural Poetics

each other, and subject them henceforth to their conventions instead of allowing the latter to be challenged.

In the poetics of the oral African text *everything can be said*. The dense mystery that surrounds the figure of Chaka does not originate in what the epic narrative hides from us but from the process of accumulation.

The poetically unsayable seems to me tied, in the West, to what one calls the dignity of the human being, in turn surpassed since the historical appearance of private property. This daring leap allows us to argue that poetic passion, insofar as it requires a self, assumes, first, that the community has abandoned its basic right to be established and has been organized around the rights of the private individual. The poetically unsayable reflects the ultimate manifestation of the economics of the right to property. Paradoxically, it is characterized by transparency and not by obscurity.

I have constantly contrasted this keen awareness of the individual with the no less intense feeling for the dignity of the group, that appears to be characteristic of many non-Western civilizations. In contrast to the progression: private property—dignity of the individual—the poetically unsayable, I placed another that seemed to me equally fundamental: indivisibility of the land—dignity of the community—the explicitness of song. Such an opposition between civilizations also helped to explain the ruptures in Caribbean culture, in which the African heritage (the feeling for the dignity of the group) came up against an impossible circumstance (the collective nonpossession of the land) and in which the explicitness of the song (the traditional oral culture) was impeded by Western education (the initiation into the poetically unsayable). We have surrendered to a fascination with poetic obscurity that it is long and painful to get rid of: Rimbaud did more than trade in Abyssinia. And I have known so many young French Caribbean poets, desperately unable to accommodate this obscurity and yet fascinated by the success of Aimé Césaire in this area, who exhausted themselves in negotiating its dazzling power, without knowing that they had the potential for creating *another way of organizing language.* Neutralized, made impotent by this dream of poetic brilliance, they paid no heed to the throbbing within them of the notion of time that had to be possessed.

But these kinds of parallel oppositions are as well founded as they are misleading. I think, for instance, that from the distinction between collective ownership of the land (in Africa) and private property (in the West), one has been able to construct the theory of African Socialism, which would appear to be more natural (and thus more "human"), whereas Western Socialism would not have been anything but a *reaction* against the received idea of private property. These theories that emphasize the natural (always more attractive than a reaction) are justifiably reassuring. We know the amazing misdeeds, ideological as well as physical, of this African Socialism, in those countries where it has become established as a principle as much as a reality.[5]

I maintain, however, that there is a profound relationship between the poetics of the moment and the belief that emphasizes the dignity of the human individual, and also the shaping influence of private property. The logic of these ideas contains implicitly the limitation of individual interests. It is difficult to separate theoretically the notion of individual dignity from the oppressive reality of private property. This makes sublimation necessary. This explains why Western philosophy and ideology all aim for a *generalizing universality.* (Even today,

5. These variations on Socialism are not to be scorned, however, or rejected categorically. In his study of Indianness, the Mexican anthropologist Guillermo Bonfil Batalla ("La nueva presencia política de los Indios," *Casa de las Américas,* October 1979) distinguishes four ideologies in his version of the future of South America: Restoration of the past, by excluding Western civilization; the reformist position, which adapts the existing system; Indian Socialism, which applies the model of Indian societies modified by the universal elements provided by the West; and finally, Pluralist Socialism, a revolutionary transformation of the capitalist mode of production.

the part of M. Léopold Senghor's formulations most easily recognized in Western intellectual circles is that of the general idea of Universal Civilization.) A generalizing universality is ambitious enough to allow for the sublimation of individual dignity based on the reality of private property. It is also the ultimate weapon in the process of depersonalizing a vulnerable people. The first reaction against this generalizing universality is the stubborn insistence on *remaining where you are.* But for us this place is not only the land where our people were transplanted, it is also the history they shared (experiencing it as nonhistory) with other communities, with whom the link is becoming apparent today. Our place is the Caribbean.

Caribbeanness, an intellectual dream, lived at the same time in an unconscious way by our peoples, tears us free from the intolerable alternative of the need for nationalism and introduces us to the cross-cultural process that modifies but does not undermine the latter.

What is the Caribbean in fact? A multiple series of relationships. We all feel it, we express it in all kinds of hidden or twisted ways, or we fiercely deny it. But we sense that this sea exists within us with its weight of now revealed islands.

The Caribbean Sea is not an American lake. It is the estuary of the Americas.

In this context, insularity takes on another meaning. Ordinarily, insularity is treated as a form of isolation, a neurotic reaction to place. However, in the Caribbean each island embodies openness. The dialectic between inside and outside is reflected in the relationship of land and sea. It is only those who are tied to the European continent who see insularity as confining.[6] A Caribbean imagination liberates us from being smothered.

It is true that, among Caribbean cultures, we in Martinique

6. Both on the Right and on the Left, there are those who will claim that you "vegetate" in these islands; they will seek, preferably in Paris, to improve their minds.

have only been allowed access, and for historic reasons, to language. We have so many words tucked away in our throats, and so little "raw material" with which to execute our potential.

This is perhaps why I was so moved when I discovered the rhetorical power of black American speech. I remember having heard, at Tufts University, an exposé on Afro-American literature and having discovered with great surprise and feeling the spectacle of this audience that, rhythmically swaying, turned the lecturer's text into melody. I also saw the television film on Martin Luther King and discovered the doubling of the voice, the echo placed behind the speaker to repeat and amplify his speech. As in the tragic text, here repetition is not gratuitous. Therein lies a new management of language.

And just as poetic brilliance is the supreme state in exalting the self, I can also speculate that repetition in speech is a response to the group. But this group is not a form of transcendence. One can even state with justification that by its very nature it is derived from that basic symptom of the cross-cultural process that is Creolization.

If we speak of creolized cultures (like Caribbean culture, for example) it is not to define a category that will by its very nature be opposed to other categories ("pure" cultures), but in order to assert that today infinite varieties of creolization are open to human conception, both on the level of awareness and on that of intention: in theory and in reality.

Creolization as an idea is not primarily the glorification of the composite nature of a people: indeed, no people has been spared the cross-cultural process. The idea of creolization demonstrates that henceforth it is no longer valid to glorify "unique" origins that the race safeguards and prolongs. In Western tradition, genealogical descent guarantees racial exclusivity, just as Genesis legitimizes genealogy. To assert peoples are creolized, that creolization has value, is to deconstruct in this way the category of "creolized" that is considered as halfway between two "pure" extremes. It is only in those countries whose exploitation is barbaric (South Africa, for instance) that this intermediary category has been officially

Cross-Cultural Poetics

recognized. This is perhaps what was felt by the Caribbean poet who, in response to my thoughts on creolization in Caribbean cultures, said to me: "I understand the reality, I just do not like the word." Creolization as an idea means the negation of creolization as a category, by giving priority to the notion of natural creolization, which the human imagination has always wished to deny or disguise (in Western tradition).[7] Analyses of the phenomena of acculturation and deculturation are therefore sterile in conception. All societies undergo acculturation. Deculturation is able to be transformed into a new culture. Here it is important to stress not so much the mechanisms of acculturation and deculturation as the dynamic forces capable of limiting or prolonging them.

We realize that peoples who are most "manifestly" composite have minimized the idea of Genesis. The fact is that the "end" of the myth of Genesis means the beginning of this use of genealogy to persuade oneself that exclusivity has been preserved. Composite peoples, that is, those who could not deny or mask their hybrid composition, nor sublimate it in the notion of a mythical pedigree, do not "need" the idea of Genesis, because they do not need the myth of pure lineage. (The only traces of "genesis" identifiable in the Caribbean folktale are satirical and mocking. God removed the White man [pale] too soon from the oven of Creation; the Black man [burnt] too late; this version would lead us to believe that the mulatto— with whom the Caribbean would therefore wish to identify— is the only one to be properly cooked. But another version of these three baked creatures claims that the first was in fact not dark enough, the second not sufficiently cooked [mulattoes], and the third just right [blacks]. The Martinican consciousness is always tormented by contradictory possibilities. These parodies of genesis do not seriously claim, in any case, to offer

---

7. "Cross-cultural contact" has also become an argument for assimilationist propaganda. Young Martinicans are told in 1980: "It is the age of cultural exchange"—which implies: "Do not isolate yourselves therefore in an outmoded and inflexible nationalism, etc."

an explanation for origins; they imply a satirical attitude to any notion of a transcendental Genesis.) The poetics of creolization is the same as a cross-cultural poetics: not linear and not prophetic, but woven from enduring patience and irreducible accretions.

Also a cross-cultural poetics could not constitute a science, that is, to be generalized by laws and definitions of distinct processes. It is not known; only recognizable.

Neither the formula from Parmenides, "Being never changes," nor the related view by Heraclitus, "All is in a state of flux," through which Western metaphysics were conceived, but a transphysical poetics that could be briefly expressed as—that which is (that which exists in a total way) is open to change.

Total existence is always relative.

It is not certain that in the West materialism does not sometimes appear as the metaphysical adjunct of idealism. Since it is the same view of history, it can support the most intolerant form of transcendentalism.

Any transphysical poetics of creolization contributes to undermining this blind solidarity.

This means that creolization and history could not lead us to any belief in cultural exclusivity, nor be expressed in terms of its poetics.

Because the poetics of the cross-cultural imagination turns up in a plowing up of phenomena that acquire significance when put together, and in the domain of the unseen of which we represent the constantly shifting background.

The accumulation of the commonplace and the clarification of related obscurity, creolization is the unceasing process of transformation.

· · · · ·

Complementary Note
concerning a pseudo-encounter

This example of negative cultural contact is offered by the short story "Music for Chameleons" by Truman Capote, totally concerned with a vision of Martinique and published in the *New Yorker* of 17 September 1979. The author recounts in it his visit to an old female member of the aristocracy (*béké?*) in Fort-de-France, and the text offers a survey of many commonly held views (pertinent or false) of Martinique from the perspective of a tourist (T) and a colonialist (C).

"The whole island floats in strangeness. This very house is haunted" (C).

"Martinique is the only island in the Caribbean not cursed with mosquitoes" (T).

"My paternal grandmother was from New Orleans" (C).

"People from Martinique seem so preoccupied. Like Russians" (T).

"Martinique is *très cher*" (T).

"Martinique could not exist without subsidy from France" (C).

"The troublemakers [and] their independence" (C).

"The women. . . . Supple, suave, such beautifully haughty postures" (T).

"The men are not appealing . . . they seem . . . without character" (T).

"It belonged to Gaugin. . . . That was his black mirror" (C).

"[Your restaurants] are better than others in the Caribbean. But too expensive" (T).

" . . . foreign ladies . . . wearing nothing above and very little below. Do they permit that in your country?" (C).

"Usually, I leave the island during Carnaval" (C).

"As spontaneous and vivid as an explosion in a fireworks factory" (T).

"We are not a violent people" (repeated) (C).

"Madame is toying with the same tune. A Mozartian mosaic" (T).

This noncontact results from the fact that no reader could imagine the true Martinique under this fantasy version; that this fantasy is of no value (artistic or ethnological): it is entirely superficial and verbal. In other words: that neither the thoughts nor the "substance" offered by the writer are pertinent. He is on one side; the subject of his story is on the other side.

"*The Novel of the Americas*"

I will attempt to bring to light a few of the themes common to the concerns of those whom we classify here as American writers. Using my own work and my own preoccupations as points of reference, I will try to state the assumptions around which I feel the work of writers in the Americas instinctively revolves.

Certainly, one essential obsession that I characterize in these terms: a tortured sense of time.

I think that the haunting nature of the past (it is a point that has been widely raised) is one of the essential points of reference in the works produced in the Americas. What "happens," indeed, is that it is apparently a question of shedding light on a chronology that has become obscure, when it is not completely effaced for all kinds of reasons, especially colonial ones. The American novelist, whatever the cultural zone he belongs to, is not at all in search of a lost time, but finds himself struggling in the confusion of time. And, from Faulkner to Carpentier, we are faced with apparent snatches of time that have been sucked into banked up or swirling forces.

We have seen that the poetics of the American continent, which I characterize as being a search for temporal duration, is opposed in particular to European poetics, which are characterized by the inspiration or the sudden burst of a single moment. It seems that, when dealing with the anxiety of time, American writers are prey to a kind of future remembering. By that I mean that it is almost certain that we are writers in an embryonic phase and our public is yet to come. Also, that this exploded, suffered time is linked to "transferred" space. I have in mind African space as much as Breton space, the "memory" of which has become stamped on the spatial reality that we all live. To confront time is, therefore, for us to deny its linear structure. All chronology is too immediately obvious, and in the works of the American novelist we must struggle against time in order to reconstitute the past, even when it concerns those parts of the Americas where historical memory has not been obliterated. It follows that, caught in the swirl of time, the American novelist dramatizes it in order to deny it better or to reconstruct it; I will describe us, as far as this is concerned, as those who shatter the stone of time. We do not see it stretch into our past (calmly carry us into the future) but implode in us in clumps, transported in fields of oblivion where we must, with difficulty and pain, put it all back together if we wish to make contact with ourselves and express ourselves.

For us, the inescapable *shaping force* in our production of literature is what I would call the language of landscape. We can say that the European literary imagination is moulded spatially around the spring and the meadow. Ernst Robert Curtius has proposed this in *European Literature and the Latin Middle Ages*.

In European literature an intimate relationship with landscape is primarily established. From this has evolved a stylistic convention that has for a long time focused on meticulous detail, exposition "in sequence," highlighting harmony (exceptions or extensions constitute reactions to this rule). Space in the American novel, on the contrary (but not so much in the physical sense), seems to me open, exploded, rent.

There is something violent in this American sense of literary space. In it the prevailing force is not that of the spring and the meadow, but rather that of the wind that blows and casts shadows like a great tree. This is why realism—that is, the logical and rational attitude toward the visible world—more than anywhere else would in our case betray the true meaning of things. As one says that a painter at work sees the light on his subject change with the movement of the sun, so it seems to me, as far as I am concerned, that my landscape changes in me; it is probable that it changes with me.

Caribbean Discourse

I could not say like Valéry: "Beautiful sky, true sky, look at me as I change." The landscape has its language. What is it in our world? Certainly not the immobility of Being, juxtaposed to a relative notion of what I could become, and confronted with an absolute truth that I could reach out for. The very words and letters of the American novel are entangled in the strands, in the mobile structures of one's own landscape. And the language of my landscape is primarily that of the forest, which unceasingly bursts with life. I do not practice the economy of the meadow, I do not share the serenity of the spring.

But what we have in common is *the irruption into modernity.*

We do not have a literary tradition that has slowly matured: ours was a brutal emergence that I think is an advantage and not a failing. The finished surface of a culture exasperates me if it is not based on the slow weathering of time. If the glossy surface of a culture is not the result of tradition or sustained action, it becomes empty and parochial. (That is the weakness of our intellectuals.) We do not have the time, we are everywhere driven by the daring adventure of modernity. Parochialism is reassuring to one who has not found his center in himself, and to my mind we must construct our metropoles in ourselves. The irruption into modernity, the violent departure from tradition, from literary "continuity," seems to me a specific feature of the American writer when he wishes to give meaning to the reality of his environment.

Therefore, we share the same form of expression. And I will forever oppose the notion of language to that of self-expression.[1]

---

1. "Ah ah, said the countess in Portuguese and to herself, for she spoke these two languages . . .": this passage from a story told in France fascinates me because of its meaningful ambiguity (its obscurity). There is an inner language that surpasses any acquired language (the interior monologue *cannot become external speech.* It has meaning only in obscurity: that of Benjy, at the beginning of the novel *The Sound and the Fury*).

Cross-Cultural Poetics

I think that, beyond the languages used, there is a form of expression specific to the American novel[2] that is at the same time the product of a reaction of confidence in words, of a kind of complicity with the word, of a functional conception of time (consequently, of syntactical time), and ultimately of a tortured relationship between writing and orality.

One of the effects derived from my own literary activity is concerned with precisely this interest: I am from a country in which the transition is being made from a traditional oral literature, under constraint, to a written nontraditional literature, also equally constrained. My language attempts to take shape at the edge of writing and speech; to indicate this transition—which is certainly quite difficult in any approach to literature. I am not talking about either the written or the oral in the sense that one observes a novelist reproducing everyday speech, using a style at the "zero degree of writing." I am referring to a synthesis, synthesis of written syntax and spoken rhythms, of "acquired" writing and oral "reflex," of the solitude of writing and the solidarity of the collective voice—a synthesis that I find interesting to attempt.

The fact is that we are in the midst of a struggle of peoples. Perhaps this would then be our first "axis."

The issue (experienced in the specific struggles that take place more or less everywhere along the chain of the Americas) is the appearance of a new man, whom I would define, with reference to his "realization" in literature, as a man who is able to live the relative after having suffered the absolute. When I say *relative*, I mean the Diverse, the obscure need to

---

2. I realize that I am now referring to the novel of the "Other America" (the Caribbean and South America) and not so much to that which is fixed (by word and gesture) in the urban, industrial world of the north of the United States. I also tend to relate Faulkner's work (the furthest from northern America as far as his ideas are concerned) to this group, in defiance of reality, and I need to clarify this. Such a clarification was attempted when I spoke of the *desire for history* in literature and the tragic return, which Faulkner has in common with us.

accept the other's difference; and when I say *absolute* I refer to the dramatic endeavor to impose a truth on the Other. I feel that the man from the Other America "merges" with this new man, who lives the relative; and that the struggles of peoples who try to survive in the American continent bear witness to this new creation.

The expression of class struggle has sometimes been "deadened" through the existence of zones of nothingness so extreme that even the perspective of a class struggle has appeared utopian or farfetched (Peruvian Indians, tribes of the Amazon). In other places, depersonalization has been so systematic that the very survival of an autochthonous culture can be questioned (Martinique). The "novel of the Americas" uses an allegorical mode that ranges from blatant symbolism (the peasant novels of South America, or, for example, *Gouverneurs de la rosée* [*Masters of the dew*] by J. Roumain) to heavy descriptive machinery (Gallegos or Asturias) to the more complex works that combine an exploration of alienation with the attempt to define an appropriate language (García Márquez). What is perhaps missing is the perspective of those zones of culture that are more threatened (by total dispossession as in the case of the Quechuas of Peru, by slow depersonalization as in the case of Martinicans), therefore more "exemplary," in which the experience of the Diverse is played out at an unknown pace that is comfortably or desperately tragic.

I am summing up what I have discussed too briefly—it is interesting to avoid sustained expositions and to try to propose points of discussion—while formulating a concept one may suspect of being designed to please. (Whom? I do not know.)

I wish to speak of the question of lived modernity, which I will not simply add to, but which I will link directly to the notion of a matured modernity. By this I am opposing, not a kind of "primitivism" to a kind of "intellectualism," but two ways of dealing with changes in contemporary reality. *Matured* here means "developed ove. extended historical space"; *lived* means "that which is abruptly imposed." When I witness from a little distance the very interesting work being done on a theoretical level in the West, it seems to me that two reactions are formed: I experience at the same time a feeling of the ridiculous and a feeling of the extreme importance of these ideas. For instance, on the subject of the destabilizing of the text and "its" author.

The text is destabilized (in the matured modernist theories of the West) to the extent that it is demythified, that one tries to define the system that generates it. The author is demythified to the extent that he is made into, let us say, the site where these generative systems manifest themselves, and not the autonomous creative genius he thought he was. If I say that it seems ridiculous to me, it is because (in our lived modernity) these issues have no bearing on us. We need to develop a poetics of the "subject," if only because we have been too long "objectified" or rather "objected to." And if I say that this seems important to me, it is because these queries relate to our deepest preoccupations. The text must for us (in our lived experience) be destabilized, because it must belong to a shared reality, and it is perhaps at this point that we actually relate to these ideas that have emerged elsewhere. The author must be demythified, certainly, because he must be integrated into a common resolve. The collective "We" becomes the site of the generative system, and the true subject. Our critique of the act and the idea of literary creation is not derived from a "reaction" to theories which are proposed to us, but from a burning need for *modification.*

I am suggesting that it is relevant to our discussion to try to show—if possible (and I do not think in any case that I have demonstrated it)—that "American" literature is the product of a system of modernity that is sudden and not sustained or "evolved." For instance, was not the tragedy of those American writers of the "lost generation" that they continued in literature the European (or "Bostonian") dream of Henry James? The United States thus combined two kinds of alienation in a great number of its reactions: that of wanting to continue politely a European tradition to which the United States felt itself to be the ultimate heir; and that of wanting to dominate the world savagely in the name of this ultimate legacy. Faulkner's roots in the *Deep South* free him from the dream of becoming European. This is his true modernity as opposed to Fitzgerald, for example, or Hemingway, in spite of the "modern" themes of the latter. The idea, however, is that this modernity, lived to the fullest in "new worlds," overlaps with the preoccupations of matured "modernity" in other zones of culture and thought. Therefore, I think that this problematic relationship is a strong force in our literatures. (The problematic is a larger manifestation of the "lived" reality.) And, in my capacity as an American writer, I think that any dogmatic conception of literary creation (as the highest point of an evolved system) would be opposed to this force.[3]

Montreal

The *poetics* of landscape, which is the source of creative energy, is not to be directly confused with the *physical nature* of the country. Landscape retains the memory of time past. Its space is open or closed to its meaning.

Against the monolingual imperialism inherited from the West, we propose to get rid of the equation: "One people, one language." A people can also signify the dramatic lack of fulfilment of a language. The threatened potential of the landscape.

---

3. Western critics would certainly agree that we should remain at the level of the lived and the instinctive (we would be instinctive creators) and would sing our praises as long as they could so reserve for themselves the dimension of thought (they would be the look that organizes and appreciates). We are pushed, for instance, towards "intuitive art," which can only have meaning in the context of a civilization that has developed a tradition of "highly finished art." Congratulating M. Césaire on a speech that he gave at a conference held in Fort-de-France in 1979, a journalist from the Hersant

Cross-Cultural Poetics

I am from a community that has been reduced to its folklore; to whom all productions except the folkloric kind are forbidden. Literature cannot "function" as a simple return to oral sources of folklore.

But we feel, we writers of this America that is the Caribbean, that we put together simultaneously reflexes in our expression that come from an oral culture (the oral means of accounting for reality) and from syntactic reflexes "inherited" from the language in which we write.

We have not lived a "continuous" history, a transition from the oral to the written, through accretions and transformations. We are faced with an impossible task.

One of my Trinidadian friends recounts that his parents would talk in Creole when they did not want the children to overhear their conversation. Today this friend is unable to understand our language. A similar situation exists almost everywhere in the world, among migrants as much as among those who experience internal exile. Local dialects disappear under pressure from the lingua franca. "Diversity is losing ground" (V. Segalen). But it matters little that here or there in the Caribbean the oral language has lost ground. We all share the same experience in the confrontation of written and oral cultures.

---

group declared his pride in having as a compatriot this "Frenchman from the Caribbean," in being charmed by his "incantatory flourishes," by the impeccable form of his speech, after which he revealed that none of the ideas of the speaker were worth retaining, even if the latter is more Latin and Cartesian than he thinks, and no more Caribbean than a former journalist from *Le Figaro*.

On the notion of modernity. It is a vexed question. Is not every era "modern" in relation to the preceding one? It seems that at least one of the components of "our" modernity is the spread of the awareness we have of it. The awareness of our awareness (the double, the second degree) is our source of strength and our torment.

The task becomes impossible in the abrupt nature of this confrontation. We are coming to grips with the impossible.

(In the Western Middle Ages written and oral cultures are inseparable. The written text was meant to be *recited aloud*. Its rhythms are deeply marked by this. But it is a matter in all cases and above all of a writing that conforms to oral modes. In the African tradition, the text is outside of writing. The restrictive force of the scribal creates in the West a poetics of the instant, against which a few poets struggled. Because of the need to recreate the rhythms of speech, there develops in oral literatures a poetics of duration: reversion and diversion are therein activated.)

I met in Montreal two quite different variations of the writer. I first heard them speak. Their speech before their writing. Jacques Ferron launched into complex ironies, admission of skepticism, and even naive digressions, solely in order to maintain a distance from the man of letters, fearing to be seen as such. There was a kind of reticence in this provoking speech. It was a perpetual practice of diversionary tactics. This public display was the last resort, like a ritual umbrella. Gaston Miron went so directly to his subject that he appeared to be swollen with it, like a ball in a game of skittles. He was so possessed by his subject, by his material (Quebec) that he refused to let go. He heard nothing. No matter how loudly you spoke, he would calmly speak more loudly. Yes. Ferron drew on the humanities. Miron reverted to a kind of savagery. They are alike. These are two strategies of diversion. Tactic and need to be at the same time. I am speaking about them for contradictory reasons. First of all, I felt I recognized in them two kinds of voice (one fluent, the other thundering) that have the same force here, but that have a greater echo in the open spaces of Quebec. We are also shifting from the roundness of a proposition to the most slender of nuances. Then, because I feel that a people is at one with its language, which in this case is the Quebecois language. The fact is that the aggressive bilingualism of Quebec keeps these two languages forever apart. "Speak white," say the anglophone Canadians. Which will not make the Quebecois more black or more red. (The cultural militants in Quebec have been criticized for ignoring the Indian minorities of Quebec.) Economic disparity has established only one kind of separateness, that is linguistic. French and English do not combine to create a multilingual culture. These two languages confront each other. The participatory and integrating bilingualism in Martinique treats Creole as an object of folklore, tolerates it, *understands* it. The only foil to this process of absorption here is to *enter into bilingualism* and to come to grips with its principle and its resolution, both of which are derived from moving to the stage of a true multilingualism.

Where the mother tongue and lingua franca are not in contact (in Africa, where Swahili, for instance, has nothing to do, in any way, with English or French), the use of the lingua franca by a writer certainly risks the danger of dilution to a much smaller extent. Perhaps it is also less exciting, given the very extraneous nature of the adopted language?

What I wish to say again about these Quebecois writers is that, paradoxically, whatever the nature of their speech and whatever they might think of the relationship I have formulated, *they are on the same side as we are in dealing with writing*. Ruralization and *Joal* have had the same effect that the plantation and Creole have had on us.

Our landscape cannot be *de-scribed* but narrated in our special approach to writing.

Poets from Here

Jan Carew has written an article on "the Caribbean poet and exile," and we know George Lamming's book on *The Pleasures of Exile*. Neither is it insignificant that the first cry of Caribbean negritude was for *Return*. The truth is that exile is within us from the outset, and is even more corrosive because we have not managed to drive it into the open with our precarious assurances nor have we succeeded all together in dislodging it here. All Caribbean poetry is a witness to this.

How has this loss been confronted?

The explosion of the primordial scream. The impulse of birth did not allow the details of the real country to be articulated but rather comprehended in a flash. This is why Césaire in his *Cahier,* without for one moment describing it, could present us with Martinican space and time in a reconstituted form. This "function" of poetry is inevitable at the creation of a people.

The patience of landscape defined. I have already said that this landscape is more powerful in our literature than the physical size of countries would lead us to believe. The fact is that it is not saturated with a single History but effervescent with intermingled histories, spread around, rushing to fuse without destroying or reducing each other. We see this in Roumain, or Naipaul, or Carpentier.

The imposition of lived rhythms. That is orality finally recognized as a forceful presence to the extent that it became the nerve center of Damas's or Guillén's writing, thereby giving birth to the movement that would support the great thrust in Creole writing.

We are finished with the fight against exile. Our task today is reintegration. Not the generalized power of the scream, but the painstaking survey of the land. And also this convergence of histories that we must today recognize in the Caribbean. Finally, the difficult duty of considering the function of language and the texture of self-expression. In particular, the handling of time and medium that forces us not to use Creole in a mindless fashion, but to ask in all possible ways *our* question: How do we adapt to the techniques of writing an oral language that rejects the written? How do we put together, in the dimension of self-expression, the use of several languages that must be "mastered"?

More than the declaration of principle, I believe in the production of "opaque" works. Opaqueness imposes itself and cannot be justified. Certainly, it allows us to resist the alienating notion of transparency. I think again of the theatrical performance give in Fort-de-France by Haitians (in exile) of the *Kouidor* company. No doubt a significant part of the text in Haitian Creole (so "dramatic," so measured at the same time as being urgent and passionate) eluded us. But this very opaqueness made us feel that this was *our* theater. There are unknown ways of understanding: the Martinican public had a profitable experience that evening.

On Haitian Painting

The painted symbol coexists with the oral sign. It is the tightly woven texture of oral expression that is introduced into (and the key to) Haitian painting. The Creole language in Haiti does not suffer the repercussions of the radical ambiguities created by writing, because of an early confrontation with writing and the creation of a dense cultural "hinterland." Haitian Creole is practically insulated from *transformation*. The painted symbol is its refuge.

To this extent any picture painted in this style is also a form of writing. It is created, for instance, on the earth in front of houses, in the manner of East Indian women on the occasions that honor the cycles of life; with natural products (starch, indigo, flour); on perishable material or as records in leather that put together the chronicles of the Indians of North America; or on the human body, in order to prepare for ceremonies or ritual exercises. That is a form of painting that produces a schematic version of reality; the beginning of all pictography. A painting that makes memory significant through symbols: the essentials of a kind of historiography of the community.

But this writing does not transcend reality. It is not a kind of literary process. It is the symbolic notation of a seldom-seen side of reality. It is both a means of communication and a transfer of knowledge for the very people who cannot write. It demonstrates by its visual form the specific nature of orality. All so-called naive painting proceeds by simplification, in which the lack of technical expertise is part of its success. When a shepherd from the Landes or a Yugoslav peasant produces pictures, it is the same process at work: nothing contrived in the perspective, nothing artificial in the silhouettes, nothing watered down in the colors. The same thing happens in Haitian painting. But it comes all at once, in a massive accumulation.

The element of the marvelous. This ability to create fantasy from a difficult, even wretched, reality is the principle that J. S. Alexis had called the marvelous realism of the Haitian people. I feel that Haitian literature in French has striven to duplicate this sense of the marvelous, which is immediately conveyed in painting. The fact is that the French language often deforms— (even in the creolized improvisations of Roumain and Alexis) because of a kind of contrived naivete—what is immediate (sudden) in the marvelous. The marvelous is first and foremost an oral phenomenon. Caribbean humor, which is one of its manifestations, is difficult to transfer to written expression. Let us reiterate this fact: Haitian painting is derived from the spoken.

Next, the use of enlargement. That the real can be represented on an "enlarged scale" allows an ingenious rendering of the visible (diversion) to replace tampering with perspective. Those children who bear the weight of a fruit as large as they are, are really related to the idea of bearing a load as practiced by the Haitian peasant. This vision is neither idealistic nor "realistic."

Haiti's pictorial discourse thus proceeds by the piling up of the visible. I am aware of its capacity to represent crowds, huge piles, profusion. *Markets* by Felix or Wilmino Domon, *Creole Festivities* by Casimir Laurent, *Paradise* by Wilson Bigaud or Gabriel Levêque, *Rice Fields* by Bien-Aimé Sylvain. Accumulation is the jubilant display of totality. In contrast, certain interiors (like those that are painted by the Obin family: the painter's house *The Famous Painter Philomé Obin Receiving a Few Foreign Clients, The Artist's Studio* by Antoine Obin, and by the same painter *Antoine Obin Visits His Uncle,* or the *Caricature of George Nader in His Gallery* by Gervais Emmanuel Ducasse) treat emptiness as a kind of fulfilment.

This emptiness is never "metaphysical." It is actually "swollen," like Hector Hyppolite's pregnant women (*Reclining Woman; Nude and Birds; Blue Angel*). One senses that the flatness of space is both shrewd and naive. That the "naive" element is necessary. For it conveys and allows the emergence of a basic feature: redundancy. There is an art of repetition that is characteristic of the oral text and of the painted sign described as naive.

Such a discourse therefore gains from being repeated at leisure, like the tale recounted evening after evening. Each of the "masters" of this pictorial art has "apprentices" who reproduce his style perfectly. Tourism has increased the production that has become more schematic without becoming an industry. The discourse is reproduced on its own but its vulgarization (the countless canvases exploiting the naivete of tourists) does not differentiate between "valid" paintings and an undistinguished pile of tourist art. We think we recognize from a distance the suspended cities of Prefette-Duffaut, when these images of levitation could be the work of an apprentice. Haitian painting challenges the magical notion of "authenticity" in art. It is a community endeavour. An entire people's discourse. The measure of its dynamism. This is a fitting conclusion to this cross-cultural poetics that we have tried to outline.

An Exploded Discourse

THE UNCONSCIOUS, IDENTITY, AND METHOD

Poetics and the Unconscious

The main idea in this essay is that the Martinican as such is limited by a poetics that is incapable of *realizing* anything from a collective and time-honored body of knowledge. This poetics produces, on the contrary, in fits and starts a kind of pseudoknowledge through which an attempt is made to deny the Other's total and corrosive hold. An anti- (or counter-) poetics. One consequence is that the state of mind created in this way is untenable and that being untenable makes it an exemplary phenomenon, serving as an example, in the modern drama of creolization.

From the point of view of method, this discussion will perhaps be marked by passion and subjectivity, which I feel can be considered as part of the problem. It could end up being obscure, which would perhaps not make me unhappy, if you were willing to be my accomplices in obscurity.

In what "space" and in what way is this poetics articulated?

Space, Earth, Landscape

Martinican space is an antispace, limited to the point of gnawing away at one's being, but diverse enough to multiply it into infinity. It is an island that is like an anthology of landscapes defined as tropical. But it is not irrelevant to repeat at this point the statement that the Martinican never has the foresight or the unconscious urge to take control of this space. Any group that is limited by the stubborn inability to take control of its surroundings is a threatened group.

The land of suffering is abandoned. The land is not yet loved. The freed slave prefers the area surrounding the towns, where he is marginalized, to working for himself on the land. The land is the other's possession. The poetics of the land cannot then be a poetics of thrift, of patient repossession, of anticipation. It is a poetics of excess, where all is exhausted immediately. That is what was generally referred to when it was said, not so long ago, that we are overgrown children. We know that we must exhaust the rhythms of the land and expose the landscape to those various kinds of madness that they have put in us.

This boundless dimension in the landscape is also true of all the poetics of the New World. If this limitlessness is characteristic of the Americas, it is not so much because of an infinite variety of landscapes as of the fact that no poetics has been derived from their present reality. The solid virtues of the patient peasant are perhaps quickly acquired, but leave traces less quickly. The monster of industrialization has perhaps broken the link with the land (elsewhere), or else it is dispossession that (here in my land) has obliterated the link. But a scream is an act of excessiveness. Our land is excessive. I know, since I can in a few steps take it all in but can never exhaust it.

Our Relationship with the Context

In such a context, I feel we are faced with a seething inevitability, which does not necessarily make up our collective unconscious but certainly gives it direction. You will pick up a few examples that result from our history, and all of which unleash the counterpoetics that I referred to.

First the slave trade: being snatched away from our original matrix. The journey that has fixed in us the unceasing tug of Africa against which we must paradoxically struggle today in order to take root in our rightful land. The motherland is also for us the inaccessible land.

Slavery, a struggle with no witnesses from which we perhaps have acquired the taste for repeating words that recall those rasping whispers deep in our throats, in the huts of the implacably silent world of slavery.

The loss of collective memory, the careful erasing of the past, which often makes our calendar nothing more than a series of natural calamities, not a linear progression, and so time keeps turning around in us.

The "liberation" of the slaves created another trauma, which comes from the trap of citizenship granted; that is, conceded; that is, imposed.

The only source of light ultimately was that of the transcendental presence of the Other, of his Visibility—colonizer or administrator—of his transparency fatally proposed as a model, because of which we have acquired a taste for obscurity, and for me the need to seek out obscurity, that which is not obvious, to assert for each community the right to a shared obscurity.

To which other determinant factors, some more useful than others, become attached.

The one and only season, for instance, this rhythmic plainsong, which denies us the pattern of seasonal change, that Western cultures benefit from but which allows us to live not only another rhythm but another notion of time.

The trap of folklore, to whose temptation we are so happy to succumb, relieved as we are thereby of not having to turn our folkloric existence into painful awareness.

Consequently, this is not a minor aspect of our counterpoetics, our lived history, to which we are introduced by our struggle without witnesses, the inability to create even an unconscious chronology, a result of the erasing of memory in all of us. For history is not only absence for us, it is vertigo. This time that was never ours, we must now possess. "We do not see it stretch into our past and calmly take us into tomorrow, but it explodes in us as a compact mass, pushing through a dimension of emptiness where we must with difficulty and pain put it all *back together.*"

We see that the residue of our troubled unconscious is deposited in the structures of speech. That excess to which we must become accustomed. The word as uncertainty, the word as whisper, noise, a sonorous barrier to the silence imposed by darkness. The rhythm, continuously repeated because of a peculiar sense of time. Time, which needs to be undated. Opaqueness is a positive value to be opposed to any pseudo-humanist attempt to reduce us to the scale of some universal model. The welcome opaqueness, through which the other escapes me, obliging me to be vigilant whenever I approach. We would have to deconstruct French to make it serve us in all these ways. We will have to structure Creole in order to open it to these new possibilities.

But how do "we use" these languages? What is in our context the relationship with the other (the link to the group) that creates a communal fraternity and authorizes the link with others? This link with the other is itself uncertain, threatened. Our expression suffers as a form of communication.

There has been much comment on the use of antiphrasis in Martinican speech. It appears that the Martinican is afraid of expression that is positive and semiotically straightforward. To my mind, a possible explanation can be found in what I call the phenomenon of immediacy—that is, in this: the fact that the relation to the outside is never filtered for us by exposure to a technical environment. Because he does not know how to handle tools, the Martinican is unwilling to consider expression as a tool. He uses it, therefore, as the ultimate medium and makes it into a strategy for diversion. This allows us to understand how such a "small" people can contain such an overarticulate elite. That is where we must begin. We use ornate expressions and circumlocutions (a diversionary tactic) in order to better demonstrate our real powerlessness. The poetics of Creole uses this ploy of diversion in order to clarify.

An Exploded Discourse

The French Caribbean elite apply it to French in order to obfuscate. The word must be mastered. But such a mastery will be insignificant unless it is an integral part of a resolute collective act—a political act.

The counterpoetics I spoke about, and which indeed we never stop referring to at every turn, does not spring spontaneously and innocently from how we express ourselves in everyday communication. It is literally its unconscious rhythm. That is why I call it a counterpoetics. It indicates the instinctive denial that has not yet been structured into a conscious and collective refusal.

Rather than carrying on endlessly about this, which would be a pleasant possibility but not a practical one here, I prefer to illustrate this counterpoetics with a small study I did of the deformation of an inscription that is put on automobiles. I will offer my impressions, as a writer involved in this venture and not as a specialist who is elaborating an argument. I will try to summarize a few points of this study.

Creolization

This concerns the warning (printed on a sticker): "NE ROULEZ PAS TROP PRÈS" distributed by the road safety association. Statistics show (we should distrust them) that approximately 20 percent of Martinican drivers have stuck it to the rear windshield of their cars, after collecting this sticker when they pick up their cars. About 20 percent of the latter make some adjustment, if necessary using scissors, to this command "NE ROULEZ PAS TROP PRÈS" by creolizing it.

What is interesting is the number and the significance of the variations in rewriting this warning. I must point out that the drivers have as reference the expression in French and that consequently the variations are extremely revealing. Here are a few: (1) "PAS ROULEZ TROP PRÈS." I note that in Martinican Creole one ought to be able to write: "PAS ROULE TRO PRE." The significance of doing without the *s* in "pas," the *z* in "roulez," the *p* in "trop," and the *s* in "près" is great, and is not only related to the phonetic transcription, but to the very structure of Creole. We can therefore identify a certain number of examples, ten out of a total twenty-five, with "PAS ROULEZ TROP PRÈS." We also find: (2) "PAS ROULEZ TROP PRÉ"; (3) "PAS ROULÉ TROP PRÈS"; (4) "PAS ROULÉ TROP PRÉ"; (5) "ROULEZ PAS TROP PRÈS." This last variation is extremely Creole (it affirms the command and warns you, before modifying it with the limiting negative), and that is a more significant manipulation of the expression than simply removing a few letters.

There are also some dramatic variations. That is, the individual can cut several stickers and amuse himself by combining them. So you can get: (6) "OU TROP PRÉ." Which is not a warning but an aggressive command. I have also picked out: (7) "PAS OULE TRO PRE," in which the *r* in "roulez" has disappeared. I will comment on this version later. Finally we find: (8) "ROULEZ," which is the opposite of the original warning. And one of these stickers even exclaimed: (9) "ROULEZ PAPA!"

This example of a counterpoetics is valuable. First, keep in mind that we are dealing with people who have cars and not with dispossessed peasants. When we are considering these variations, we cannot therefore put them down to ignorance. Second, Creole really appears to be derived from French. Third, there is evidence of deliberate cultural opposition to, if not the established order, at least the order as given. Fourth, there is a noticeable variety in these formulations, with a marked preference for the expression "PAS ROULEZ TROP PRÈS," with no change in the French spelling. The version "PA OULE TRO PRE" intrigued me. It was at the exit of a Monoprix discount department store. And it was a mixed couple, this time a young Frenchman recently arrived in Martinique and who had married (or lived with) a Martinican female. Because he had been told (or he had noticed) that Martinicans do not pronounce the *r*, he had reduced the sticker to "PA OULE TRO PRE." It is an extremely interesting example not only of a French formulation but of the interference of a French formula. The belief that it is necessary to suppress the *r* because Martinicans do not pronounce it is a ludicrous mistake. Militant promoters of Creole have nevertheless taken the same approach; in many cases they suppress the *r* and replace it with a *w*, for example. So they will write *pawol* for the Creole equivalent to the French *parole*. Even if this *w* seems valid (almost all the writers replace *moin* with *mwin*), it introduces an extra difficulty in reading that I do not feel is justified.

Let us summarize the conclusions to this rather rough inquiry. This is an example of counterpoetics: a silly exercise; an attempt to escape the French language by using variations, neither agreed on nor thought through; the inability to settle a common way of writing; subversion of the original meaning; opposition to an order originating elsewhere; creation of a "counterorder."

Caribbeanness

What do such practices reveal? Naturally, the ambiguities of the relationship between Creole and French, to which we will return presently. But also for the community an awareness of the ambiguity, and that therein lies a problem that has to be solved. And, if the Martinican intuitively grasps the ambiguity of both his relationship with French and his relationship with Creole—the imposed language and the deposed language respectively—it is perhaps because he has the unconscious sense that a basic dimension is missing in his relation to time and space, and that is the Caribbean dimension. As opposed to the unilateral relationship with the Metropolis, the multidimensional nature of the diverse Caribbean. As opposed to the constraints of one language, the creation of self-expression.

The islands of the Caribbean, no matter how idealistic such an assertion appears today, are in the world of the Americas no less of an entity, threatened before coming to light, conceived only by intellectuals and not yet taken into account by the people. It is no less true to say that this is the framework, the support, that would ensure the domination of uncertainty and ambiguity. What interests us now is the possibility for the Caribbean people, whether Creole-speaking, francophone, anglophone, or hispanophone, to attempt the same process beyond the languages spoken, a process that is related to expression. Let us then examine this problematics of self-expression.

Self-Expression

There are, as we have seen, no languages or language spoken in Martinique, neither Creole nor French, that have been "naturally" developed by and for us Martinicans because of our experience of collective, proclaimed, denied, or seized responsibility at all levels. The official language, French, is not the people's language. This is why we, the elite, speak it so correctly. The language of the people, Creole, is not the language of the nation. I do not simply mean that Creole is the victim of the conditions of its existence, but that because of that, Creole has not been able so far to reflect on itself— neither as popular wisdom nor as a conscious decision by the elite; that Creole falls short of its potential; that perhaps in the host of proverbs and sayings that it communicates, at least in Martinique, there is none to provoke the sort of turning of language on itself, that critical or mocking attitude to its glossary or syntax that causes a language, literally or by reflection, to become a form of self-expression.[1] Creole is also a concession made by the Other for his own purposes in his dealings

---

1. *On the other hand,* we often take great pleasure in ridiculing our use of the French language. As in this popular refrain (in 1977) in the dance halls when a woman dancing the tango whispers (ungrammatically, with respect to French):
Quand je danse la tango
je me sens tourdir
j'ai envie de vome
ma pié me font mal
j'ai lasse.
This play on the original form of expression is not given in the Creole text. Furthermore, it uses the creolization of the French text to produce the bilingual play. A metalinguistics (insofar as it is an analysis of grammar, etc.) could not compensate for such a deficiency, but rather simply risks rationalizing it. Self-scrutiny emerges from the constant exercise of responsibility, first and foremost. It is perhaps political before being "linguistic."

An Exploded Discourse

with our world. We have seized this concession to use it for our own purposes, just as our suffering in this tiny country has made it, not our property, but our only possible advantage in our dealings with the Other—but having seized it does not make it into a means of self-expression, nor has our only advantage become a nation.

They claim there is no real bilingualism in the French Lesser Antilles because the Creole language is nothing more than a deformation of French. The dilemma is really that we note the absence of both a responsible use of the two languages and a collective exercise in self-expression. What is called bilingualism finds here a rather special manifestation. We are collectively spoken by our words much more than we use them, whether these words are French or Creole, and whether each individual can handle them properly or not.[2]

Our problem is therefore not to create an awareness of an obvious linguistic phenomenon—Creole—that could have preceded the disfiguring influence of French and would await the moment of its rebirth. Creole was not, in some idyllic past, and is not yet our national language. To claim that Creole has always been our national language is to even further obscure, in this triumphant version, the disturbing self-doubt that is the source of our insecurity but that also establishes our presence. We know that for Creole to have the chance of becoming the national language of Martinicans, such a complete change in structures would be required that it is idle to talk about it at this time. We also know that such a promotion of Creole could not result from a decision made by the elite. We know, ultimately, that at that time the ambiguity of the relationship of French to Creole would disappear and that each Martinican would have access to the sociocultural means of using French without a sense of alienation, of speaking Creole without feeling confined by its limitations.

2. That is why one of our most frequently used rhetorical strategies is that of association: one word releasing through assonance or by inner logic a series of other words, and so on.

On the other hand, the definition of a common form of expression beyond the languages used, in keeping with the reality of a multilingual Caribbean, is, in my opinion, now possible through a kind of intellectual and necessarily elitist choice.

A popular revolution would certainly make Martinique an integral part of the Caribbean, and, by freeing us from an antipoetics, would allow the Martinican people to choose either one of the two languages they use, or to combine them into a new form of expression. But in the more embattled present circumstances, the challenge of an antipoetics, deliberately creating new forms of expression, with a more limiting, less developed, less free function, would allow us from this very moment to engage in the quest for self-expression and prepare for the future.

Our aim is to forge for ourselves, by either one of these not necessarily mutually exclusive ways, and based on the defective grasp of two languages whose control was never collectively mastered, a form of expression through which we could consciously face our ambiguities and fix ourselves firmly in the uncertain possibilities of the word made ours.

We must, however, in formulating this alternative that questions the past, take note of the use of Creole in popular protest movements. Such an activity, in fact, releases Creole from its irresponsibility and makes it into a weapon in its own struggle. But the world lives its history too quickly; we do not have the time to slowly "meditate" on Creole. All the people together or an elitist group, liberated poetics or defiant antipoetics, we must force self-expression into existence because it does not have the time to mature through some slow evolution. Perhaps we do not have the time to wait for the precious linguists. When they catch up with us, it could well be to explore the traces of what has already happened.

Like a strange planet, self-expression beckons. For those who have never seen words bloom, the first articulations are unpromising and clumsy. The second will be daring and selective. If this does not happen, we will not have a voice. I mean

An Exploded Discourse

that passion would preserve us from a concern for minutiae—inevitable, perhaps, but easily avoided—that would allow us perhaps to "study" the Creole language, but by depriving it of its own sense of organization. A systematic linguistics can uselessly entangle a threatened language.

Identity

This is what I call cultural identity. An identity on its guard, in which the relationship with the Other shapes the self without fixing it under an oppressive force. That is what we see everywhere in the world: each people wants to declare its own identity.

The Space, the Poetics

Is there anywhere else in the world where such human waste takes place and that the world has no time to notice? Not great catastrophes that are like monumental phenomena in the history of the world, but the shadowy accretions of misfortune, the unseen erosion of a cornered people, the unnoticed disappearance, the slow loss of identity, the suffering without consequence?

If we posit that the issue of this collective and silent death must be removed from the economic dimension, if we argue that it can only be dealt with on the political level, it also seems that poetics, the implicit or explicit manipulation of self-expression, is at the same time the only weapon that memory has against this human waste and the only place to shed light on it, both in terms of an awareness of our place in the world and our reflection on the necessary and disalienated relationship with the Other. To declare one's own identity is to write the world into existence.

If, therefore, when we deal with our own history, we adopt (we Caribbean people) the various European languages and adapt them, no one will teach us how to do this. We will perhaps be the ones to teach others a new poetics and, leaving behind the poetics of not-knowing (counterpoetics), will initiate others into a new chapter in the history of mankind. In-

Caribbean Discourse

deed, we may be the ones (except in the eventuality of some monolithic language that suddenly descends and covers over all our countries[3]) who will fuse, one with the other, these new forms of expression through our combined poetics, and far removed from abstract universality, with the fertile yet difficult relationship with our willed, collective need for obscurity.

3. For instance, a "universal English": *francophonie* is also built around (that is beyond our concerns) the obsession with such domination. The linguistic imperialisms of the West continue to struggle for control *through us*.

LANGUAGES,
SELF-EXPRESSION

On the Teaching of Literatures

We are dealing in this instance with literatures in French from outside of France. Teaching them poses a problem, especially at the university level. The temptation is great to treat them as parallel to French literature and to draw limiting conclusions from the comparison. I have had occasion to protest against some assertions, curiously enough advanced by the very ones whose mission ought to have been to fight for these literatures. Here are a few of them.

These are not literatures that allow a human being to understand himself and to be himself.

This is not, sir, the "humanist" objective of these literatures. If you take "understand himself" to mean rediscovering one's raisons d'être in the world, these literary works certainly have their contribution to make. We do, yes, opt for indulging one's individuality. Such luxuries are open only to those who know who they are and are not alienated from themselves.

The lecturer will describe as classics works that are not.

The idea of a "classic," pertinent in the context of European literatures, comes from teaching a "cumulative" notion of cultures. A people's quest for themselves is an equally absorbing object of scrutiny. The false starts and the fumblings will be discounted later.

We are using an instrument (the vehicle of communication) that does not correspond completely to who we are.

To say that is to dignify a language beyond its due. In our present world, the equivalence between self and language is an aberration that disguises the reality of dominance. Let us challenge the latter with the weapon of self-expression: our relationship with language, or languages which we use.

The individual (in our countries) is painfully divided between two cultures.

We reject that pain. It only strikes those among us who, because they are held in subservience, are incapable of conceiving the new cross-cultural relationship and are in any case prevented from really being a part of it. We now repeat for your sake that there is no acculturation in which division is maintained of necessity, nor deculturation that one cannot escape.

A Montaigne, a Pascal, is expected from Africa (or the Caribbean).

Right, if you mean: a great writer, the definition of greatness can come from no one except the African people (or the Caribbean people), *first and foremost.*

*

But the (common) ideological denominator for all these questionable positions is formulated in an international forum in the notion of "*la francité* as the multiple echo of the voice of France." When you are caught in that multiple echo, you are, in fact, divided, you cannot understand yourself or be yourself.[1]

Quebec

It is valid to introduce into our vision of Caribbean landscape—mountains and seas, sand flats, contorted hills—the same swirling movement of the Quebecois landscape. It is said that in certain parts of northern Quebec, as no doubt in the

---

1. M. Jacques Berque, who was the first to propose this concept of "francité," certainly did not define it in as wretchedly functional a way as those who used it subsequently. (Jacques Berque, a professor at the Collège de France and a specialist of North African literature, prefaced the author's collection of poems *Le sel noir* in 1959. *Trans.*)

steppes of Russia, you lose a sense of direction and have no sense of moving forward. I am curious about how the imagination functions there. Just like the child who would wish: "I would like to boil like water just to see how it feels"; I say to myself: "I would like just once to feel myself part of such unrelieved vastness, to experience what rhythm of life it imposes." What rhythm of speech rises in you.

And then Quebec is a land that provides asylum for Haitians: an asylum that, I am told, is more or less comfortable. When I was there, a group of young people wanted to fight against a new law prohibiting the entry of illiterates into the country. They were planning the creation of literacy centers for those who were already there. There are subdiasporas in the Caribbean diaspora.

A Quebecois writer told me one day—we were discussing the eternal problem of language: "Indeed, all you have to do in the Caribbean is to let yourselves be colonized by Quebec." To which I replied: "In practice, colonizers who appear to be chasing each other off are in fact replacing each other and even supporting each other. A number of rich people from Montreal have acquired property around Anse-Mitan and Anse-à-l'Ane in Martinique, and it is not the Martinicans who gave them the right to administer the area."

We were then quite distant from a contrastive poetics.

Pedagogy, Demagogy

I

This article attempts to examine what conditions exist for an education system suited to Martinique, not by proposing warmed-over solutions, but by entertaining, if possible, an indepth discussion of the problem. The main idea is that any partial reform will be unable to bring about major change and that intermittent reforms inevitably depend on a total transformation of social and mental structures in Martinique. That will be the price of their success.

We will begin our discussion by focusing on two aspects of all teaching: the technical development of the individual, that is his ability to play a role in society that in practical terms is no more and no less a long-term investment; the general molding of the individual, that is, his cultural, emotional, and intellectual equilibrium, without which no human being would know how to "play his role" in society, and without which, furthermore, there would be no society to plan its objectives or to fulfil them more or less. The fact that in reality these quite necessary categories are never fully taken into consideration, that quite often the individual is crushed by the dominant forces of the society, should not prevent us from tackling our problems in this area.

We will begin with aspects of the historical background, taking as a rough starting point the date 1946, first, because at that time we have the beginning of the postwar period and the spread of new ideas, radical technical change (learnt or passively received), the emergence of peoples who express themselves, new relations between the peoples of the earth, and, second, also because this date, and the law that assimilated Martinique into an overseas French department, corresponds to a profound change in the way Martinicans see themselves and conceive of their relationship with the other.

This is how the discussion is organized:

A. *"Technical" development of the Martinican:* (1). before 1946, during what is called the colonial period; and (2). at present.

B. *"Cultural" development:* (1). before 1946, and (2). at present.

A. *From the perspective of "technical" development*
  1. *From "liberation" in 1848 to assimilation in 1946.*
      Here we are faced with an agricultural society based on a monoculture and organized into a plantation sys-

An Exploded Discourse

tem, increasingly threatened by competition with beet sugar. There is an urgent need to form an elite capable of "representing" this system. The school responsible for this is:

a. singlemindedly elitist (with controlled entrance by Scholarships);
b. the tip of a steep pyramid (by limiting scholarships and the number of graduates);
c. based on individual success (merit and luck);
d. intensive (overpreparation of students);
e. nontechnical (the "humanities," as in France).

This system functions very well. It creates two kinds of individuals:

a. Members of the liberal professions and functionaries (teachers, academics, doctors, lawyers, etc.) generally smug in their alienation—that is, who do not ask questions (except at the level of unconscious reflex) about the teaching they were offered and that they in turn retransmit. (The French language. A solemn and vibrant eloquence. Elite control of political representation.)
b. A small number of individuals, who, "through the grid created by the system," and in a more or less lucid way, begin to question it.

And it leaves behind an excluded majority that, after some formal training in elementary school, reverts to chronic illiteracy.

This illiteracy is strengthened, first, by the isolation of the country, and then through the absence of any kind of cultural organization to encourage the curiosity and passion for learning in an informal context. Popular culture is not one of development or transcendence (of either concepts or techniques), it is a culture of survival, parallel to the economy of survival established by Martinicans *alongside* the organization of the plantations. A culture limited to survival, in spite of the intensity of its possible manifestations, is not able to develop into a national culture, except through revolution. This possibility was clearly out of the picture in Martinican society during the period being considered.

This system, therefore, works well: because it trains those who are needed for the jobs defined *from the outside* and which they accept without question. There are factories, but we do not seem to need Martinican engineers. We are given instead a middle class with no link to an economic system that they could never be called on to direct or control. We even export, to Africa, individuals trained for these modest elitist needs, which has the advantage of widening the area of usefulness of this elite. Because those who are formed in this way, except for a small minority that I have mentioned, are "happy" with their education. As we have said, challenging it is an unconscious process through frantic caricature of imitative behavior and by redundant excess in speech. Finally, because this system operates within a relatively stable basic social structure, troubled, nevertheless, by popular, indecisive revolts, which we have indeed acquired the habit and the means of suppressing regularly.

 2. *Since 1946*

 The plantation system has collapsed completely. It is neither replaced by industrialization nor by a complete restructuring of the economy. From the point of view of collective response, the depopulation of the countryside is not followed by either the monstrous development of an intolerable lumpenproletariat or by the emergency of a bourgeoisie that would have controlled for its own benefit the social and the economic dynamic. Instead, we witness three noticeable changes in the social structure:

 a. The creation of an indeterminate class, with no defined "professional" status or vocation, emerging from those who were called *djobeurs* and who settle around cities and towns.

 b. A class of civil servants often unable to attain key posts in the various branches of the public sector,

An *Exploded Discourse*

a class that is an enlargement (made necessary because of the need to administer assimilation) of the
old elite.

c. The less fixed class of young people, trained in skills,
meant to function in the context of migration to
France.

Education in Martinique has been tailored to these
needs.

a. Under the pressure of assimilation, this system of
education has become extensive. The registration of
children in classes up to a higher and higher age
limit has made indispensible (as in France) the creation of pseudo-classes (for extra tuition or improvement) that can only feed this social group of *djobeurs*
that we have mentioned.

b. Secondary schools have filled their function: feed-
ing the second group (in the Civil Service, the Post
Office, Social Security, etc.). Similarly, the bank
workers and those in the tertiary sector have also
done so extensively. The official screening of an elite
that once existed has yielded to a screening that
depends on privileges or credentials determined by
"class."

(The liberal professions as a group have today
arrived at saturation point. Consequently, Martinicans say that their country is not underdeveloped! It
will become increasingly difficult to find a job as
teacher, lawyer, dentist, pharmacist, or doctor. Especially since another consequence of the law of assimilation, and perhaps the coming integration of
Martinique into the framework of the European
Common Market, is to open Martinique increasingly to French nationals and soon to those from
other European countries. All the same, we are re-
assured that it will be possible for any Martinican to
set up practice in the Pyrenees and soon Milan or
Brussels!)

c. There remains basic technical training, rounded off by skills training acquired during the modified military service, and which, as we have observed, fed in particular the group of people holding lower-level jobs, in a modest way, in France. Naturally, I do not take into account here those who migrate without even the benefit of this training.

Let us also note that, just as in the old elitist system a few individuals escaped their limiting background and began to question the system, so the new educational opportunities offer possibilities, beyond the spread of basic training, of acquiring a superior competence in the technical areas. There are engineers, but most are not in Martinique. In the preceding period there were factories but no Martinican engineers; today there are Martinican engineers but no factories.

This system is therefore well adapted to the social reconstruction of today's Martinique, but, as we shall see, that is why it does not function well. Here is the explanation.

B. *From the perspective of a general or cultural background*
  1. *"Colonial" Period*

Let us examine the paradox: why did a completely alienated schoolteacher in the 1930s or 1940s—who has his pupils sing the praises of their ancestors the Gauls, as was done to me: "Valiant Allobroges"—succeed in giving them an intensive education, while the most serious, most lucid, most courageous teacher today feels discouraged because of his inability to overcome academic backwardness and to motivate his students?

In the preceding period, the educational system is dealing with a community that has not yet experienced the massive impact of world events, which have since, without it being fully realized, marked this community. The politically naive Martinican elite laughed at the

An Exploded Discourse

Arab peasant, but the Algerian war changed something here. Martinicans continue to call the inhabitants of St. Lucia English—that is, foreigners—but they have been deeply affected by liberation movements in Africa, by the struggle of black Americans, which make them sense that there are other ways to conceive of the world or to live it than through imitation. We continue to give tacit approval to the expulsion of Haitian workers from Martinican territory, in the very place where any European can operate without hindrance and enjoy many privileges; but we are more and more ashamed of our complicity. It is becoming hard to find collective acquiescence. Elite complicity in the past, which apparently was not troubled by occasional popular revolts, would provoke unconscious, individual, compensatory reactions: "literary" preciosity and the sumptuous excesses of Creole have always, let me repeat, seemed determined by this unconscious and individual need *to be other than who you think you are.* Colonial excess would here be an unintended festoon of self, a supplement to the impossible. The addition is excessive in order to be more persuasive. Today, this unconscious awareness of alienation is not felt only by the elite; it is more widespread. Also more commonplace. It excludes baroque ostentation and manifests itself in a tawdry anguish, an everyday inertia. The extravagantly ridiculous performers who were our schoolmasters in 1939 have disappeared. Nothing is left but minds fatigued by what they convey. It is difficult to be ostentatious, but it is exhausting to be lackluster. Today, this apparently widespread complicity unleashes collective compensatory reactions that are of two kinds: everyday indifference and periodic uncontrolled impulses.

2. *The present inertia.*

The real drama today for the Martinican, when it comes to the educational system, is:

a. That he feels that this education is no longer a means

Caribbean Discourse

of escaping, even at the individual level, a situation that hardly allows for individual survival and that puts everyone in the same boat indiscriminately. The son of a lawyer or a doctor has a much greater chance of getting his school diploma than the son of a *djobeur*. But what price will he have to pay and what will it bring him?

b. That he subconsciously realizes that this education creates contradictions that become a part of him.

The problems recorded in our analysis of academic backwardness can be linked generally to the insignificance of the Martinican in his own land, to the resulting anguish in the student, to the everpresent awareness that there is no future other than the lower levels of the Civil Service (which has besides become an ideal kind of promotion), the pseudotechnical areas that are both unstable and always threatened, or the entry into the insecure day-to-day existence of those who survive by their wits.

We certainly realize that such problems are also part of the general disaffection of young people all over the globe (that is, where they are not simply crushed by extreme physical poverty) as they confront the modern world. But this process is accelerated in Martinique by the frustrating difficulty of finding the route to some kind of *collective* responsibility in one's own country. It is aggravated by the absence of any general cultural background: the oral culture is disconnected from the real rhythms of existence; the written culture is psychically and materially beyond their reach. The transition to writing is simply "a form" that exists, with no possibility of meaning. Fatigue irritates our eyes, both teachers and taught. Year after year, you can face this erosion of self.

II

We think we have demonstrated, by this simplified discussion:

A. That partial improvements of the educational system in Martinique will certainly be welcome: it is not a matter of

An Exploded Discourse

folding one's arms and hoping things will get better; but Martinicans as a whole must know that:

1. If the community does not by itself come up with a new program of work, the teaching profession will "rot" in its present impasse. We define as a new program of work, not the occasional alleviation of unemployment in one sector or another, but the organization of a collective program of production, so that Martinican society can escape the tragedy of *djobage*, underdeveloped technical skills or the already saturated "opportunities" in the junior Civil Service.

2. If the community does not pay attention to its own psychological and social dilemma by lucidly isolating the contradictions that torment it and trying to resolve them—that is, by collectively entering the world of cultural responsibility—the revival of dynamism among the youth will never happen. I do not call "revival of dynamism" an acceptance of what already exists, or of some future order, but for the youth the aggressive and, if necessary, unregulated activity of an age group that, as such, *understands* what is going on in the country.

B. That, consequently, if we continue to reexamine the problem outside of the "structural" context, we will have simply reinforced the process of depersonalization of our community.

C. That in this matter no director, no teacher—no matter how competent and skilled they are—should willfully underestimate the absence of a consensus, or the positive advantage of a revolution at the mental as well as the structural level.

III

We will only truly begin our discussion of the problems of education in Martinique, at least this is my suggestion, when we examine the structural problems that emerge from this general approach:

A. In what kind of society do we wish, or do we hope, to live? (I do not refer to the eternal social choices with which we are bothered: liberalism, self-determination, Socialism? I refer to the concrete options open to us: will we or won't we have a society of self-sufficiency, organization of public services, orientation and development of skills, relations or no relations with the Caribbean, development and orientation of specialized technology: projects for the involvement and organization of Martinicans according to these choices.)

B. To what extent do these questions—to which I could not give a personal reply a priori—depend on our political choices? Does a collective will exist to orient or simply to promote a unanimous decision?

Creole

The prejudices shared by Martinican parents and teachers on the question of the teaching of Creole and teaching in Creole is perhaps a crucial area of concern. It seems that the forces of deculturation no longer need to incite these prejudices. We have all taken over this responsibility. Because Creole is not strong in particular areas of knowledge, parents fear (and they are partly right) that a child speaking Creole in his formative years would be disadvantaged in comparison with another who only spoke French, the language of knowledge. The training of teachers accustomed to pedagogical methods over which they have absolutely no control leads to an attitude of passivity, or to panic in the face of a need for creative daring. Thus an inhibited response is automatically spread because of the existing situation.

According to traditional textbooks, Creole is a patois that is incapable of abstract thought and therefore unable to convey "knowledge." We should state that, taken in this sense (as an exclusive privilege of *superior* languages), abstraction is a presumption of Western thought, a presumption based on technological expertise and the means of dominating nature.

An Exploded Discourse

There is no other way to organize knowledge that would be linked to both the power of abstraction and technical domination, which are being questioned almost everywhere in today's world.

The appearance of new teaching methods based on multilingualism opens original possibilities for treating linguistic contact. Based on this, a methodological synthesis can be envisaged, which can perhaps permit a creative transcendence of the concept of the uniqueness of abstract thought.[1] In multilingual teaching, the child learns, along with his mother tongue, one or several languages considered acceptable (containing a technical potential not found in the mother tongue). But it is not a question of superiority. The language that has the potential to convey "technical information" is not offered as superior to any other. For instance, the English language is not considered "superior" to the French language, and yet the technical information transmitted in the world and constituting an integral part of this language is far superior to what the French language explicitly or implicitly conveys.

If it is assumed that today's universal languages are necessary for technical development (even though one is aware, for instance, of the ravages caused in Africa by the uncritical adoption of Western agricultural techniques), it has been demonstrated that the mother tongue is indispensable in all cases to psychological, intellectual, and emotional equilibrium among members of a community. If one continues to compel the Martinican child to have a French experience in school and a Creole experience at home, the process of collective irresponsibility that afflicts the Martinican community will be reinforced. The principle of multilingualism increases the child's learning capacity because he is free from the kind

---

1. On the subject of the linguistic universality of "abstraction." Abstraction in the Indo-European languages little by little became apparent, not as method, but as end result. Audio-visual media today seriously undermine any pretentions to transcendent universality. All language "abstracts," but this process is not the highest achievement of the language.

of dissociation that emerges as inhibitions, complexes, retardation, and sometimes opens the possibility of mental instability. In the context of the persistence of this dissociation and this collective irresponsibility, the whole pursuit of qualifications will continue to be an impossible exercise, because it is empty and pointless.

A university president has publicly declared in the French Caribbean, with the ethnocentric arrogance of his conservative attitudes, that Creole is not a language. It is almost impossible to argue with such a position, because it is based on deepseated ideological self-interest. Linguists have in general dealt harshly with such declarations. However, different tendencies can be noted when it comes to appreciating the nature of this language. Thus, in Haiti two directions emerge: the first, a traditionalist one, represented by M. Jules Faine, author of, among other things, a work entitled *Philologie créole* awarded a prize by the Académie Française—which argues that the Creole language is an off-shoot of French (before acquiring a separate existence); the other, represented by M. Pradel Pompilus *La langue française en Haiti* (Paris: Institut des Hautes Etudes de l'Amérique latine, 1961), which defends the hypothesis of the independence of the Creole language. Here are the basic data available on Creole in the "francophone" world— naturally the *cultural phenomenon of Creole* can relate to other Creoles (anglophone, portuguese). The table showing Creole in the francophone world does not take into account marginal Creoles (Louisiana, etc.). Variations in Creole dialects (Haitian, Martinican, Guadeloupean, etc.) and their variety make possible an attempt to derive general laws regarding their creation, if not rules concerning the emergence of a specific dialect. The creative thrust of written Creole has not waited for the formulation of general regulations: plays, poems, novels exist.[2] The Haitian writers Morisseau-Leroy, Franketienne, Frank Fouché, Paul Laraque, the Kouidor

2. The first novels published in Creole, as far as I know, are: *Desafi* by Franketienne (Port-au-Prince, Fardin, 1975), and *Lanmou pa jin barye* by

An Exploded Discourse

Creole in the Francophone World

Extent of influence	Number of speakers
Francophone Creole-speaking Caribbean (including Haiti)	6,900,000
Anglophone Creole-speaking Caribbean (including immigration to Trinidad and Jamaica)	500,000
Creole speakers from the Caribbean living in Europe (France and England)	600,000
Other Caribbean emigrants in America and Africa (including Haitians)	500,000
Creole speakers in the Indian Ocean	1,500,000
Total	10,000,000

troupe, the Guadeloupean Sony Rupaire, and the precursor, the Martinican Gilbert Gratiant.

In most countries, the languages taught in a multilingual situation are not "homogeneous": the consequent risk of syntactical ambiguity is minimal. It is obvious that Creole is a "francophone" phenomenon, that essentially its lexicon is derived from a French vocabulary for the most part. This, in addition to the constraints imposed on the Creole language, has led to the controversy over "origins": is it a language with its own syntax (in particular, derived from Africa), or is it a dialect of French speech deformed in the eighteenth century (such as the speech of Breton and Norman sailors)?[3]

Emile Célestin-Mégie (Port-au-Prince: Fardin, 1975). M. Raphaël Confiant publishes in Martinique novels which are typed and bound and among which is a Creole version of *L'étranger* by Albert Camus (turned into Creole). Title: *Mun andéwo-a*. A worker from Réunion island has published a bilingual narrative of his experiences in France: *Zistoir Christian* (Paris: Maspero, 1977).

3. The example of St. Lucia confirms that Creole is not always treated as simply a dialect of French, despite their linguistic proximity. Creole is the

Caribbean Discourse

I proposed in 1975, in a conference in Milwaukee on the possible framework for an ethnopoetics, that the only practical way to proceed in this situation is to make these two languages, linked in this way, *separate* from each other when they are taught.[4] This separateness, which is important to me, must not be achieved by some contrived transcription that will make written Creole ultimately appear to be some kind of derivative of Greek or Polish. It is not by wishing to make Creole distinct from French at all costs that we will best preserve the specific linguistic nature of Creole. Concern with a specific poetics must be of greater urgency than the question of devising an original spelling.

Giving the language a fixed form also raises some pertinent issues. Are modern civilizations not becoming more oral? Today's approaches to language teaching tend to reduce the imperious, even imperialist, domination of the written and to emphasize the oral.[5] Will not oral languages be more at ease (because of their very flexibility) in this new cultural climate? Some Haitian linguists have claimed that attempting to formalize the Creole language will only reduce its creativity. It is perhaps more useful to enlighten students on the real relationship between oral and written than to enclose them in the relative sterility of two grammatical systems, one of which would be in the process of being developed, or of two lexicons,

---

mother tongue widely used among St. Lucians and Dominicans. They do not speak French and are incapable of "deducing" it from its so-called patois. Explaining to FR3, on the day of St. Lucian independence, why Martinique should be the "instrument" of French business in this new country, M. Stirn (22 February 1979) declared that the two islands spoke different languages (English and French) but the same patois (Creole). M. Stirn appeared to be in his right mind, serious and smiling.

4. Edouard Glissant, "Free and fored poetics," *Ethnopoetics: A First International Symposium,* ed. Michel Benamou and Jerome Rothenberg (Boston: Boston University / Alcheringa, 1976), pp. 95–101. (*Trans.*)

5. M. Pompidou had commissioned research teams to devise a simplified version of French orthography (*ortograf*), that is, in fact, to "oralize" the language which has resisted this.

one of which would be made as distinct as possible from the other. The necessary inclusion of both Creole and French in the school system does not imply a laborious teaching of syntax, but rather a creative confrontation of two worldviews.

All poetics have implications for a general politics. That is why I say that, as parents and teachers, we are guilty of the same lack of responsibility. Our prejudices reinforce those of the Martinican child. In class he is exposed to the world of the serious, of work, of hierarchical relationships, with which he naturally associates the French language. At play, he reverts to Creole, with which he associates the world of recreation, freedom, and lack of restraint. This would be all well and good if he did not in addition make the link between Creole and irresponsibility. We help to strengthen this association.

The main source of our prejudice is that we clearly see that indeed in Martinique today the Creole language is one in which we no longer produce anything. And a language in which a people no longer produces is a language in agony. Creole is impoverished because terms relating to professions disappear, because vegetable oils disappear, because animal species disappear, because a whole series of expressions that were linked to forms of collective responsibility in the country are disappearing as this responsibility diminishes. The sociolinguistic study of terms fallen into disuse and that have not been replaced reveals that this happens because Martinicans as such no longer do anything in their country. The linguistic impoverishment that results echoes throughout the entire syntactical continuum of the language. This is how we move progressively from the impasse in the school system to the disappearance of Martinique as a community—nothing but a collection of individuals without links, to either their land or their history, or themselves.

That is why any reform that envisages the introduction of the teaching of Creole in a technical way in our educational system will be futile and ambiguous if it is not conceived, discussed, agreed to, by Martinicans themselves.

Caribbean Discourse

COMPLEMENTARY NOTE

—The objective of this meeting (of parents of students in Lamentin) was to isolate the main problems and to propose solutions. The scandal created by such discussion in our concrete situation is one aspect of the problem.

—Haitians have invented the neologism *oraliture* to replace the world *literature,* thus indicating their insistence on remaining in the realm of the oral.[6] It is enough to say that at the very least the strategy of fixing an "oral" language in the modern context is not clear-cut or finished once and for all.

—The clarification of the approach to a contrastive method of teaching, the teaching of a written language (French) or an oral language (Creole): this, for instance, is the responsibility to be shared between linguists and teachers.

—It is not enough to denounce the creolisms of which Martinicans are "guilty" when they use the French language, nor the deformations of Creole through the uncontrolled use of French. It must be recognized that in both cases the Martinican is a passive speaker who makes no contribution to the evolution of these languages of which he is essentially a "consumer," with no capacity for self-assertion. (In such a situation the reciprocal contamination of these languages is not an indication of creative evolution or the emergence of something new.) In other words, the Martinican has no language.

(It is felt, for example, that French is the second language

6. I often use the expression "oral literature," which many claim contains a contradiction in terms. It has the advantage of conveying that one is writing a text that was meant first and foremost to be read aloud and that could benefit from the techniques of oral expression. Such an oralization has, for instance, characterized the poetic discourse of American writers of the Beat Generation (Kerouac and Ginsberg). In these texts, the shout becomes written word without ceasing to be shout, or even scream. In the same way, oral literature will not cease reflecting the specific quality of spoken language even when transcribed. As for the formalizing of language, see what Rousseau says in his *Essay on the Origin of Language:* "Writing, which seems to be the method of formalizing a language, is precisely what

An Exploded Discourse

of Martinicans, in relation to Creole, which is their mother tongue. I suspect that the linguistic situation is complicated by the fact that this second language has become the natural language, but without first having been actively possessed by the community, then subjected to the constraints of the mother tongue. The destabilizing and dramatic conflict arises from the opposition between the falseness of the natural and the reality of nonassimilation.)

—The absence of an autonomous language compels us to consider in a new light the role and function of the writer, who can forge a new language. Particularly as a response to the question: "Why not write exclusively and immediately in Creole?"

1. The written version of Creole, as long as it does not result from a collective consensus, runs the risk of drifting fatally towards a folklorism that is all the more naive because it is done conscientiously.[7] This does not exclude the necessity of providing a number of works in Creole that will give it the necessary validity. These works need not necessarily be "literary."

---

alters it; it does not change the words but the spirit; it substitutes precision for expressiveness." He does add, it is true: "You convey feelings when you talk and ideas when you write." We could ask ourselves today if the major preoccupation of any Creole text ought not to be (against folkloric sentimentality) how to *transmit ideas?* I rediscover this Rousseauesque distinction (the division between expression of feeling and expression of ideas) in a declaration by M. Aimé Césaire: "Then, for me, each speech is a matter of reflection, it is a conceptual exercise, and so must be done in French. You see Creole is the language of the immediate, of folklore, of intensity," (interview with Jacqueline Leiner in an introduction to the reedition of the magazine *Tropiques*, 1978). Senghor's ideas are not really different (on emotion and reason.) And this is also perhaps a declaration that contradicts what M. Césaire says later: "For me it is the image that is strong and the idea that is weak." Because the Creole imagination has not yet been explored.

7. As the use of the French language increases the risk of following the vagaries of universality. Might we perhaps fear even more the initial risk that would be more decisive and catastrophic for us?

2. The present defense of Creole is perhaps primarily taken up by teachers, political militants, sociologists, linguists, the activism of a popular consciousness. We must find out why Creole is in decline in Martinique. What can its role be in a system of renewed productivity? How do we formalize it without neutralizing it? How to integrate it into the school system? All these questions have less to do with literary production than with sociolinguistic analysis, an educational policy, a political program.

3. In the face of the numbed linguistic sterility imposed on Martinicans, the writer's function is perhaps to propose language as shock, language as antidote, a nonneutral one, through which the problems of the community can be restated. This function could require the writer to "deconstruct" the French language that he uses (and that is one of the fundamental aspects of the situation); first as a means of demystification in relation to any automatic reverence for this language, then as a tool for locating major themes, cultural projections that from within the French language will be able to facilitate (by clarification) the future use of a written or revitalized Creole.

   (I argue in this sense that our present works are the "preface for a literature of the future." A Martinican academic proposes that it is really a matter of "archeological" texts: dead and out of date. That is an exorbitant claim and one that misreads the necessary and dynamic links that stretch from our present repressed, forced poetics to the "liberated" poetics of tomorrow's Caribbean. No one can determine today what this poetics will be (for instance, monolingual or multilingual) nor, consequently, can designate what will be the unreadable relic or the unlikely monument.)

4. It is not a matter of creolizing French but of exploring the responsible use (the creative exercise) that Martinicans can make of it.

An Exploded Discourse

5. The function of the writer in such a context, function of researcher and explorer, often isolates him from the language in use "at present" and consequently from the reader trapped in "the everyday." A regrettable but necessary condition with which he must come to terms if he wishes to bring his work to technical fulfilment; without feeling that he is, in some messianic way, the representative of anyone at all.

Man gin-yin an zin

With this opening line taken from a Creole sentence that I imagine has often been pronounced by the fishermen of Martinique, during the period of what I call "functional" Creole, I will try to convey my thoughts on how a language could possibly slip into decline.

Man gin-yin an zin. "I have bought a fishhook." Two features of Creole are represented here. The French verb *gagner,* (to earn) used with the meaning of *acheter* (to buy). It is very possible that this is inherited from old French; that is not important: its appropriation by the Creole language has been complete. The word *zin* used for the word *hameçon,* (fishhook) and I am not here interested in the process of substitution or adaptation: if, for instance, it might originate in the French word *zinc* and if, consequently, the material (or something like it) is meant to represent the object.

What interests me is that the expression has achieved, while maintaining a kind of linguistic integrity, an independence such that it is only heard under specific conditions. It is also true that this expression is—both for the community and for a group of fishermen—an expression of solidarity. What is the "context" for this expression? Not the ideal situation of a happy fisherman, earning his livelihood in an unexploited way. But at the very least that of a fisherman still master of his technology, capable of transforming it, finding someone to transmit it to. Catching his fish "in Creole" and buying his *zin* in the same way: I mean that the language is not only applicable when fishing takes place but to what happens before and after.

J'ai acheté un hameçon. "I bought a fishhook." How does a fisherman today say this coming out of one of these modern department stores or these "specialist" shops where the tools of his trade are mixed up with the rigging needed by tourists for their chartered sailboats or by those who like one-man crossings of the Atlantic? He says: *Man acheté an amson.* Why? Because the fishhook is not, in his mind, a *zin;* because the salesman speaks to him (or he speaks to the salesman) in French; because the very traditions of his trade elude him. Is there anything wrong with this? Cannot a community become usefully acculturated, make the transition from an oral mother tongue to a prestigious written language without being ruined? Of course it could be done if this transition were made by *an autonomous movement of the society on its own.*

But the Martinican fisherman says: *Man acheté an amson* because he has no control over the technical aspects of his trade. At the same time the language of prestige has both established its values in the wider community and imposed itself on the practical world of the fisherman. It has imposed a written form, integrating its linguistic structure in a form of expression that then ceases to be expressive.

That is the inadequacy that is referred to sometimes when it is pointed out that some languages like Creole "have missed the boat of the industrial revolution." There are, apparently, great universal languages, historically destined to develop because they "provide" machines (for counting, measuring, constructing, writing), and there are others already marked for extinction because they "serve" no purpose.

I do not support this point of view. It is not necessarily true that the future of mankind depends totally on the domination of the technology of the developed world. Without reverting

An Exploded Discourse

to an ecstatic vision of this future, and without succumbing to the idyll of eating fruit washed in spring water and riding our mules once again, we are justified in visualizing, in those countries where this is possible, a restoration of the balance between man's domination of nature and the way he lives nature, a new order that would naturally presuppose the victory of popular struggles over dominant injustice and inequality, that of a popular consciousness over elitist authority. Within this possible framework, use of language would match the relationship with the wider community, without being alienated because of its contact with a distant culture.

This is not the case with Creole today. It has stopped being a functional language: it is being undermined by a dominant language. M. Husson's black patois is the next step. Not in the way M. Husson used it, but now "integrated," normal, unnoticed. All that the Creole language has achieved: the transcendence of linguistic compromise, the sublimation of the activities of childhood, the art of the diversionary image, rhythmic camouflage—all of that risks being lost in this process of marginalization, produced by both an absence of productivity and an absence of creativity.

In such a circumstance, the limitations of any attempt to standardize Creole are obvious. It is of no consequence whether you choose to write *Man acheté en hameçon* or *Man acheté en lanmson*, or *Mã ãste ã amson*: the method of transcription that you will have used, no matter how distinct from a French transcription, will not prevent the weakened form of this language from already existing in your expression. We must begin by going back to the poetics of the language: the mechanism it uses to avoid the potential danger of linguistic compromise. It is based on this poetics and the consequent exercise of creativity that little by little the future forms of writing in Creole will emerge. That is the job of the storyteller, of the performer within the language—but one who cannot envisage his role except when the common will puts in place the economic, social, and political conditions for the development of the language. In the meantime, the work done by linguists offers us useful guidelines. It must be understood for what it is: a preparation for future growth, not any essential and exclusive need for some pseudoscientific study of linguistic dynamics.

THEATER, CONSCIOUSNESS
OF THE PEOPLE

(In the Street)

And so we enact for ourselves theatrical scenes, on the stage of our continued wandering, such that it can appear ridiculous to recommend to us the value of that form of self-analysis provided by theatrical activity.

But the simple "street scene" does not provide us with the vital mechanism of the popular consciousness; in it energy intensifies in nothing but an everyday delirium. The street scene as a rule *does not create* popular consciousness but reinforces it and contributes to structuring it in those places where it already exists—that is, really, for a community already secure in its history and its traditions.

Or else it is also an everyday manifestation of *theatralization* that in the street feeds on our impulses. The theatralization of our impulses makes theatrical activity useless. The creation of theater "in real life" makes it unnecessary to have theater as spectacle in a chosen arena.

Community theater, on the other hand, diverts energy from the individual manifestation of delirium or from the collective tendency to the theatrical, so as to orient it towards the shaping of a popular consciousness.

But individual delirium and collective theatralization, as forms of cultural resistance, are the first "catalysts" of this consciousness.

(It remains to be said that theatrical performance is often satisfied with the complacent *reenactment* of the street scene; we have abandoned spontaneous impulse for the lure of repetition: simply another kind of folkloric devaluation of our culture.)

Theater, Consciousness of the People

I. THEATER AND NATION

Concerning a few scattered proposals, conventional since Hegel

(*On the danger of playing here the black man in a Greco-Latin mode*)

But a historical perspective, no matter how fleeting—and in any case it will only focus on History (with the capital letter implied and which is the creation of the West, leaving out of account our history)—is nevertheless rich in what it teaches us: in a negative way, to provide contrast.

Therein lies a striking vision of the birth of a people, meant for a people becoming aware of itself. Since we are involved in a process of liberation, we tend to believe that every people in the beginning was like a version of black people. The birth of a people (their emergent consciousness) is a fascinating spectacle. The theater that accompanies it is a moving experience.

1. *When a nation is taking shape, it develops a theatrical form that "duplicates" its history (gives it significance) and provides an inventory.*

   a. Theater is the act through which the collective consciousness sees itself and consequently moves forward. At the beginning, there can be no nation without a theater.

   b. Theater involves moving beyond lived experience (dramatic time takes us out of the ordinary so that we can better understand the ordinary and the everyday). The ability to move beyond can only be exercised by the collective consciousness. There is no theater without a nation at its source.

This creative expression, which starts as folklore and then becomes a transcendence of folklore, is probably at its origin the vestige of an intention (a becoming) whose manifestations (state, religion, language) are organized around a common

An Exploded Discourse

objective. What this objective means is not primarily (in History) recognized as such. Folklore "reveals" and theater "reflects" this objective. They are the original circuits of knowledge, but which can neither shape nor limit it.

2. *This form of theatrical expression is particularly vibrant, fertile, free when the collective consciousness is being formed.*

   a. The collective impulse is experienced in all its urgency, not simply lived as a given.

   b. It is threatened, not alienated: it has to be expressed.

   c. It is dynamic, nontechnical; it is not subjected to the pressure of rules, which are beneficial at a later stage.

   d. It is therefore "totally" expressed.

A necessity—"total," yet threatened: that is the essential tragedy of our Caribbean situation. Yet there is a deficiency in "our" theater. What is this necessity that cannot find expression, this threat that remains invisible, this totality that fragments? Our tragedy is not resolved. The reasons for the deficiency are cumulative: the traumatic conditions under which the Caribbean was settled, structures (based on taboos) of the slave's world, self-repression provoked by depersonalization, etc. But the fact that the Martinican is incapable of representing himself only makes the need more intense for the opportunity offered by the theater, through which he could be made to come to terms with himself.

3. *Theatrical expression is structured from the forms of common folkloric background, which then ceases to be lived in order to be represented, that is, thought through.*

   a. This folkloric background is represented but also "represents itself."

   b. The effect, emotional and conceptual, is echoed back

to the collective consciousness, which reacts critically to this representation.

Two forms then emerge—the sacred and the profane— which become one, or rather a whole. (It is not unlikely that two forms of Western theatrical activity: tragedy and comedy, are initial responses to this twofold necessity.)

What is needed is a hardy tradition of folklore. To go beyond lived experience is to go beyond folklore, which, because it is hardy, can only be transcended by providing on its own the means of its transcendence. This hardy folklore is at the source (of theater).

The folkloric background represented, reflected on, given a cultural thrust, is raised to the level of consciousness, shapes it, and—strengthened by the very action of reinforcing consciousness—criticizes itself as a consciousness in its new "form" as "culture." Culture never simply comes into existence or imposes itself.

Representing itself, thinking itself through: these two are simply the very process of forming a whole.

4. *This form of dramatic expression becomes that of the (entire) community because it moves beyond its folkloric origins while not undermining them. (The marketplace and the amphitheater are essentially the same Site where Greek drama is acted out, where Socrates has himself condemned in order to see, and where blind Oedipus defies the capricious gods.)*

When Socrates drinks hemlock and when Oedipus gouges out his eyes—one in a real prison, the other on the tragic stage—folklore is left behind. The setting of Socrates' trial then becomes the same as the celebrations at Eleusis, in order to constitute, beyond spectacle (beyond the indictment of the one and the decree of the gods in the other), the basic features of consciousness.

A politicized people is one that transcends folklore.

An Exploded Discourse

5. *What the theater expresses in its early stages is not the psychology of a people, it is its shared destiny: through the investigation of why it acts and how its forward movement unfolds.*[1] *In other words, its place in the world and not so much the conditions (distinctiveness, separateness) of its existence.*

Naturally, its role is dependent on these states. But priorities are fixed as light is shed. Coming to terms with the world (finding where one must establish one's place in the sun) is certainly of primordial importance in this period when man almost always confused the world and what he knew of it. History was the result of this confusion.

Origins therefore relates historically here to the creation of any people. Theatrical beginnings are not just the early stages of dramatic form (which in itself would not necessarily be a frame of reference) but the origins of a people (for whom the theater is part of a larger pattern.)

6. *Psychological analysis, the technical mechanism of "dramatic form," the shaping force of rules are progressive indications that a collective consciousness has been created, giving rise to "specialization." At this point the nation has taken shape—that is, it has a past it fully recognizes.*

This moment of nostalgia is the mark of any people who have come of age: that fragile moment when the nation, already structured, is not yet solidly fixed. The memory of this trembling hope directs the excesses and the audacity of national feeling. Equally pernicious, however, is the absence for a community of this troubled hope. Here we do not have a sense of the past; consequently, we cannot move beyond it (beyond ourselves). What rules would obtain, since we cannot even define our "specific" identity? Thus, any specialization is for us absurd (but) necessary. It must be managed (that is here and for the moment,

---

1. This unfolding is a continuation of what has been said about the infolding of myth.

constantly presupposed). "Objectivity" (the misleading claims of another scientific method) is one of the major reasons for our tragedy.

7.   *Finally, this form of a people's dramatic expression, in its early phase, is "harmonious" as far as the peoples formed before modern times are concerned: the transition process from lived experience to conscious reflection is not "forced."*

This means that there is no voluntarism in the collective form of expression adopted by one or several poets, who themselves may be praised or vilified. That consequently the links (for instance, between masses and elite) are "autonomous": that is, they are not subjected to the imposition of a force external to the given society, even when their structure is built on the real alienation of a large part of the community by a small group. That, in other words, this (dialectical) manifestation of alienation is related to collective progress (generates history).

Nothing like that here.

R E S U M E
What happens in History

—*Transition from lived folklore to the representation of knowledge.*
—*Transition from the beliefs of folklore to the consciousness of "culture."*
—*Harmonious, unforced transition.*
—*Force: collective impulse.*
—*Form: Not specialized, or, rather, to become specialized.*
—*Factor: links between elite and group.*

This transition from lived folklore to represented culture emerges as a process of enlightenment (which reinforces the movement from belief to consciousness); can we not conceive of the chorus in Greek theater as primarily the basic revelation of the esoteric and elite mysteries of Eleusis? Progressive and obscure revelation is the principle of tragedy: the difficult journey to consciousness. To shared consciousness. This revelation has its own way of proceeding. Tragedy does not resort to any contrived process. On the other hand, it is an elite that reveals and shares (is forced to share) the elitist force of tradition. The criticism of this elite comes later: when Aristophanes laughs at Aeschylus or Socrates (intellectual criticism), or when the society is dissolved or remade (structural criticism).

All of this eludes us: an impulse, a representation, an elite dialectically linked to a people, an internal possibility of criticism and transcendence: a freedom.

II. ALIENATION AND REPRESENTATION

(Unperceived and unassumed in our unexpressed history)

(Let us therefore leave History and go down into the gully course that is our future—our difficult becoming. Hegel does not enter with us.) The rupture of the slave trade, then the experience of slavery, introduces between blind belief and clear consciousness a gap that we have never finished filling. The absence of representation, of echo, of any sign, makes this emptiness forever yawn under our feet. Along with our realization of the process of exploitation (along with any action we take), we must articulate the unexpressed while moving beyond it: expressions of "popular beliefs" are a nonpossession that we must confirm; to the point where, recognizing them as a nonpossession, we will really deal with them by abandoning them.

A

1. *Expressions of "popular beliefs" in Martinique: these are the rituals of festivities and ceremonies, dances (*bel-air, laghia *or* damier*), folktales.*

2. *These forms of expression no longer correspond to "beliefs" except in a dramatic and deep-seated way.*

3. *These forms of expression have been constantly distorted. They are therefore the dramatic manifestations of a cultural legacy that has, moreover, been deformed.*

The exploitation of this kind of colony requires depersonalization. At the servile stage, the slave, after having been deported, must be mentally dislocated. The Caribbean person must be persuaded that he is different (in order to prevent him from representing himself). Initially, the imperialist objective is to do everything first to cut the slave off from his former culture (the vestiges of this culture become survivals), then to cut the Caribbean person off from his true world (vestiges of a former culture are turned into an ornamental folklore). Both these processes have in common a lack (carefully cultivated) of history. Everything must grind to a halt so that exploitation can take place; the elite is given the responsibility of "maintaining" this condition of stasis. It is only through an evolution of the historical consciousness that a transition can be achieved, from the beliefs before the rupture, to the realities of deportation, to the consciousness of a new people. It is, for example, normal that a member of the elite should dismiss any reference to his past as a sign of obsessiveness or an attempt to be divisive (he will claim that he is Indian, European, and African at the same time, that all of that is irrelevant): capitalist exploitation creates the ideology of the *assimilé* (the deculturated, assimilated person). Isolated, uncertain of its own values, a people gradually and profoundly becomes more French.

4. *It follows that the "harmonious" transition from the representation of "popular beliefs" to that of the collective consciousness was difficult, let us say even impossible: the spontaneous birth of a theater was out of the question.*

5. *For one cannot transcend in one's consciousness (even if it is only to take the opposite view) what is nothing*

but the expression of a deficiency, of an experienced inadequacy.

6. *Our conclusion is based on the (imposed) collective inability to evolve from folklore to theater, belief to consciousness, lived experience to the reflective act.*

Cultural expression—such as the community's involvement in poetry (the cry), collective action, or a dance—does not immediately achieve self-representation in the way that theater (in its articulation), painting, the essay form, or reflective thought can do. An alienated poetry is easier to conceive than the systematic deformation of a theater or any other literature. The elite poetizes but treats any kind of reflection as contempt of the other (feeling itself inadequate in this reflection that eludes it). But this reflection remains intellectual as long as the people, who can ensure collective involvement, remains absent from the process; the lack of history, discontinuity, sterility are all symptoms. One could ultimately conclude that we cannot produce a "theater" because we do not (yet) act collectively.

B

1. *Beliefs are not productive in cultural terms:*

   a. They are experienced as exile and suffering, not as presence and happiness. This is so because they primarily challenge and recall; they do not affirm.

   b. They do not over time have the benefit of the support of a collective consciousness that they would in turn help to reinforce.

In addition to the initial rupture (the slave trade), the conditions of settlement aggravated the isolation of the group. Centuries of suffering and struggle would be needed before communities of Africans, transplanted in the Americas, dare to claim this new land for themselves. In small, isolated communities, continual revolts would invariably be undermined. In the case of Martinique, a transition will be imposed from African beliefs, gradually emptied of meaning, to the aspiration to be French in a meaningless way. It must perhaps be noted that the impulse toward representation, if not fulfilled in literature, tends to become part of the everyday. The life of the Martinican is certainly filled with drama, and the theater is in the street.

2. *The expression of popular beliefs is maintained at its most elementary level:*

a. This is so because of the violence of the act of colonization, which obliterates the sense of a shared past. This wiping out of the past does not mean that, along with memory, the nation has disappeared. The nation is erased, obscured, but not abolished.

b. Also because of the subtle colonial creation of an artificial elite whose role is to take charge of the function of representation.

The system was established and reinforced by maintaining the vacuum separating the elite from the rest of the community. We have cause to wonder whether this face-to-face contact between masses and elite did not exist undisturbed in the town of St.-Pierre before 1902. (The dependent nature of theater in St.-Pierre before the eruption of Mt. Pelée, which is evident in the documents of the time, does not prevent us from seeing in it a kind of disturbed originality or debased authenticity—similar to the definition given by Alejo Carpentier of the colonial theater in Havana, for example—and which cannot be compared with the wretchedness of Fort-de-France stricken with assimilation in 1971. Old St.-Pierre formed a context that allowed elite and masses to confront each other directly; perhaps an investigation of its cultural institutions would show this.)

An Exploded Discourse

(Elite and Representation)

Every elite is created on the basis of class differentiation in which a small group has real control over the majority. This real control is what allows an elite to claim the right to representation (in it and through it) of the entire social system, on which it lives. The function of representation is like the consummation, the worthy and formal consecration of material privilege. (Thus, all representation means the alienation of the represented.) The French Caribbean elite is distinct in that the function of representation precedes that of exploitation. In other words, it has been systematically created to take control of—literally, to represent (in the fullest application of the notion of representation)—the alienation of the collective whole.

The elite exploits the Caribbean masses, not because it is driven to by its dynamism, but because its role (of representing the appearance of progress) requires it to live off colonial handouts. To some extent, the elite practices a kind of secondary exploitation.

The precarious and absurd nature of this elite in the French Caribbean is based on its ability to represent one manifestation of "culture," as opposed to the "uncultured" masses:

—this representation is not based on any material footing (since the elite does not represent for itself and does not really represent itself);

—this representation is only performed as parody, since (despite assertions that are even more fierce because they are "defensive" and compensatory) the elite is not responsible for what it represents: in other words, it has absolutely no role in the development of this official "culture" that it claims to represent formally;

—this representation does not develop (even clandestinely) with the "uncultured" masses the relationship between exploiter and exploited whose tensions would have provoked a collective transcendence of oppositions (because in our case the elite does not exploit for itself—despite the tremendous advantages and privileges that it is granted—and remains as much slave as it is master).

One unforeseen consequence of this state of things is that "emancipation by the elite" is out of the question.[2] The so-called national bourgeoisie is for us an aspiration and not a reality. Besides, the system strategically maneuvers the elite into a position where it must maintain dialogue with it in the name of the people.

C

1. *The expression of popular beliefs is restricted, as performance, to the everyday existence of the people, a silent existence.*

2. *The elite "express" (themselves); the people are silent.*

3. *The expression of popular beliefs dwindles because they do not have the resonance we mentioned—the ability to transcend.*

They become, when taken over by the elite, a kind of entertainment (and no longer serious activity) that allows the elite to assert itself only insofar as it can smugly project its superiority.

Intellectuals "go into" the countryside, for instance, in order to listen to ("drum up"?) the *bel-air;* but as the intention behind this act is never clearly thought out, the most obvious result is to achieve an "official" promotion of "*bel-air*" dancers for the pleasure of tourists (and the "renown"). Everything here is "reclaimed."

2. For the members of the elite who wish to help make changes in existing relationships, there is an absolute obligation to deny there is such a group so as to undermine the system. If they declare their commitment to liberation without also denying themselves (calling themselves into question) as a group, they cannot fight against the system that created their class and will only fall into step with the system.

An Exploded Discourse

Therefore, in a situation where the people do not have the resources (either social or cultural) to express themselves, the elite, who ought to take charge technically of guiding that society, to outline in a specific historical period the reasons for making the move from folklore to consciousness, are precisely that part of the social body whose function here is to be both alienated and alienating.

4. *The expression of popular beliefs never "includes" the total expression of the community, because it has no perspective: no leverage or dynamism.*

In other words, the community presents itself, but does not reflect on itself (does not represent itself): folklore never moves beyond that phase. There emerges, in the worst meaning of the word, folklorization. That which (within the "culture") changes is that which comes from the outside: from the floats at carnival to teaching techniques. Nothing else changes; it disappears.

The expression: "the community has no leverage or dynamism," means that in its unconscious history the community has not managed to develop a common vision, and not that the impetus (the popular spirit) was lacking.

RESUME
What does not happen here

—*Harmonious transition from beliefs to consciousness.*
—*Expression of collective thought or experience.*
—*Independent organization of the society and consequently "productive" (dialectical) links between various classes.*

Over this collective failure constantly falls the shadow of the colonial strategy to reinforce the break with the past. The very nature of colonialism in Martinique (the insidious kind) requires, not that Martinican or Caribbean originality should be clumsily crushed, but that it be submerged, that it should be watered down in a cleverly instituted "natural" progression. Thus, we have the official defense of folklore. It seemed shrewder to neutralize it while giving it apparent support than to suppress it: it becomes cloying, silly, too much. The elite, which has never assisted in the positive evolution of folklore, will assist in paralyzing it.

D

1. *The artificial revival of forms of popular belief is particularly misguided and harmful as long as:*

    a. those who live these beliefs do not have the means of defending their true nature;

    b. the elite, who could guarantee the possibility of their technical renewal, have no idea of their importance.

Besides, it is a widespread strategy of depersonalization to paralyze a people, alienated from its folklore, in a state of confusing stasis. The fact is that here this strategy is facilitated by all kinds of known historical circumstances, which we have outlined. It is one of the fundamental issues that must contribute to considering "cultural" activity in our political program and must not lead to its neglect (or its being rushed over) because we have no time for it. Urgency is always fundamental and "includes" individual events.

2. *We become witnesses to the following:*

    A folklore in decline (or paralyzed): the people increasingly uncertain of the truth of their experience.

    Parodies of folklore that flourish: the elite are further and further removed from the dignity of folk expressions, of which they are ignorant.

The first official who comes along will defend indigenous cultural manifestations, and their "enchanting" quality. In the same breath, Martinicans are said to be pleasant and welcoming (it is true that when they are grouped as an elite they ap-

An Exploded Discourse

plaud any speech given to them, precisely where they are insulted): this fossilization of everything is (linked to) the very process of folklorization.

Folkloric displays are therefore never part of a program of self-expression, which is what paralyzes them. Invariably, the "artist," forced to resort to the circuits already established or in a hurry to exploit them, depoliticizes his art (that is, removes all expression or any vision capable of preventing access to these circuits—we see that this depoliticization is not an ideological choice, never possible in this case, but a form of amputation akin to castration of the self) and, having entered these circuits, becomes in turn a part of the folkloric.

E

"Theatrical" expression is necessary, however.

a.   In its critical dimension: in order to help destroy alienated forms of representation.

b.   In its dynamic dimension: in order to contribute to the basic process whereby a people escapes the limitation of folkloric expression to which it has been reduced.

It is frightening to see what the system offers the Martinican public in the name of "theater" and which goes well beyond simple mediocrity. It is useless to state that, after all, it is entertainment for the elite and that the majority of the people do not have general access to the theaters. The whole of this study is based on the feeling that, in this case, the objective circumstances impose the same alienation on the masses as on the elite. Experimentation is for us the only alternative: the organization of a process of representation that allows the community to reflect, to criticize, and to take shape.[3]

3. All political activity is theater (just as all caricature of political life becomes a circus). If politics for us gives meaning to that which is being

Caribbean Discourse

R E S U M E

—*The theater "remains" folkloric (the folkloric stage is not left behind).*
—*Aggression and exploitation paralyze folklore.*
—*There are visible signs that the community is threatened by slow suffocation, by gradual disappearance.*

In the remarkable process of cultural alienation that is likely to succeed here, it is noteworthy that there is a celebration of folklore at all levels (radio, television, carnival, tourist entertainment), but a carefully depoliticized folklore—that is, cut off from any general application or meaning. It is, moreover, amusing to note or to track down (in the newspapers or even at the level of the few institutions of cultural activity that have been set up) a single-minded effort to Indianize the folkloric background, which fits in with an extreme repugnance on the part of the Martinican *assimilé* to think about his real past (because of slavery). This Indianization is totally understandable: the Carib Indians on the francophone islands are all dead, and the Indians of French Guiana pose no threat to the existence of the system. Indianization thus has advantages: it glosses over the problem of Martinican origins, it appeals to one's sensitivity, it offers a pseudohistory and the illusion of a cultural (pre-Columbian) hinterland, all of which is rendered harmless in advance (from the point of view of collective self-assertion) because the Caribs have already been exterminated. (The pre-Columbian heritage in Caribbean and South American cultures requires an in-depth examination that we will attempt elsewhere.) The entire depersonalizing policy of the system aims at emptying expressions of popular culture of their historical significance: cut off from the meaning of the past, folklore becomes neutralized, stagnant. Therefore, it contributes to the collective drift to oblivion.

---

represented, theater can be considered as representation (or the signifying expression) of politics.

An Exploded Discourse

III. THEATER AND ACTION

(Toward a Theater of Disorder, in accordance with a Dynamic
Order, embryonic and emergent, within Our Community)

The imposed cultural vacuum creates urgent areas of concern
and in particular the following one is more perplexing than
any other: Does necessary and irreplaceable political action
logically and inevitably involve a cultural revolution?

Yes. When this political action aims to overturn an "established" cultural "order" or to reinstate an alienated national
culture. It is in creating the conditions for revolution that cultural revolution makes sense and becomes possible.

No. When alienation has taken hold of a collective body
with no cultural reserves, with no fixed point of reference capable of stabilizing (that is, capable of bringing to fruition) a
struggle to emerge. Perhaps it is then necessary, simultaneous
with the conduct of political activity, to develop the hidden
potential of this cultural hinterland, or at least work toward
this. Among the factors linking cultural emergence and political activism, dramatic dialogue (between speaker and listener,
a storyteller and his audience) appears to be one with the
greatest potential.[4]

A

1. Since the *"harmonious" transition (from belief to consciousness) has not been possible, it is necessary to create
it by force.*

2. Since the community's *potential for action is submerged,
we must be made to face the community's ability and
need to act.*

4. It is certain (in contrast to an excessive belief in the autonomy of culture) that it is political choice that determines the direction of culture: that
the latter could never result from a decision taken by the elite, but must

3. *Since the collective impulse, based on which the community represents itself in dramatic performance, is threatened, we must consciously reanimate this impulse at the level of theatrical representation.*

4. *Since the elite does not "play its role" as part of a natural circuit, we must question its present usefulness as a social class and declare on the political (and therefore cultural) level its harmfulness as a group.*

What remains constant is that a certain petrified, almost quantifiable vision of "culture" (which could be imported like merchandise) will here be officially and persistently promoted; what also remains constant is that all artistic production in Martinique falls generally into a kind of vacuum: it is then salvaged for use by the system. The will to keep one's distance from any form (whatever this distance may be) produced by the system is therefore one of the most useful ways to prepare for true creativity. Any artist who does not abide by this rule is condemned to neutralize his creativity (consciously or not) in the "business as usual" colonial scheme of things. This veritable deformation is not avoided even by works that are apparently (and in an immediate way) "militant." For it is difficult to be constantly on the alert, especially in a generally static situation, incrusted at every turn with tempting contradictions. Such a neutralization involves a crippling discontinuity; political action lies in continuity.

---

proceed from a process agreed to by and within the majority of the people. But it is also true that political action that does not concern itself with cultural reform runs the risk of being reduced to deadly abstractions. In this way, the introduction of a popular theater will *really* be incorporated into the social system, that is, it will (critically) enfold the latter; but (in order to respond to the charge of having no sense of timing or of being too abstract in my argument) this process must be implanted in each performance, and not theoretically determined in terms of some anticipatory, global perspective.

An Exploded Discourse

B

1. *Therefore, it is not primarily on the technical level that the theater's necessary activity must be reconsidered.*

2. *(Except when the technique is based on the natural impulse of the group: for instance, if it is a question of adapting for political performance, or for the effectiveness of theater in the round in adapting the popular ritual of the* lagghia *dance.)*

The theater, if it is not an integral part of the society (a "natural emanation") and if it is, however, necessary, can only be a "willed act." It is a matter of breaking through each individual's silence and solitude. This means that this theater cannot simply be the reflection of the community's activities, for it would be solely the expression of a vacuum, of an emptiness. It must do more than just point to this loss. Such a role has been negatively taken over by the excuses for drama now in evidence. A functional popular theater, through as fierce an exploration as is necessary of ways and means, must contribute to overcoming this emptiness and, in its own limited domain, to filling the void.

In this sense, the work that, in our context, does not unceasingly put the movement of history on a new footing only serves to reinforce the alienation. Begin with the first slave ship that unloaded its first cargo and, from that point onwards, fill in the void. This implies that economic exploitation should be denounced from the outset and consistently. That denunciation is linked to the clarification of history. Without this, it invariably serves the interests of the elite that has emerged, by usurping the victories won by popular struggle.

(On the notion of the "willed act")

No one could ever live folklore as a willed act (it always is the product of an unconscious process), but one can exercise

Caribbean Discourse

one's will to facilitate the transition from lived folklore to the representation of consciousness. Our (obvious) hypothesis is that the French Caribbean people do not progress "unconsciously to a consciousness of themselves," as would have been the case (which is what I mean by harmony) with a people who would have created themselves in former times. It is a sign of our modernity that we are created out of suffering.[5] It is the willed effort toward consciousness itself that produces the community. The theater ought to represent this process, give meaning to this effort.

C

1. *This dynamism is not (ought not to be) of this or that kind, nor in one group but a product of the whole group (of the community as such): and consequently must not result from a progressive approach to problems but from the very unexpectedness of the cultural revolution.*

2. *The specific manifestation of this cultural revolution can only be for us that of establishing or constituting a culture (a struggle converts individual activist initiative into a genuinely collective expression).*

3. *It is no use saying that the elite is cut off from the masses. The elite is also alienated from itself. And the masses also suffer from alienation produced by depersonalization. What, in this case as in others, constitutes the advantage of the people's cultural force is, first, its fundamental role in any creativity; it is, second, that it lives and suffers the expression of beliefs (in a negative way), whereas the elite can only parody this expression.*

Even when the people and the elite are affected by the same alienation, the former are not subjected to the added obliga-

5. This modernity negates any nostalgia for the past: the reconquest of history is not a matter of turning backward.

tion of "cultural representation": they are not in addition required to project (to represent) this alienation—which is the main function of the elite.

On the other hand, even as they dwindle, the forms and expressions of popular beliefs are lived by the people, at least in this tragic phase of their disappearance. This is what explains the popular distaste for mass cultural demonstrations, which, like the carnival, are increasingly reduced to small gatherings and limited to parades in which we detect the representation of alienation that we mentioned and the restricted, pejorative, deformed, dead meaning that we now give to the word *theater.*

(Scenes depicted in the Martinican carnival: the court of Louis XIV, Napoleon and Josephine, etc. We should note that the same kinds of scenes occur in carnivals that are apparently more lively and authentic, those of Brazil and Trinidad, for example. We should examine too whether it is also a case of assimilation, or whether, on the contrary, this phenomenon—the reproduction of the world of the former master—is not now neutralized by an intense and authentic indigenous culture). We must also emphasize that the slightest sign of revival of the dying carnival in Martinique is greeted by the official media (radio, television, newspapers) as a victory, and furthermore is encouraged in all possible ways. The carnival (which was the implicit focus for reversing this decline in self-expression) becomes an explicit instrument of alienation.

Ultimately, the cultural dynamism of a people paradoxically results from its prolonged repression. They have suffered from deculturation as they have suffered from not possessing the land to which they were deported. Their right to possession of the land is an acquired right: collective ownership of the land is won through suffering and not the law. The power of a culture is born of suffering and not learned.

D

The problematics of a Martinican theater can be presented in this way:

a. Participation in a collective existence:
—consciously focused, at the level of drama, on the expression of a popular cultural base.
—consciously made to move beyond, always at the level of drama, this spontaneous form of expression.

b. Development not so much of partially critical themes (which would permit all kinds of compromises to slip in: "analysis," "allusions," psychological "subtlety," witty "words": the range of techniques from an inculcated dramatic form) as of a general critical perspective on the situation (a revaluation of history).

c. Becoming, through its dynamism, the moving force (in its area) of a collective dynamism that must be constantly reanimated.

d. Avoiding being clad in social finery but being endowed with the seriousness of the people.

e. Seeking its technical inspiration in the source of the community's existence (possible examples: the nonnecessity of the stage, the importance of voice as opposed to dialogue); seeking its theoretical inspiration in the strength of the collective expression, not of beliefs any longer, but of the very basis for existence.

The unrelieved caricature found in our "theater houses" would be enough to produce a dynamic reaction favoring the popularization of theatrical performance. This popularization, which must tactically burst into life far from the theatrical auditorium, becomes vital when it is a question of combating in the Martinican mentality the intrusions and impositions, on the technical and ideological level, that create a self-inflicted castration. A genuinely popular art is therefore not only one that denounces the existing reality (any sort of paternalism could be at work here) but an art capable, because of the way it is incorporated, of changing this reality: of contributing to historical revaluation. This art can only be the product of Martinicans themselves, involved in their own process.[6]

(Theater and action)

Such a theater, as opposed to the currently orchestrated and imposed version, therefore offers an internal capacity to challenge and refute. It is not a matter of shouting down or applauding a particular actor but of discussing the significance of the performance. (In order to combat what any representation contributes to the alienation of what is represented?) To discuss the performance is to make it less sacred. This phenomenon would perhaps correspond (for a modern consciousness) to what was meant by the comical farce in the fourth period of the Greek tetralogy: a revaluation from the inside.

This raises the problem of "comprehension" (a too elaborate theater that might go "over the heads of the people"). Typical intellectual pretentiousness! The problem is not one of whether or not the form is accessible, but whether or not the representation is adequate. In terms of being adequate, representation cannot be "beyond" the represented. In the performance of popular theater, we feel there is nothing (in expression, form, complexity) that the people cannot master; and that only its critical consciousness (not that of the elite) can determine the appropriateness of the shape and the content of the dramatic performance.

One of the most frequently heard comments (made invariably by intellectuals) relates to the exclusive and necessary use of Creole in the elaboration of a popular theater. Even if no one can deny the value of this orientation, we must nevertheless be wary of too dogmatic an approach to this issue. The objective conditions of the liberation of Creole are determined

6. At the theatrical level, this art form presupposes a resolute desire to express what is (because fear of criticizing oneself often leads to a temptation to deny oneself).

by the social revolution and popular initiative: it is possible that a prophetic and "a priori" use of Creole, whether written or declaimed (in relation to the true liberation) could produce folkloric deformations, in which the greatest risk of caricature would be, because of populist sentimentality, a kind of leftist "folksiness." Backward and reactionary attitudes, in fact, can fit in very well with a dogmatic insistence on Creole, behind which they could be concealed. In other words: one can be tempted to insist on Creole (or to demand here and now its exclusive use) simply to conceal a real inadequacy in one's analysis of existing reality. Thereby, unwittingly falling into the trap of the "official" strategy of promoting folklore. This issue is important enough to deserve separate examination.

RESUME

1. *Can one, here and now, create a national economy?*

   —If the answer is yes, theatrical reform becomes unnecessary: collective expression is channeled elsewhere (which sometimes is the source of the formal conception of internationalism) and the community no longer needs to represent itself.

2. *Can one achieve a kind of "consciousness" without the experience of a collective impulse?*

   —If the answer is yes, the people can be harmlessly maintained in a static folkloric condition—and the depersonalization of everyone is not a source of alienation.

One can understand how the theater can help call into question the concept of the nation, in a community that has undergone the excesses of nationalist ideology. One can reject the nation, if one already has one. Thus, the opposition between theater as communication (the sacred phase) and theater as revaluation (the sacrilegious phase) will take on a different significance depending on whether one takes the perspective of an overdeveloped society or the perspective of an under-developed society. But the nature of representation (always involving the possible alienation of the represented) compels us here, in an underdeveloped country, to create communion from revaluation, and collective participation out of collective criticism. The energy and the impulse that then evolve are the kind that promote a common destiny and favor at the same time and constantly the transcendence (but conscious, consequent, and unanimous) of what emerges and what will necessarily emerge as a "limitation" (or divisiveness) in the concept of the nation.

NOTE
Concerning a modern tragedy that no longer
requires the sacrifice of the hero

Yes, modern man has learned not to abuse faith in the community (and the resulting tensions) to the point of offering in its name the ritual sacrifice of heroes. The tragic rite of sacrifice is predicated on confidence in the dialectical opposition (individual-community) whose reconciliation is deemed beneficial. Modernity assumes the rupture of this dialectic: either the individual is frustrated and History turns to pure negation, or the communities develop and there is a new pattern of histories that take over (consciously) from History. In both instances, the mediating role of the heroic sacrifice becomes useless. Political consciousness does not assume the need for a victim that the naive (or intuitive) consciousness needed. This is why the great periods of political and revolutionary crisis have not, as ought to have been the case, produced great tragic works.

The transition has in this way been made in the West from the "representation" of tragic sacrifice to the "reflective" political consciousness implied in modernity. In principle the alienation technique in Brecht is an index of this transition. Mother Courage is not a propitiatory victim nor an exemplary heroine; she represents a phase of the alienated consciousness that "develops" through situations.

Our community will not achieve this progressive transition from sacrificial tragedy to political tragedy. This is because all tragic theater requires, except in the rules of classical French theater (where the tragic element is subsumed in the longing for universal truth), a hero who *takes unto himself* the destiny of the community. Our drama (which is not tragedy) is that we have collectively denied or forgotten the hero who in our true history *has taken unto himself* the cause of our resistance: the maroon. This historical lapse leads to the absence of tragedy.

Therefore we have not exploited these gaps either—the feverish nature of the sacred—which are the links between the tragic and the political. Neither the systematic release of Cyrano, nor the tortured obsessiveness of Artaud. In this area we know nothing but the folkloric debasement of self-expression.

A theater springing from a "collective politics" would banish such debasement. It is emerging everywhere in South America with the same provisional characteristics: a schematic conception of "character" (there is no "profound" psychological examination), exemplary situations, historical implications, audience participation, elementary decor and costume, importance of physical gesture. If this process (regularly reported in the theater review *Conjunto* from Cuba) is maintained, it is possible that a new art form is in the process of being shaped. In cross-cultural contact, the tragic element would be one of the most easily replaced phases. A single cosmic origin is not its driving force, but its ancestral raison d'être. It must be left behind. In order to rediscover it in the distant future, in those unexplored zones where atoms never die.

A Caribbean Future

TOWARD CARIBBEANNESS

The Dream, the Reality

In 1969

The notion of *antillanité,* or Caribbeanness, emerges from a reality that we will have to question, but also corresponds to a dream that we must clarify and whose legitimacy must be demonstrated.

A fragile reality (the experience of Caribbeanness, woven together from one side of the Caribbean to the other) negatively twisted together in its urgency (Caribbeanness as a dream, forever denied, often deferred, yet a strange, stubborn presence in our responses).

This reality is there in essence: dense (inscribed in fact) but threatened (not inscribed in consciousness).

This dream is vital, but not obvious.

I

We cannot deny the reality: cultures derived from plantations; insular civilization (where the Caribbean Sea disperses, whereas, for instance, one reckons that an equally civilizing sea, the Mediterranean, had primarily the potential for attraction and concentration); social pyramids with an African or East Indian base and a European peak; languages of compromise; general cultural phenomenon of creolization; pattern of encounter and synthesis; persistence of the African presence; cultivation of sugarcane, corn, and pepper; site where rhythms are combined; peoples formed by orality.

There is potential in this reality. What is missing from the nation of Caribbeanness is the transition from the shared experience to conscious expression; the need to transcend the intellectual pretensions dominated by the learned elite and to be grounded in collective affirmation, supported by the activism of the people.

Our Caribbean reality is an option open to us. It springs from our natural experience, but in our histories has only been an "ability to survive."

We know what threatens Caribbeanness: the historical balkanization of the islands, the inculcation of different and often "opposed" major languages (the quarrel between French and Anglo-American English), the umbilical cords that maintain, in a rigid or flexible way, many of these islands within the sphere of influence of a particular metropolitan power, the presence of frightening and powerful neighbors, Canada and especially the United States.

This isolation postpones in each island the awareness of a Caribbean identity and at the same time it separates each community from its own true identity.

II

This dream is still absurd on the political level.

We know that the first attempt at a federation, in the anglophone islands, was quickly abandoned. The conflict of interest between Jamaica and Trinidad, their refusal to "bear the weight" of the small islands caused this idealistic project to fail. What has been left behind is a serious aversion on the part of the anglophone Caribbean to any such idea. This federation had been agreed to by the political establishment and not felt in a vital way, not dictated, by the people.

It would be silly to try to unite under some kind of legislation states whose political regimes, social structures, economic potential are today so varied if not opposed to each other.[1]

The Spanish-speaking Caribbean, and in particular Cuba, is completely turned towards Latin America: believing in the intensity of the revolutionary struggle on that continent, sceptical about the potential of the small islands of the Caribbean.

The dream is kept alive in a limited way in the cultural sphere.

The region's intellectuals know each other and, more and more, meet each other. But the Caribbean people are not able to really understand the work created in this area by their sons who have escaped the net. The passion of intellectuals can become a potential for transformation when it is carried forward by the will of the people.

III

As soon as we see a political program, no matter how radical, hesitate in the face of choosing a Caribbean identity, we can offer the certain diagnosis of a hidden desire to be restrained by the limits imposed by nonhistory, by a more or less shameful alignment with (metropolitan) values that one can never, and with good reason, manage to control, by a fatal inability to have a sense of one's own destiny.

At this point the eternal question is raised: And then what? What will we do? How? This supercilious lack of generosity is the basis for the following assertion: the structures within the country will collapse. As if they are not really collapsing at the very moment when we are speaking.

The distant, uncertain emergence of the Caribbean is nonetheless capable of carrying forward our people to self-renewal and of providing them with renewed ambition, by making

1. So in 1980, to give one example, Barbados is generally presented as being with the tacit consent of the United States, "the bastion among the small islands against Communism."

them possess their world and their lived experience (wherein a Caribbean identity is present) and by making them fall into step with those who also share the same space (this too is implied in *antillanité*).

IV

But Caribbeanness is not to be seen as a last resort, the product of a lack of courage that one fears to confront alone. Seen in this way, it would be another kind of escapism and would replace one act of cowardice by another. One is not Martinican because of wanting to be Caribbean. Rather, one is really Caribbean because of wanting to become Martinican.

Island civilizations have so evolved that they then acquire a continental dimension. The oldest dream in Western culture is related, for example, to an island-continent, Atlantis. The hope for a Caribbean cultural identity must not be hampered by our people not achieving independence, so that the new Atlantis, our threatened but vital Caribbeanness, would disappear before taking root.

The problematics of Caribbeanness are not part of an intellectual exercise but to be shared collectively, not tied to the elaboration of a doctrine but the product of a common dream, and not related to us primarily but to our peoples before everything else.

In 1979

Having been invited to a gathering in Panama, I devoted an entire evening to meeting a group of Panamanians of Trinidadian and Jamaican origin. They spoke English and Spanish. Various proposals were debated on negritude, on the class struggle, on the strengthening of the nation of Panama. The following afternoon, after the working sessions for which I was summoned, I was invited by the Martinican historian René Achéen (who willingly confesses his weakness for the Mexican landscape) to visit an old lady from Martinique, who had followed her parents to Panama, at the time when the canal was completed. We found her house in a subdivision.

A Caribbean Future

Madame Andreas del Rodriguez, who was almost ninety, spoke, in an unhesitating and unaccented way, the delicate Creole of the respectable people of the beginning of the century. Panama is where I belong, she told us, but Martinique is the land of my birth. She showed us precious, yellowed photographs and offered the agreeable hospitality of former times. She told us her story and shared her anguish with us. She was still looking for her son, born in St.-Esprit (Martinique) on 28 January 1913 during a visit she had wanted to make to her homeland. M. Gatien Ernest Angeron, that was his name, left in Martinique with an aunt, since deceased, wrote her up to 1936. She blames the disorders of the Second World War for his disappearance. He is, no doubt, dead, she repeated, otherwise how could he have forgotten his mother? But she was still hopeful. She published announcements in the newspapers in 1960; she asked us to try and do something. She even intended, in her serene way, to hand over to us the documents and photographs, which we refused to take: fearful of the great responsibility this entailed. The pencils belonging to her second husband, a retired draughtsman, were carefully arranged on a small desk of whitewood. We promised to return. She embraced us again and again.

In April 1980 the second Latin American Congress of Negro-African cultures was held in Panama; unfortunately, I was unable to attend. The intellectuals, who today benefit from the exorbitant privilege of being invited all over the Caribbean region, have the responsibility to raise their voices for the benefit of those who cannot see the Caribbean world in its diversity or hear the word sung right there, just beside them.

Saint-John Perse and the Caribbean

I

We notice that in Perse's work the more he wanders, the more poetic expression is "stabilized." Almost to the point of attempting to make it harden into a seamless universe, in order to avoid having to bring it into contact (to put it off or pervert it) with a single disconcerting contingency. As if the untainted architecture of words was the first response, the only one, to the emptiness of wandering. The world is in the West and the word is in the West. That is where Perse will establish his true dwelling place. The threshold of this unlikely house, erupting suddenly from the shifting and amorphous world, is the word; and word is also its rooftop. The flesh becomes Word. In this way Perse achieves the ultimate "total" expression of the West; he is the last herald of a systematic universe. In this he is different from Segalen: Diversity can be nothing but an accident, a temptation, not his language.

II

Such a project was possible not only or not so much for a Caribbean mind as for a man born in the Caribbean. If Perse had come to another world, if he had come into the world elsewhere, he would certainly have been restrained by being rooted, by ancestral impulses, by a sense of attachment to the land that would have located him firmly. On the contrary, his being born in the Caribbean exposes him to wandering. The universe for the restless wanderer does not appear as a world limited by the concrete but as a passion for the universal anchored in the concrete. One is not sufficiently aware of the fact that Perse in this is reliving the dilemma of the white Creole, caught between a metropolitan history that often does not "include" him (and that he, in reaction, claims meticulously and energetically as his legitimate ancestry) and the natural world of the Caribbean, which engenders new points of growth that he must perhaps deny. In spite of himself, Perse has experienced this stress, to a degree unsuspected by either his Creole contemporaries or his French supporters, who ultimately establish his reputation. It is not surprising that for those French Caribbean individuals who, on the contrary, are devoted to reconciling—beyond the disorder of colonialism—

nature and culture in the Caribbean, the relationship with Perse should be hesitant and ambiguous. How do we recognize his Caribbean nature, when he wrests himself free from our history and so denies it?

Nevertheless, a fragile Caribbeanness is there. That is, in him, that part of us that goes away. We too shudder from the need to remain and the temptation to leave. Perse shares with us only that temptation, on which he acted. No doubt a small island sheltered within a port is the most secure repository of the urge to wander. Ilet-les-Feuilles in the port of Pointe-à-Pitre. A small island in the anchorage of a larger island, bordered, not by sandy beaches twisted with mangrove, but by the scrawl of tall ships that keep tugging at it. For those who like Perse's work, there is nothing so moving as this closed site where the poet places himself at the edge of his birthplace. For the French Caribbean mind, there is nothing as obvious as this inexorable separation, through which Perse both turns his back on us and is one of us.

Ilet-les-Feuilles. Sea and forest. This natural world that engenders and dictates his style. There is in Perse's work the recurrence of surging waters, countless arrivals from the sea, tents with no stable mast, the forever-future skies over roads forever windswept: the shifting, the fragile, the fluid, the sea. At the same time, an excessive sense of structure, rotting vegetable matter, luminous salt clinging to violet roots: growth and permanence, flesh, stump, forest. Perse is Caribbean because of the primal, intertwined density of his style. It is nature that first and foremost speaks in us. In him, nature is the language of dense growth; but his history is that of the pure desire to wander.

For he is not, after all, Caribbean. He is not involved in this history, in that he was free to walk away from it. The shaping force of his surroundings did not require of the child that he was to have to stay. It became the will to leave. Perse chose to wander aimlessly, to "head West," where the Western world was not only a concrete reality but an Ideal. Perse became what

Dante had become. He sublimates history and nature in the single History of the Logos. *Eloges* (*Praises*) still deals with the word; *Amers* (*Seamarks*) is about nothing but the Logos. We should never resent him for this. That he did not wish to be Caribbean, he whom his political enemies described as "the mulatto from the Quai d'Orsay"; that he could justify the ravages of conquerors, by having regard for their work as synthesizers; that his poetics crystallized (from *Anabase*—*Anabasis*—to *Amers*) into an anonymous universality—What could be more natural? The writer today in these French Caribbean islands waiting to be born is logically part of the export trade; precisely where Perse, through sustained choice, stands separate from and taller than the rest. In this way he turns into a life's ambition what for us is a source of anguish. But the passion is the same.

III

We realize that these two reactions are liable to leave something unexplained in Perse: the reaction that makes us want to drag him back forcefully to his Caribbean roots (him, the inveterate wanderer); the other one that makes us eager to whiten him as a French Creole, with that twisted legacy from which he secretly suffered. In the first hypothesis he is attributed a history that he could not consciously conceive (he fell in step with another History); in the second we deprive him of a nature that even sublimated, universalized by the Winds [see his *Vents*, 1946] of the absolute to which he ultimately yielded, had nevertheless a shaping power over his language. Perse's greatness is that he longs to transcend the hiatus between history and nature. Perse is exemplary in that his longing demonstrates the divided nature of the Western mind, suddenly concerned with a world no longer made in its image.

IV

For, as colonizer of the universe, Perse does not suffer from a guilty conscience but, on the contrary, signifies (through remoteness and restlessness) the double ambiguity of his relationship with the world; to the point of having a total commitment to the word of the absolute.

V

This poetics of remoteness and restlessness exposes the poet to the "movement" of the world. He knows that he must today and tomorrow *spread* his language. But nostalgia for an impossible architecture (to suddenly emerge, from words themselves) forces him to turn his back on this movement. Fascinated by glorious journeys (these travels through eternity, through which nothing changes), he chooses, perhaps, to ignore the humble or mediocre vegetation that is permanent yet changing. He sees, in the distance, how the world will change, but not the effort of those through whom it will be changed. The last herald of world-as-system; and no doubt Hegel would have loved the passion for "totality" in Perse. But the world can no longer be shaped into a system. Too many Others and Elsewheres disturb the placid surface. In the face of this disturbance, Perse elaborates his vision of stability. To stabilize through language what through it is dispersed and is shattered by so many sudden changes. Since universality is threatened to its very roots, Perse will, with one stroke, transcend everything through the light of universality.

The stubborn attempt to construct a house of language (from the word, a reality) is his reason to the world's "lack of structure," at the same time that it boldly refuses to recognize the value of lowly vegetation. Perse realizes what is happening to the world (the poet's privilege); he nevertheless chooses not to accept it, not to be a part of it.

VI

The longing for stability. The desire to turn pulp and flesh into word. I notice that the West is hypnotized by these two impulses: rejecting the world by a denial of the salt of the earth, withdrawal from the world by stamping the flesh of the world with an absolute ideal. You choose either the schematic or the hallowed. Therein lies an extreme openness: through refusal or transcendence, the Western mind admits the disturbing presence of the Other. Saint-John Perse is part of the world, even if he must dazzle it with glory. In the drama of the modern world, his work, which is to construct through language a pure reality (which would then engender any possible reality), is as striking as the ambition of those who wish to elaborate the pure reality of language. Like them, he rejects the eruption of histories; but he feels he should glorify History instead. Rootlessness provides the space for this glorification. He who never stops leaving, whose route is the Sea, and who unleashes the pent-up squalls of the High Plateaus, he is the one who breathes in pure History. Yes. The more intense the wandering, the more the word longs for stability.

VII

French Caribbean people clearly realize that this "need to stabilize" concerns them; but that they still have perhaps to invent a syntax, to explore a language that is not yet *theirs here and now*—before they could give its explosive force a shape. Just as Perse often appears in the clearing created by words. I likewise think that if he happened to think of Guadeloupeans or Martinicans, of whom he knew so little (he who dedicated such rare praise to our lands), it was with arrogance, certainly, but also with regret. History is fissured by histories; they relentlessly toss aside those who have not had the time to see themselves through a tangle of lianas.

VIII

Beyond all this, Saint-John Perse is still vital to everyone, and this is the most deserving tribute to be made to the poet. When, at the most dense flowering of language and the web woven from countless strands of languages, man wants to return to the sources of light, he will understand that this light, from the depths of the French language, has managed to create (extending Segalen the Divided, exceeding Claudel the Catholic) a reference for stability, a model for permanence, which our Diversity (without exhausting itself in this) will no doubt one day need—in order to be more completely fulfilled.

Cultural Identity

I now summarize in the form of a litany the facts of our quest for identity. The litany is more suitable in this domain than a discourse.

The slave trade that meant rupture with our matrix
(the mother beyond our reach)

Slavery as a struggle with no witness
(the word whispered in the huts)

The loss of collective memory
(the swirl of time)

The visibility of the other
(the transparent ideal of universality)

The trap of folklore
(the denial of consciousness)

The trap of citizenship
(the obsession of the name)

The linguistic trap
(dominance)

Lack of technical expertise
(the tool, a strange object)

Immediacy
(the direct effect of pressures)

Political timidness
(fear of contact with the world)

Passive consumption
(flood of imports)

Oblivion
(neither doing nor creating)

Barter system
(Martinique, a country you pass through)

The ruse of diversion
(popular "wisdom")

Survival by subsistence
(life at the edge of limitations)

Multilingual potential
(the final stage of bilingualism)

The lure of the Caribbean
(the outer edge of space and time)

The past recognized
(absences overcome)

The troubling reality of the nation
(the autonomous resolution of class conflict)

The oral—the written
(the release of inhibitions)

A people finding self-expression
(the country coming together)

A politicized people
(a country that acts)

and at the end of our rooted wanderings, the unrestrained will
to propose for this collective action specific paths, woven
from our reality and not falling out of the blue ideologically;
the no less firm resolve to resist being locked into the premedi-
tated ideological dogma of those who do not focus on the

cross-cultural contact between peoples; the ideal being a unified whole, a collective and creative daring, to which each one will contribute.

This litany does not come to an end with an amen: for we visualize, dimly apparent in the void, deep in the depths of ridicule, this new night for the huts under whose cover we put our voices, first in whispers, a rasping deep in our throat, together.

The one and only season

The creative imagination is a function of desire, yes. But when desire is forbidden because its aim is irretrievably lost in the depths, the soaring of the imagination is contrived. The use of the word *summer* in French Caribbean writing, formerly in my own, shows how this works. For this word, *été*, not the participle but the season, left its remote resonance in me: remote in my case. I can also see its other side where it leads to oblivion. I used to write *été* automatically as a synonym for fire, warmth, passion. Then one day I happened on the word in *La Lézarde* (The ripening) and I was amazed. When I became acquainted with the text of *Légitime Défense*, one of the symptoms of alienation seemed to me to be the frequent use of this word, among people who come from a land of only one season. But how is this possible? They had migrated some time ago. Winter takes its toll. The nimble voice runs in pursuit of the wind in the streets. The sun has shut off its salt marshes. We learn to measure the seasonal changes. The word *summer* brings necessary hope. It happens unconsciously.

I have said that, in my experience, the difference between the one and only season and summer lies totally in the secretive chill of autumn, which shudders in the warmth of summer. I remembered that this hoped-for intensity (the appeal of the word *summer*) ran its blind course, uttered its scream burnt dry, in *Le sel noir* (Black salt). I wanted to see how it happened; I reread the text. Alienation beyond a doubt: hope that is nothing but hope; in spite of the poem's pretext and its trajectory, which are supposed to be general. I later looked for the same word in my "Martinican" poems: *Boises* (Shackles); *Pays rêvé pays réel* (Land of dream, land of reality): I could not find it. This reminds me that a piece of information provided for Mme Maude Mannoni by Georges Payote concerns the difference he establishes between the four seasons in Europe and the two seasons in the Caribbean, which he does not give a name to and which are not really seasons: the dry season (*carême*) and the rainy season (*hivernage*).

What does the poetic imagination tell us in this mechanical way? The unfulfilled desire for the other country. One Martinican woman who read *Malemort* (The undead), I think, criticized me for having too many references to "the former country," which she thought referred to France. But she was mistaken; the text referred beyond any possible doubt to Africa. An unfulfilled desire, reluctantly buried in my reader, had brought her imagination to life. She had read what she both feared and longed to read.

Just as political action shapes reality, the poetic imagination struggles against the marauding shadows within us. Not by interrupting the text in order to confer authenticity on it; but the sustained project that is entirely devoted to self-expression and the changes that come from fidelity to this project. When one rediscovers one's landscape, desire for the other country ceases to be a form of alienation. I once dreamt of a character on a mountainside, and I called him Ichneumon. No doubt this word haunted me. I learned much later that it is the Egyptian (so, so ancient?) name for mongoose. Like it, but in the fissure of a dream, "it sought its own short-cut."

And as we must again and again raise these ideas, approach them in all possible ways, I here reproduce the notes found in my papers, as a form of recapitulation.

A Caribbean Future

1. The creation of a nation in the French Caribbean and the creation of a Caribbean nation.

When one considers the artist's contribution to the creation of the nation of the French Caribbean, the question is also posed of the possible creation of a Caribbean nation.

One can indeed think that the countries of the Caribbean will develop an original Afro-Caribbean culture whose cultural reality is already in evidence.

The problem is that this cultural reality has been activated at the same time it was fragmented, if not totally shattered, by the antagonistic tensions of European nations in the Caribbean. The artist articulates this threatened reality but also explores the often hidden workings of this fragmenting process.

If at present Caribbean countries experience or are subjected to social, political, and economic regimes very different from each other, "artistic vision" creates the possibility of cementing the bonds of unity in the future. The nation does not then appear as the product of divisiveness, but as the promise of a future sharing with others.

2. Intellectual creativity and popular creativity

The artist's ambition would never be more than a project if it did not form part of the lived reality of the people.

Building a nation means today thinking first and foremost of systems of production, profitable commercial exchanges, betterment of the standard of living, without which the nation would quickly become an illusion.

But we discover daily in the world that one also needs a sense of a collective personality, of what is called dignity or specificity, without which the nation would precisely be stripped of meaning.

The value of artistic creation in developing countries, where the imperatives of technological orientation and returns have not yet overwhelmed all areas of life, remains vital.

This is what we mean when we state that the beginnings of all peoples (from the Iliad to the Old Testament, from The

Book of the Dead of the Egyptians to Europe's chansons de geste) are poetic. That is, one needs a voice to give expression to common ideals, just as one heeds the realizations without which these ideals would never be fulfilled.

3. *The poetics of resistance and the poetics of natural expression*

The language of the Caribbean artist does not originate in the obsession with celebrating his inner self; this inner self is inseparable from the future evolution of his community.

But what the artist expresses, reveals, and argues in his work, the people have not ceased to live in reality. The problem is that this collective life has been constrained by the process of consciousness; the artist acquires a capacity to reactivate. That is why he is his own ethnologist, historian, linguist, painter of frescoes, architect. Art for us has no sense of the division of genres. This conscious research creates the possibility of a collective effervescence. If he more or less succeeds, he makes critical thought possible; if he succeeds completely, he can inspire.

VOICES

From the perspective of Boises (Shackles)

I

On disembarking, elusive utterance. The secret resin of our words, cut short in our mouths, uprooted from their night. A kind of hope for those who prey on the people. A whole desolate Creole, twisted in the murky depths of mangrove.

Then, this other language, in which we keep quiet. (It is the timid owl frightened by the speech of Domination.) Nip it in the bud. Weave it, not into the greenness that does not suit it, but into the stripped truth of our contradictions.

The unrevealed (always dared) defeat of the cross-cultural imagination! Through which from a windy island you advance into the world's babble of voices, with your throats of dried cassava, and the faint trace of earth on your forehead.

II

Vegetation. Terror to be burnt like the earth that must be scorched before it can be tilled. Land adrift in a sea of derision. Gasping the leaf like a bomb explodes. Dead with a shudder of writing and a hidden beat: all is history.

From the North, the dark blue of the rain. From the Center, the earth with its tree-bearing rocks, and the scent. From the South, the mirage of thorns bleached like sand. A spray of nettles.

The spoken narrative is not concerned with the dead. We stand our mouths open under the sun like bagasse, silenced from elsewhere. We encumber our moons with ceremonies that lack fire.

III

The storyteller's cry comes from the rock itself. He is grounded in the depths of the land; therein lies his power. Not an enclosed truth, not momentary succor. But the communal path, through which the wind can be released.

Purify the breath until it reveals the harsh taste of the land: bring breath to the death of rocks and landscape.

Those who shattered tribes; exiled drowned dried up; turned away, in riotous masquerades from their truth. Those who extend, above their minds on fire, a very official hand. Those who crush until nothing is left. Even the sun and the air we drink in.

IV

The closed texts of *Boises* resemble the formula of the *Tim-tim boiseche* riddles: "—A barrel with no bottom?—Wedding ring!" They trace the void, through overly measured explosions. Our one and only season closed in on itself, by the disorientation of assimilation. The islands now are opening up. The word requires space and a new rhythm. "I see you moving forward through the land the inspired people that we are."

Seven Landscapes for the sculptures of Cárdenas

I entered through the *Gate of the Sun,* which is an opening to one of the highroads of the Americas. There I feel the wind's bracing force. It swallows up our exploded history; it unweaves the icy tresses in their air over the colossal cities; it spreads down to the infernal flatness of the favelas, on the coast. Cárdenas has sculpted this gate, which is not the creation of an individual's narrow demands but brings an infinite dimension to every object the sculptor erects. In it our space coils and twists. The Andes where Tupac Amaru pulled against four horses, the Grenadines with their concentration of stunned sands in the Caribbean. Diversion and reversion, the still-moving eye of the center from which passion is released. You turn around what you see, which looks back at you and controls you. It is what they call the Heights.

I also saw spread before me a jungle of stumps, roots, bulbs. The art of tying the night to revelation. But we do not acclaim the overwhelming stature of any one tree, we praise this language of the entire forest. Cárdenas's sculpture is not a single

A Caribbean Future

shout, it is sustained speech: unceasing and deliberate, which is forever creating and at every turn *establishes* something new. In our lands and to the furthest reach of the sun, these profound revelations take root. In the sheltered space of La Tracée, between the path of Deux-Choux that rises to the heavens and the tortuous road, winding towards St.-Pierre, streaks of mauve and blue flash through the heavy silence. I could discern in the dark the marble sculpted by Cárdenas, the dazzling portent he planted in the primordial mud.

How long have we been waiting, on the High Plateaus, for this Door to receive us? The object before us (a work of art: a *constantly changing sign*) takes us away from the gaping void of the past to our future action in this fiery present. Its intense ambiguity moves through time and summarizes it. Our history made visible, that, therefore, is the meaning of the passionate project of Cárdenas's sculpture. His interior landscape is just like ours. From Trinidad and Antigua, man and woman (the Caribbean couple) are scattered on windswept paths, in a profusion of transplantation, in the uncertainty of speech; they wait to *focus their eyes*. With Cárdenas we indeed turn our faces to this wind. I mean it revitalizes us. Yes. It reveals in us hidden energy. Cárdenas gives us life. The foaming form of his marble is rooted in the sky. His bronze, projected upwards, oozes new blood.

There is no doubt that he also needed the expansive thrust and the hardy appeal that have been shaping forces in Western art. Let us not hesitate to identify at this point the syntactical features of his style, elements of Arp and Brancusi, for example. Modern art in the West is filled with the blind faces of dream that peoples from elsewhere carried within them, it has reflected that shattered light that today allows us to see the world. Cárdenas is a cultural crossroads. The encounter between this movement of form and this passionate existence placed him at this crossroads, marked him with the invisible, which in the depths of Guadaloupe is called simply, in a littered and mysterious expression, a four-roads. The red earth is hemmed in by the dense thrust of cane; its path is worn flat in an even way by bullock carts and diesel trucks. Heat fixes its waves close to the earth, a favorite haunt of our zombis. Cárdenas's bronzes are inextricably part of this world and they show us a new way forward.

I have a great piece of sculpture by him, which was done here in Martinique. He came, for our communal festivities, to see where the heliconia grows whose *three times heaving heart* was examined by André Breton, and whose delicate and rough stalk, with its ornate outgrowths, he has so often concealed in a sculpted form. But we could only find, for him to work on, tall narrows pieces of mahogany that we collected on the heights of Morne Pitault, just above the plain of Lamentin where the Lézarde River trickles in agony. We had not the time to find him thick chunks of wood or stone, which, moreover, we may never have found. Our lands do not contain treasures that can be transformed. We have deserted our massive trees; they stand watch on the inaccessible heights of the Pitons. Our hills are scattered with dead acacias and lifeless mahogany. We are no more dense than the stalks of sugarcane. First Cárdenas joked: "I asked you for wood. Wood is something thick, it takes up space, it is long!" But his hands did not resist the hard, brown mahogany for long, even if it was not thick this time, and there soon emerged the undeniable figure of *an Ancestor who is broken in silence*. In it, the flatness of the original wood became patience and transparency, the tiny opening became the *eye of lineage*, lost time took shape in our consciousness. I like the fact that this work was so born of a twofold imperative. Those who admire it instinctively ask: "Is it African?" The misreading of form behind such a question presupposes a number of fixed responses. This sculpture, spirit of the wood bringing new rhythm to our reconstituted time, is alive in the marbles and bronzes, which transform it before our eyes.

Now the storyteller pauses. The rustle of branches in his speech, when at night the scent of logwood slowly makes its way up from the burnt interior. The man who chants has tamed with his hand a spiral of words. He becomes sculpture

A Caribbean Future

in motion, sowing his seeds in us. He does not release us. His rhythms fill the space in which we tremble as we listen to a primordial age rising through time. The poetics of Cárdenas is woven in this passage of time, where the uniqueness of the sculpted object is forged. It connects with the tradition of oral celebration, the rhythm of the body, the continuity of frescoes, the gift of melody. From one work to the other, the same text is articulated. Structuring to this extent into discourse the art of the unique object, that is where Cárdenas is at his most striking. In this way he puts together a poetics of continuous time: the privileged moment yields to the rhythms of the voice. Memory is forced to abandon its diversions, where unexpected forms lurk and suddenly emerge. In the same way, the storyteller suddenly sweeps us away with a gesture: but it is because he has taken us so far. And we are struck by his incantation whose meaning we have lost, but whose force has remained among us.

I also remember (Is it an illusion?) the white dust that, in certain roads of our towns, at the edge of barely constructed slopes, suggests so much care and neatness. This was now in a section of Havana, where I was going to visit the sculptor's family. His father, with the restrained self-assurance of one who receives his son's friend, which is both understandable and yet not so. Being introduced to the household, the language barrier, the difficulty of establishing the link. But also, this immediate sense of welcome. An unaffected tranquility, like relatives who meet once a year. The lacework of sunlight across the room. And beneath our quiet efforts to communicate, the companionable silence to which we would have liked to surrender. Cárdenas is familiar with this silence. We see that it takes the forms that make it visible. He protects himself from it, perhaps, but he especially allows it to enrich his work and sometimes to infect us. It is the punctuation of discourse. It is the quintessential landscape. Perhaps I took it with me when I left this house, in which we so naturally discovered ourselves to be from the same land and the same race. Land of converging cultures, race of many ideas. Outside, the sun banged away at its drum, and Cuba was a shimmer of palm trees.

Scatterings

All mimesis presupposes that what is represented is the "only true reality." When it involves two realities of which one is destined to reproduce the other, inevitably those who are part of the process see themselves living in a permanent state of the unreal. That is the case with us.

*

We have today "neutralized" the force of the baroque, by discouraging the continuation of former "excesses." Deviation becomes more and more secretive. The language of the street is now forced back down our throats.

*

The preoccupation with being "considerate" has replaced the impulses behind the frenzy of public speech. It is even more underhand. If you want to work with anyone at all, begin with an ostentatious display of your esteem for that person. If not, work will be hampered.

*

This agony does not justify an escape into the future (when we no longer know what to do), which happens when "proletarian" is used disparagingly by "intellectuals." In our context, the work of the intellectual is invaluable. Only his claim to leadership is to be condemned.

*

I am in a car with friends, and one of them suddenly says: "What a great country." Meaning that we do not cease to discover it within ourselves.

A *Caribbean Future*

*

But what about French Guiana? An inexhaustible space that in our imagination is filled with rivers and forests. The Guianese ask Martinicans and Guadeloupeans to leave them in peace. We have had our share of colonizing in that area. Yet there is a secret bond that links us to the continent. A poetic bond, even more passionate because we renounce it. Even stronger because Guianese leave their stamp on their land. Songs like rivers against whose rapids we journey upstream, poems like so many endless forests.

*

Martinicans of East Indian origin arrived here mostly with their families. It is claimed that their collective solidarity is greater than among those of African descent.

*

We must, however, think about a systematic renewal of ancient forms of survival. Create in the country a network of as many productive units as is possible. Put them together. Maintain them through interdependence.

*

A magical notion of reality is based on beliefs hidden deep in the collective past. It forms part of the present. But it proliferates also because the present is elusive and slips away from you. We do not know which of its motifs will be important to us.

*

The theory of "slow evolution" by the progressive education of a people. Such an education increasingly strengthens the process of becoming accustomed to dependency.

*

We love beetroot. It is sweet, it is red like blood.

*

We do not dare admit that we like hurricanes. They bring us so much. The periodic shudder originating out there in the sea, the announcement that follows that we're an official "disaster area."

*

Earthquakes terrify us. First of all, we have no warning: it is neither annual nor decennial. Then, it is too brief to be understood. Also, it sometimes causes too much damage.

*

Mimesis operates like an earthquake. There is something in us that struggles against it, and we remain bewildered by it.

Concerning Literature

So we raise the question of writing; we ask a question of writing, and each time it is through writing. In this way trailing behind our own discourse on orality. Will we ever invent those forms of expression that will leave the book behind, will transform it, will adapt it? What had we said about oral techniques of expression, of the poetics of Creole, for example? Repetition, tautology, echo, the procedure of accumulating the spoken. Will we dare to apply this, not to a speech uttered by the light of torches, but to books that require correction, reflection, care? Or alternatively, shall we abandon the book, and for what?

If I could return to the poets who have appeared in our midst, I would tend to choose an oralization of the written. The rhythm is that of the folktale. Their language consists of a humorous use of words, meant to be sung. And then, there is all the confusion of our relationship to time, a ruined history, which we must give shape, restructure. The book is the tool of

A Caribbean Future

forced poetics; orality is the instrument of natural poetics. Is the writer forever a prisoner of a forced poetics? Literature, insofar as it produces books and is the product of books, bears no relationship to outgrowths that are natural, anonymous, suddenly emerging from the composts. But that is precisely what we want: a literature that does not have to be forced.

In my case, for some time I have tried to master a time that keeps slipping away, to live a landscape that is constantly changing, to celebrate a history that is documented nowhere. The epic and the tragic in turn have tempted me with their promises of gradual revelation. A constrained poetics. The delirium of language. We write in order to reveal the inner workings, hidden in our world.

But could Creole writing reconcile the rules of writing and the teeming, irrepressible element in "oraliture?" It is much too early to reply, and the countless publications I have read have not for the most part abandoned the facile effects of a folkloric naivete. But those who persist in this experiment, no doubt are preparing the way.[1]

This discourse on discourse, situated at the confluence of oral and written, has attempted to adapt the form of one to the subject matter of the other. It was expressed in me as a

1. Young Martinicans show nothing but their imitativeness in the way they speak ("it's super," "it's heavy," "tough, tough," etc.). There are also signs of a persistent creativity, based on the systematic interdependence of Creole, French, and also English or Spanish. This is a simple example. Based on the French expression: "arrête ton cirque" ["stop clowning"] the Creole produced: "pa fé sic épi moin" (literal translation: "ne fais pas de cirque avec moi") ["don't do your circus number on me"]. But as the Creole word *sic* can mean both "circus" and "sugar" (we do not pronounce the *r* in the middle of words!), Martinican students currently use an expression they have invented: "Don't make sugar with me!" This anglicism has its final formulation in: "Stop sicking!" [in English in the text], which is the ultimate deformation of the French: "Arrête ton char."

These maneuvers are amusing, perhaps fascinating, to study. They contain a derisive use of language, but also the prescience that comes with an adapted language.

melody and picked up again as plainsong, has been slowed down like a great drum, and sometimes has been fluent with the high-pitched intensity of small sticks on a little drum.

Event

The French press was disturbed by a collective nightmare in March–April 1980. Countless articles appeared. Concern mounted. French Caribbean persons living in France telephoned their friends in great distress. The place is in a bloody uproar. What is happening?—Nothing is happening. A few strikes and the blocking of roads (but Paris was witnessing many more, *at the very same time*), acute social conflict, the refusal of civil servants to give up their 40 percent cost-of-living allowance. The machinery of authority got into the act, there were innumerable shattering announcements, while most Martinicans continued to occupy the roadways. There was, deep down in the French attitude, something subtly changing with regard to the French Caribbean. Is nothing happening? One would be blind to be taken in by this calm. The intolerable pressure of our contradictions is behind it all. We have become accustomed to living like this. But cracks emerge that are thresholds of explosion, and we feel today that we will soon have to move beyond this stage. The wild imaginings of public opinion, that really there is nothing to warrant this, are not as unfounded as one might think.

I balance it against the systematic refusal to see. I was amazed to hear a couple of French civil servants, charming individuals, admit, with complacent sighs, that things were fine in Martinique and that they could not understand why everyone else spoke so anxiously about the social climate and conflicts in the country. The subtle assimilation of the colonial complex is what explains this level of naivete.

Another "classic" reaction from the French section of this

population is objectivity. "The problems are the same in the Ardèche or the Roussillon. These are the symptoms of remoteness from central authority. The school children of Savoie are as decultured as those from here."

This now pushes us toward a new permutation, a universal humanism. In 1979 a Martinican branch of LICA was formed, "against all racism, white or black." A young Martinican, Jovignac, was killed? We read on the walls of Fort-de-France: "Jovignac could have been white!" "Martinicans, Metropolitans, the same racism! Stop the massacre." As the minister says, "we are brothers."

OVERTURES

People and Language

We know and we have said that before the arrival of Columbus the Caribbean archipelago was constantly linked by a system of communication, from the continent to the islands of the north, from the islands to the continent in the south.

We know and we have said that colonization has balkanized the Caribbean, that it is the colonizer who exterminated the Carib people in the islands, and disturbed this relationship.

Slavery was accompanied by reification: all history seemed to come to a halt in the Caribbean, and the peoples transplanted there had no alternative but to subject themselves to History with a capital *H*, all equally subjected to the hegemony of Europe. Reification was systematized in racism: "All blacks look alike; the only good Indian is a dead Indian."

My exposé tends to demonstrate what the people of the Caribbean have preserved and deployed against this oppression; for example, their own particular histories, which have been opposed to the claims of History with a capital *H*, and whose synthesis today contributes to the creation of a Caribbean civilization.

I will not elaborate on the circumstances that have already been examined earlier: the constituent parts of the Caribbean population, the structures of the world of slavery, the episodes in the struggles of our peoples and their resistance, the aberrations of our elite. I will concentrate, to begin with, on a few features that are undeniably shared. Based on these, we can establish more clearly the differences among our various circumstances.

The rigid nature of the plantation encouraged forms of resistance, two of which have a shaping force on our cultures: the camouflaged escape of the carnival, which I feel constitutes a desperate way out of the confining world of the plantation, and the armed flight of *marronnage,* which is the most widespread act of defiance in that area of civilization that concerns us.

It is nothing new to declare that for us music, gesture, dance are forms of communication, just as important as the gift of

A Caribbean Future

speech. This is how we first managed to emerge from the plantation: esthetic form in our cultures must be shaped from these oral structures. It is not a matter of claiming that writing is of no use to us, and we are aware of the dramatic need for literacy and the circulation of books in our countries. For us, it is a matter of ultimately reconciling the values of the culture of writing and the long-repressed traditions of orality. In the past, in the darkness of slavery, speech was forbidden, singing was forbidden, but also learning to read was punishable by death.

For a long time as well, the arrogant imperialism of monolingualism accompanied the spread of Western culture. What is multilingualism? It is not only the ability to speak several languages, which is often not the case in our region where we sometimes cannot even speak our oppressed mother tongue. Multilingualism is the passionate desire to accept and understand our neighbor's language and to confront the massive leveling force of language continuously imposed by the West—yesterday with French, today with American English—with a multiplicity of languages and their mutual comprehension.

This practice of cultural Creolization is not part of some vague humanism, which makes it permissible for us to become one with the next person. It establishes a cross-cultural relationship, in an egalitarian and unprecedented way, between histories that we know today in the Caribbean are interrelated. The civilization of cassava, sweet potato, pepper, and tobacco points to the future of this cross-cultural process; this is why it struggles to repossess the memory of its fragmented past.

We in the Caribbean realize today that the differences between our cultures, with their fertile potential, come from the presence of several factors.

—The more or less definitive extinction of the Amerindian people.

—The presence or absence of a cultural "ancestral" hinterland or, what is really the same thing, the systematic success of techniques of survival.

—The presence or absence of an extensive physical hinterland, that is the success of cultural accretion based on *marronnage*.

—The potential, or lack of it, to create or maintain an autonomous system of production.

—The presence or absence of compromised languages, accompanying the survival of vernaculars and the development of major languages.

These differences, reinforced by the colonial need for isolation, shape today the various tactics of the struggle that the peoples of the Caribbean are deploying. In any case the result is a new conception of the nation. The nation is not based on exclusion; it is a form of disalienated relationship with the other, who in this way becomes our fellow man

*

The time has come for us to return to the question of the baroque, which we have often discussed. Had we not observed that, in the evolution of our rhetoric, the baroque first appears as the symptom of a deeper inadequacy, being the elaborate ornamentation imposed on the French language by our desperate men of letters? Should we not abandon this compensatory strategy? But for us it is not a matter today of this kind of excess, which was wrapped around a vacuum. The unconscious striving of baroque rhetoric, in the French colonial world, is dogged in its pursuit of the French language by an intensification of the obsession with purity. We will perhaps compromise this language in relationships we might not suspect. It is the unknown area of these relationships that weaves, while dismantling the conception of the standard language, the "natural texture" of our new baroque, our own. Liberation will emerge from this cultural composite. The "function" of Creole languages, which must resist the temptation of exclusivity, manifests itself in this process, far removed from the fascines (linked facet, fascination) of the fire of the melting-pot. We also are aware of the mysterious realm of the unexpressed, deep in all we say, in the furthest reaches of what we wish to say, and in the pressure to give weight to our actions.

22 May

The political parties in opposition have been trying for some time to make the date 22 May into a "national holiday." Why? Because, on that day, the slaves of St.-Pierre in Martinique rose up and demanded the proclamation of the abolition of slavery, which was accepted in principle in Paris since 27 April of the same year 1848, but whose application was delayed in our country. Let us look again at M. Husson's proclamation, dated 31 March.

The revolt of the slaves in Martinique in May 1848 is an established fact, even if its significance is open to question. But there were other slave revolts. I think that the choice of the date of 22 May corresponds in fact to a collective delusion, through which we conceal from ourselves the true meaning of this so-called liberation. What did it really contain?

—The obvious transition from slavery capitalism to a form of capitalism in which the worker is no longer chattel but receives a salary. The hidden potential already exists in this transition for a system of exchange, and consequently the

1. We can ask ourselves, like one of my Martinican friends—a psychiatrist in fact—if it is not a question of the fear of violation. My friend argues like this: "What could we be afraid of, as Martinicans, that might unite and move us forward," since the sky cannot fall on our heads? My main argument is that even this question of violating taboos is not applicable to us, that "composite" peoples are required to reduce that dimension, and that their collective energies are rather channeled through a sense of an open *relationship to the world*, as a poetics of the recognition of diversity. Cross-cultural poetics undermines a sense of the uniqueness of the sacred, while salvaging it in the process.

inability to establish a national system of production. The present system of exchange is implicit in the "liberation" of 1848.

—The domination of the reality of "liberation" by the ideology of assimilation, whose ideological weapon will for some time be Schoelcherism.

—The adoption, without general criticism, of the slogans and the contents of this ideology: French citizenship, the republican ideal, etc.

—The bestowing of an inevitably precarious citizenship on an illiterate population, completely depersonalized because of the granting of this status.

The "liberation" of 1848, paradoxically, has nothing to do with the community. The latter lost any sense of organization or future; any ability to conceive of themselves as a group. Resistance and slave revolt, *as in all the other times,* would not have a "continuity" with the collective will, the feeling of nationalism, but are gradually diverted towards the perspective of individual social mobility.

It is possible that this conscious choice of the date 22 May as the anniversary of a "national holiday" reflects a secret, unconscious wavering; another example of the inability of the "political" elite to accept the radical idea of the nation. That would certainly be a compensatory delusion, even more satisfying because it does involve a struggle.

Naturally, a delusion can act as a catalyst in history. The solemn renewal of the memory of the struggles of May 1848 could contribute to maintaining the emergence of Martinicans as a collective whole. But I feel that such a delusion could only be functional in the context of a situation that is not itself the product of delusion. If this is not the case, it would be nothing but an unproductive tautology. That is the risk we run.

The twenty-second of May is a day of celebration for our people. The "national holiday" for Martinique is yet to come: that will be the day when the reality of the nation will have been established.

A *Caribbean Future*

Resolutions, Resolution

We have had the stubbornness and perhaps the courage to analyze the fullest possible implications of what we saw as the structure of Martinican reality. We have tried to do so, often in a collective way, because we are convinced that it is a hidden reality, elusive to the very ones who live it. I have planned for some time the wide-ranging survey that is in this book because I felt that a great number of the structures in the process of writing, considered as a form of production, particular expression of a creative impulse, are clarified (to the extent that any process of creation can be) by this analysis.

The aesthetic we have come up with is that of a nonuniversalizing diversity, the kind that seemed to me to emerge from global relations ever since the peoples of the world have realized and demanded the right to express themselves. A nonessentialist aesthetic, linked to what I call the emergence of orality: not to the extent that the latter dominates the audiovisual but because it summarizes and emphasizes the gesture and the speech of new peoples.

The Caribbean constitutes, in fact, a field of relationships whose shared similarities I have tried to point out. A threatened reality that nevertheless stubbornly persists. And in this reality, Guadeloupe and Martinique seem even more threatened by the unusual manifestation of cultural contact that is called assimilation. They are deviated from their natural course of development, zombified within their world, yet resisting an overwhelming force, given the means used to achieve successful assimilation.

Colonization has therefore not had the success that was apparent at first sight. The irresistible pressure to imitate comes up against areas of resistance whose problem is that, in a literally fragmented context, nothing holds them together. For us cultural activism must lead to political activism, if only to bring to fruition the unification of those implicit or explicit areas of resistance. Political action could manage to achieve such a consolidation of forces only if it is based on analysis derived from a notion of this reality. I do not see a conception of the whole as a uniform construct providing solutions, but as a polyvalent idea that is capable of explaining and understanding the contradictory, ambiguous, or unseen features that have appeared in this (Martinican) experience of the global relationship between cultures.

The central focus of this work is precisely that, just as Martinican reality can only be understood from the perspective of all the possible implications, abortive or not, of this cultural relationship, and the ability to transcend them, so the proliferation of visions of the world is meant only for those who try to make sense of them in terms of similarities that *are not to be standardized*. That these poetics are inseparable from the growth of a people, from their time for belonging and imagining.

A consistent concern underlying my project has been to resist the naive optimism that glamorizes "natural" poetics, structured or woven in a uniform or self-assured context. The world is ravaged, entire peoples die of famine or are exterminated, unprecedented techniques are perfected to ensure domination or death. These are part of an everyday reality that a cross-cultural poetics must take into consideration. Also, one could never fit this new sensibility into a neutral context in which political pressures miraculously vanish, and where no one dares to mention the class struggle except in low and muffled tones.

It is because social and political reality in Martinique is camouflaged in all kinds of ways—by imitation and depersonalization, by imposed ideologies, by creature comforts—that I felt it necessary to examine ourselves first, and to look at the unspeakable or irreparable effects on us. This vision is a form of our poetics.

I have spoken a lot about the system by which we are victimized. But that is a notion that would eventually become too comfortable. And what about us? Have we not contributed to our own domination?

A Caribbean Future

If, therefore, I have insisted on production and productivity, on technology and technological responsibility, it is not in order simply to modernize my discourse, nor to suggest that all "solutions" originate in this. The same need would exist to question a blind devotion to the technical and to conceive of a technology relevant to our culture: of a relating of ends to means, of an adaptation of technological levels to our world. But only a community totally free to act and to think could manage such a strategy. The independence of Martinique is vital to this process. It is a form of creativity and will generate its technology; this is where a collective sense of responsibility originates. How much frustrated effort, how many men and women arguing with their shadows at street corners, how much delirium, because this sense of responsibility is lacking.

This responsibility cannot be delegated to the dominant classes who have the desire without the power. The future of this country does not depend on the skill of those in power (we know what kinds of catastrophe ordinarily emerge from this kind of skill) but the radical nature of the change in mentality and its effect on social structure. I believe in the future of "small countries." [1] They have the possibility of achieving modern forms of participatory democracy, however much one distrusts this form of government when one considers the terrible aberrations it has produced in the past.

The need for this unanimity, not imposed by some prefabricated ideology, and possible in a Caribbean context, dictates the choices made by Martinican militants: there is no alternative to a uniting of all those who struggle for independence.

Have I, in saying this, drifted away from the idea of crosscultural poetics? No. It is built on the voices of all peoples, what I have called their inscrutability, which is nothing, after

---

1. Consider, for instance, the disproportion between the scattered communities of the Caribbean and the growing impact of their experience on the modern consciousness, without taking into account their role in world politics. But my faith is not derived from this role or this impact.

all, but an expression of their freedom. The transparency encouraged by misleading imitativeness must be shed at once.

If the reader has followed these arguments up to this point, I would wish that, through the twisting complexity of my approaches to Caribbean experience, he may manage to catch this voice rising from unexpected places: yes, and that he may *understand* it.

Appendix

Table of the Diaspora

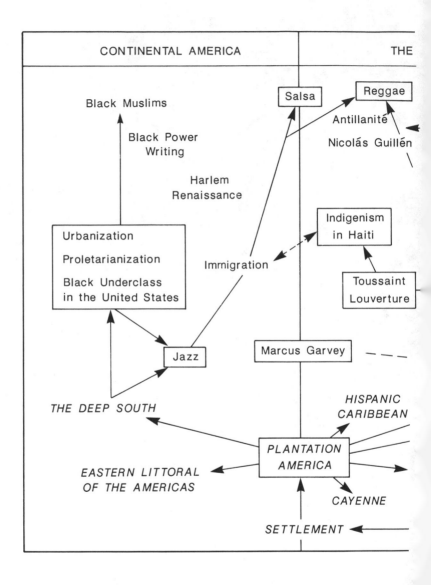

CONTINENTAL AMERICA   THE

Black Muslims   Salsa   Reggae

                                                        Antillanité
        Black Power   Nicolás Guillén
        Writing

            Harlem
            Renaissance
                                              Indigenism
Urbanization   in Haiti

Proletarianization
                        Immigration
Black Underclass   Toussaint
in the United States   Louverture

                    Jazz   Marcus Garvey

THE DEEP SOUTH   HISPANIC
                                               CARIBBEAN
                                PLANTATION
EASTERN LITTORAL   AMERICA
OF THE AMERICAS
                                                CAYENNE

                    SETTLEMENT

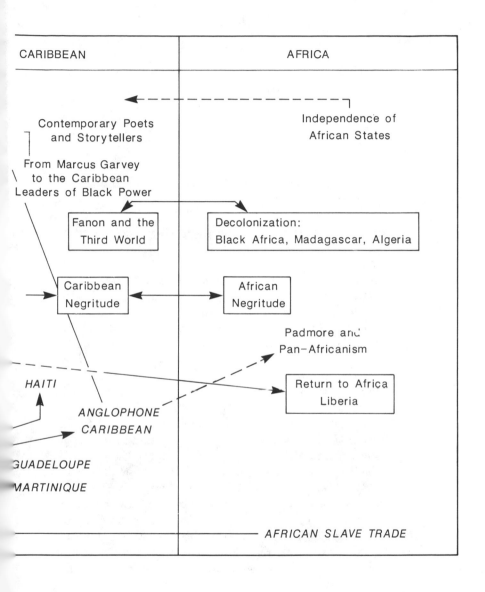

| CARIBBEAN | AFRICA |

Contemporary Poets and Storytellers

Independence of African States

From Marcus Garvey to the Caribbean Leaders of Black Power

Fanon and the Third World

Decolonization: Black Africa, Madagascar, Algeria

Caribbean Negritude

African Negritude

Padmore and Pan-Africanism

HAITI

ANGLOPHONE CARIBBEAN

Return to Africa Liberia

GUADELOUPE

MARTINIQUE

AFRICAN SLAVE TRADE

Glossary

Prepared by the author for the original French edition. Addenda are marked (*Trans.*).

Abolition ("liberation" of the slaves). 1848. The second republic chooses Schoelcher to take care of this matter. He becomes the new "father," a sublimated substitute for the colonizer. There will always be, from Schoelcher to de Gaulle, a father to fulfil Martinican fantasies. This form of alienation is derived from the circumstances of Abolition in 1848. That is why I always say the so-called liberation. This is why I place "liberation" in quotation marks.

Acoma (acomat). One of the trees that has disappeared from the Martinican forest. We should not get too attached to the tree, we might then forget the forest. But we should remember it. The review *Acoma*, 1972–73.

Aliker (André). Secretary of the Communist Party of Martinique. The sea washed up his body bound to a piece of sheet metal. He planned to denounce tax fraud among the big planters. The general verdict was suicide (1936).

(the other) America. The America of Juarez, Bolivar, and Martí. The America of Neruda. But especially that of the Indian peoples. The notion of the Other America (as formulated by José Martí) is a countervailing force to Anglo-Saxon America. But the Other America is not "Latin"; one can imagine that this term will gradually disappear.

antillanité. More than a theory, a vision. The force of it is such that it is applied to everything. I have heard *antillanité* proposed on a few occasions (without any further details) as a general solution to real or imagined problems. When a word acquires this kind of general acceptance, one presupposes that it has found its reality. (In the text *antillanité* has been systematically translated as Caribbeanness—*Trans.*)

Antilles (Greater, Lesser; the Caribbean islands). In this convergence of their cultures we may perhaps be witnessing the birth of a civilization. I think that the Caribbean Sea does not enclose; it is an open sea. It does not impose one culture, it radiates diversity.

Antilles (anglophone). So alike yet so different. They distrust the theory of Caribbeanness, or *antillanité,* but they try to make it work. The histories of the people are more apparent there than in our case. The Caribbean people from these countries are perhaps as English as we are French. But they do not want to be English.

Antilles (francophone). Confetti, dancing girls, nightmare, incomplete archipelago, specks of dust, etc. That is how we are seen. Martinique, Guadeloupe. We have not yet grasped the other image of our world.

Arawaks, Caribs. The first inhabitants of the islands. All massacred. A few thousand relocated on the island of Dominica (*q.v.*). During the period of the formation of the Martinican elite, it was good form for Martinicans living in France to have it thought that they were descendants of a Carib chief. Which implied that they were not as African as they appeared.

assimilation. The principle behind any idea of assimilation is direct contact and fusion by osmosis. The absurdity of the theory of assimilation in the French Caribbean is that what the French Caribbean claims to be assimilating—the French experience—is nothing but a deformed version of this experience, a cultureless, futureless zombie.

Which in turn zombifies the *assimilé*. He has no alternative but to cling to the deluded "truth" of a process that is invariably unreal.

autonomy. One does not quite know if it is an ideal or a stage. It will mean "conducting one's business" while counting on another to balance the books. (See also *status—Trans.*)

beetroot. It is amazing how this tuber has been an invisible force in the French Caribbean. What happened in the foggy plains of Northern France has changed the tropical landscape of Martinique.

Béhanzin. King of Dahomey who opposed the French penetration into Africa. Exiled in Martinique. He was a curiosity to us. I think he still haunts our unconscious.

béké. Creole term used for white planters and their descendants in Martinique. (See also *zoreill—Trans.*)

bel-air (bèlè). A dance; the music for this dance. (*Trans.*)

bossale. In Haiti, the recently arrived African. I translate this as the newly initiated.

Brer Rabbit (Lion, Tiger, Elephant). One of the peculiarities of the Caribbean folktale is to depict animals (generally from Africa) that do not exist in the country, but that do exist elsewhere.

Caliban. Cannibal. Shakespeare gave us the word, our writers have made it over.

carême. Dry season (from February to August). Increasingly humid, because the weather is changing. Popular belief: the Americans clean their air space around Cape Canaveral and all the debris from storms, rains, and hurricanes falls down on us. Hence the change in weather. The rainy season (September to January) is called *hivernage*.

Caribs. See *Arawaks, Caribs* (*Trans.*)

Carifesta. The greatest cultural spectacle in the Caribbean (Guyana, 1972, Jamaica 1976, Cuba 1979, Barbados 1981). Disturbs the powers that be.

carnival. Finally revived in Martinique in 1980. All is well in the country. All the same we run off to the carnival in

263

Glossary

Trinidad and perhaps to the one in Rio. (See also *Vaval.— Trans.*)

Château Dubuc (the Dubuc Great House). On the coast of Martinique, at Caravelle Point. Disembarked slaves were stocked there. No doubt the traffic took place outside of the control of the authorities at Fort-Royal.

Code Noir. Published by Colbert in 1665, regulated the life of the slave. Depending on whether you are optimistic or not, you will consider it to be a humanitarian gesture or a monumental piece of colonialist cynicism.

commandeur. In the hierarchy of slave labor or in the plantation system, he is the foreman directly in charge of the agricultural workers. Above him are the paymaster and the supervisor.

coolies. F. Ivor Case criticizes Caribbean writers in French for not dealing with the question of East Indians who arrived from 1850. The latter kept their customs; they were for a long time subjected to black racism. The term is often considered an insult. The East Indian presence poses a problem, because of their rivalry with the African community (or vice versa) in many anglophone Caribbean islands. The East Indians are called Malabars in Guadeloupe.

créolité. Theory according to which it is a matter of uniting Creolophone peoples (including Réunion Island) and promoting the exclusive use of the language. Créolité has taken up what our language has suffered from (the prejudice of monolingualism) and ignores the history of the Caribbean, which links us to Jamaicans and Puerto Ricans beyond the language barrier. (See also *antillanité— Trans.*)

croix-mission. In the towns. In theory, the first cross planted by the missionaries and the square around it. The special place for street talk. The name has remained, but its function has disappeared.

cutlass. A history of this tool, which is also a weapon, remains to be written. It is also an instrument of violence against self, of the "senseless violence" among Martinicans.

da. Black wet nurse. Has her equivalent all over the Caribbean and southern United States. Idealized protagonist (victim) in the novel. Black, slave, and yet loving and heroic.

Delgrès (Louis). Taking to their deaths a group of six thousand French soldiers who had besieged him, he blew himself up with three hundred men on the stock of gunpowder at Fort Matouba in Guadeloupe. It is debated whether he was a hero who refused the restoration of slavery in 1802, or someone intoxicated with "republican" ideas who did not dare call for total insurrection and preferred death to the loss of his ideal.

departmentalization. What was once seen as a "legal and administrative advance" has become an end in itself. Note the obsessive insistence with which official statements in the media refer to Martinique as: the department, our department. Ultimately they make it so. (The DOM—Départements d'Outre-Mer, or overseas departments—were created by legislative act in 1946—*Trans.*)

devils. Carnival characters. They used to be extravagant and all in rags: terrifying. They have been standardized. Today they sell costumes in the stores for devils large and small.

djobeurs. From English *job;* those who subsist by doing odd jobs, in particular by recycling used materials. (*Trans.*)

DOM (Départements d'Outre-Mer). See departmentalization (*Trans.*)

Dominica. To the north of Martinique. Became independent after having been an English colony. Martinicans willingly compare their per capita income to that of the Dominicans. In order to reassure themselves why it is good to "remain French." See also: *St. Lucia,* to the south.

"The East I Know." Claudel's title is symbolic of the maneuver of so many Westerners who were tempted by total otherness, without ceasing to be, above all, Western. Only

Victor Segalen, who started it all, dared to go all the way, until he died from his daring.

ecology (environment: "national park"). A recent fashion inherited like others. Will it become "functional"? The organizing bodies are all in Paris.

elite. Like the elite everywhere in the Third World; what is terrifying, given its unimportance, is its self-assurance, its smug tastelessness, its unprotesting servility, its chronic lack of productivity.

emigration. Combined with a falling birth rate, which is systematically promoted, and immigration coming from Europe. In forty years the Martinican population will have been reduced by nearly 100,000 inhabitants and will have grown by as many Europeans (about 350,000 inhabitants at present). Then there will be 150,000 Martinicans living in France. What M. Aimé Césaire's political party (PPM) calls "genocide by substitution."

fer-de-lance. This is a very poisonous trigonocephalic snake from Martinique. It haunts our subconscious. In the countryside they say: the enemy, the long creature. They go so far as to call it (in order to avoid saying the word *snake*) *la cravate*, the necktie.

gombo. Okra, one of the most widespread vegetables in that zone of plantation cultures, from the southern United States to the islands and the South American continent.

Gorée. Island off Senegal, where slaves were loaded after being seized on the African continent. We all dream of Gorée, as one dreams of a motherland from which one has been excluded: without really realizing it.

griot. African storyteller and singer. The griot has a social status, he is a "professional" as opposed to the Caribbean storyteller, who is generally an agricultural worker for whom the art of storytelling is pure recreation.

Haiti (Saint-Domingue). Possibly the new "motherland." Because there (and only there) could be found the conditions for organized survival and the political (revolutionary) self-affirmation that emerged. The extremes of underdevelopment and state terror have made this country regress beyond any possible evaluation. But Haiti retains a strength derived from *historical memory,* which all Caribbean people will one day need.

hivernage. See *carême (Trans.)*

FR3. The third national television network in France, specializing in regional programming. FR3 considers the DOM (*q.v.*), a "region" of France. (*Trans.*)

independence. The great fear of Martinicans. But which recedes under the pressures of this contradictory reality. I am told that Third World leaders snigger (at the UN, for example) when one mentions Martinique. An inevitable crisis here, we do not know what it has in store for us.

Joal. From *cheval* (horse); designates the French spoken by the urban poor in parts of Montreal and its industrial suburbs. (*Trans.*)

laghia (damier). Dance taking the form of a fight. The two dancers are in a circle of spectators, around a drum. The same dance is found in Brazil. The *laghia* is no doubt a ritual derived from initiation. There is always a "Major" (a champion) and a challenger. An exercise in regression. The *laghia* became linked to the production of sugar cane.

La Grande Patrie and *La Petite Patrie.* This is one of the most disturbing creations of the elite, during the period of its ideological conception. The hierarchical division of the notion of mother country can only be conceived in the ambiguous and confused context of this notion of the elite. Such a division has ultimately been abandoned. "La Petite Patrie" became the department. (See also *departmentalization—Trans.*)

Lamentin. Former heart of the Martinican economy. It is significant that today we find there the airport, the pseudo-industrialized areas, etc. The Lézarde River that flowed out into the sea is a trickle of water. Its delta is clogged. Its fauna has disappeared.

Lareinty. One of the most important sugar factories in Martinique, situated on the Lamentin (*q.v.*) plains. One of the last ones too. Its agony never ends. We see in it our upside-down image of what I call our inability to produce.

Corpse that the night cuts, washes
Squatting, wreck
Exposed to the stinging wind, its heart
Only bolted down by the last rivets.
The keeper of the seal, wise and one-eyed, has labelled
This disaster by decree: "died
From a natural death."

Latécoère. The seaplane operator in the French West Indies in the 1940s. (*Trans.*)
Legba (and Ogun, Damballah, etc.). Gods or Voudou loas, each having his own personality and function. Many Martinicans go to Haiti to be initiated.
Lorrain (the). Large town in the North of Martinique. Banana workers staged a determined strike (1974), interrupted by gunfire from the police. One of the leaders of this strike, M. Ilmany, was killed. The same day, the tortured body of a young man, whose murderers are still running around (or have gone underground), was discovered at the mouth of the Capote River.
macoutism. A regime characterized by terror exercised by a police or paramilitary force loyal to the dictator, as under the Duvalier regime in Haiti; from *tontons-macoutes,* (*q.v.*). (*Trans.*)
maroons (marronnage). Suffered different fates according to the topography of the islands where they operated. In Cuba in 1979 were discovered old maroon campsites containing objects invaluable for research (clay pipes, cutlasses, etc.). In Haiti, the Dokos were a community of maroons. In French Guiana, the Bonis and Saramakas are still separate communities today. In Jamaica, the epic struggle of the Trelawny and Windwards maroons was

waged by exceptional leaders: Juan de Bolas, The Great Traitor; the most inspired of all, Cudjoe, The Mountain Lion; Quaco, The Invisible Hunter. Conquered by negotiation and not by arms, the maroons of Jamaica were deported first to Halifax in Canada (1796), then to Freetown in Sierra Leone (1800), where since 1787 freed blacks leaving England had settled. There is in Sierra Leone a variety of Creole, called *Krio*.

metropole, metropolitan. I mean France and French each time, which generally is shocking to my Martinican readers and generally leaves the French themselves quite unmoved.

old francs. French francs multiplied by 100 (also called centimes) corresponding to the currency devalued by de Gaulle in 1960. A disconcerting but common practice throughout France and the French West Indies. (*Trans.*)

pacotilleuse. A market woman who sells craft items to the tourist, but who regularly goes to Haiti to buy her stock. Almost all the objects sold at the Savane in Fort-de-France come from that country.

póyós. Little green bananas, grown especially in Guadaloupe, which would never become ripe. We were quite happy to get some in Martinique. The word has become symbolic of poverty, even endemic starvation.

Quechuas. Perhaps the Amerindians of South America who most capture the imagination: by their historical silence and obstinate presence.

quimbisero. In Cuba, the *quimbisero* has the role of a sorcerer, but exclusively used for *daño:* to do harm to another person.

razié. The most appropriate French word would perhaps be *halliers* (brushwood).

reggae. "Reggae is a type of music that emerged in the mid-sixties based on the Ska and usually having a heavy four-beat rhythm using the bass electric guitar and drum, with the scraper coming in at the end of the measure, and acting as accompaniment to emotional songs expressing

Glossary

rejection of established (white man: or Babylonian) culture." A definition proposed in 1976 by Frederick Cassidy and reported by Rex Nettleford in *Caribbean Cultural Identity: The Case of Jamaica* (Los Angeles: Center for Afro-American Studies and UCLA Latin American Center Publications, 1978), p. 22, n. 40. Ska is an urban Jamaican form of music from the fifties inspired by American pop music records, traditional music, and Rastafarian rhythms.

St.-Domingue. See *Haiti (Trans.)*

St. Lucia. Island of the former British West Indies, to the south of Martinique. Creole is spoken as well as English, the official language. (*Trans.*)

Schoelcherism. Doctrine surely at the origin of the concept of assimilation. Schoelcher "liberated" us. Therefore there is a "French" route to emancipation and evolution.

Ska. See *reggae (Trans.)*

Solidarité nationale. This is the euphemism that is used to conceal the injection of public-sector credit meant, in turn, to camouflage the real nature of the exchange between France and the overseas departments.

status. Department. Self-governing region. Independent nation. The notion of "status" is absurd as long as it is not an actuality. (See also *departmentalization—Trans.*)

tim-tim boisèche. Ritual game of riddles, at the beginning of an evening of storytelling.

tontons-macoutes. The secret police used by the Duvalier regime to enforce state terror in Haiti. See also *macoutism.* (*Trans.*)

tre (tray). Platter on which items are sold.

Tupuc-Amaru. This hero of the Indian revolt in the Andes is fascinating. One of his first companions was an African. Today, the Tupamaros movement claims him symbolically.

Vaval. The king of carnival (*q.v.*) who is burnt on Ash Wednesday evening. Once signifying an event (candidate beaten in elections, individual who has had fantastic ad-

ventures, etc.), it has been trivialized to the point of being
nothing but a big effigy with no distinguishing features.

Vertières. One of the last battles of the Haitian war of independence General Capoix-la-Mort in Dessalines's army
earned there by his bravery the admiration of the racist
officers of the French army, which soon after had to surrender to his mercy and leave the island.

vèvès. Shapes drawn by those who officiate at Voudou ceremonies, before or during the ceremonies.

Voudou. See *Legba* (and *Ogun, Damballah, etc.*); *Vèvès*
(Trans.)

zoreill or *zoreye* or *zorey.* This is how whites are called in
Martinique. Perhaps because they have red ears from the
effect of the sun? The term spread to the extent that it no
longer has a pejorative connotation.

Sources of Documents Reprinted in This Volume

From a Presentation Distant in Space and Time
  Revised version of an article published in the special issue of the magazine *Esprit* on "Les Antilles avant qu'il soit trop tard" in 1962.

Acceptance and Theater, Consciousness of the People
  Originally published between 1971 and 1973 in *Acoma*.

Reversion and Diversion
  First presented at a UNESCO meeting in Panama in 1979.

The Quarrel with History
  Paper read at the Carifesta colloquium in Kingston, Jamaica, in 1976.

History and Literature
  Presented to the Centre d'Etudes de Lettres, Fort-de-France, Martinique in 1978.

Sameness and Diversity and Techniques
  Papers delivered at colloquia sponsored by the magazine *Liberté* in 1974 and 1975; subsequently published in *Liberté*. Techniques was also presented as a lecture in Boston in 1976.

Natural Poetics, Forced Poetics
  Presented at the First International Symposium on Ethnopoetics of the Center for Twentieth Century Studies at the University of Wisconsin-Milwaukee in April 1975. Published by ALCHERINGA in the volume edited by Michel Benamou and Jerome Rothenberg, Boston University, 1976.

Sources of Documents

Cross-Cultural Poetics
Lecture delivered in Madison (Wisconsin), Pittsburgh, and Toronto in 1973; and in Halifax (Nova Scotia), in 1974.

Poetics and the Unconscious
Paper presented at a colloquium at the University of Indiana in 1973.

Pedagogy, Demagogy and Creole
Talks given to the PTA in Le Lamentin, Martinique, in 1976.

The Dream, The Reality
Lecture for the Institut Vizioz de Droit in Fort-de-France, Martinique, and the Centre d'Etudes Littéraires in Pointe-à-Pitre, Guadeloupe, in 1969.

Saint-John Perse and the Caribbean
Article published in a special issue of the *Nouvelle nouvelle revue française,* "Hommage à Saint-John Perse," in 1976.

Cultural Identity
Litany read at the Carifesta colloquium in Cuba in 1979.

From the Perspective of *Boises* (Shackles)
Written in 1979 on the occasion of the publication of this collection of poetry.

Seven Landscapes for the Sculptures of Cárdenas
Written for the catalog of the Cárdenas exhibit at the Point Cardinal gallery, Paris, in 1979.